African American Women and
Sexuality in the Cinema

African American Women and Sexuality in the Cinema

NORMA MANATU

foreword by Kwyn Bader

McFarland & Company, Inc., Publishers
Jefferson, North Carolina, and London

Library of Congress Cataloguing-in-Publication Data

Manatu, Norma.
    African American women and sexuality in the cinema /
Norma Manatu; foreword by Kwyn Bader.
        p.   cm.
    Includes bibliographical references and index.

    ISBN 0-7864-1431-6 (softcover binding : 50# alkaline paper)

    1. African American women in motion pictures.   I. Title.
PN1995.9.N4M28   2003
791.43'652042'08996073—dc21   2002015421

British Library cataloguing data are available

Cover photograph: N'Bushe Wright in the 1992 film *Zebrahead*
(Photofest)

Manufactured in the United States of America

McFarland & Company, Inc., Publishers
    Box 611, Jefferson, North Carolina 28640
        www.mcfarlandpub.com

To Deta, Carmen and Ulyp

Acknowledgments

Although *African American Women and Sexuality in the Cinema* evolved from my dissertation study, this book's focus is the question of whether the emergence of black male filmmakers has altered images of black female sexuality. A complete replication of the original study was conducted to reverify findings for the more recent films. I am grateful for the contributions of numerous people who helped me complete the book.

From the time of my entry into the doctoral program in the Department of Culture and Communication at New York University, I was blessed with the guidance of a dedicated and superb teaching staff. I owe the greatest intellectual debt to the following professors there: Drs. Borisoff, Nystrom, Hauser, Boyum, Hahn and Moran. All provided an atmosphere which challenged my thinking and clarified my ideas. Dr. Borisoff helped sharpen the book's focus. Responsibility for any shortcomings remains my own.

I am especially grateful to my colleagues in the Speech and Theatre Department at John Jay College of Criminal Justice. Drs. Wallenstein, Wylie-Marques, Green, Hill, Rodriguez, Parlakian, Collins, Telesco, and Moller provided valuable support and good counsel. Mrs. E. Dean, secretary of the department, offered a wealth of support, encouragement, and good advice.

Kudos to a group of unsung heros at John Jay—the library staff! I cannot praise them enough for the help they provided in my search for books, journal articles, and the like. Their patience in the face of my computer struggles and anxieties was laudable! I especially want to thank the chief librarian, Dr. Larry Sullivan, who was the first to read parts of my manuscript and offer sound advice. His support sustained me through much of the down times. I sincerely thank Profs. Katherine Killoran, Maria Kiriakova, Marvie Brooks, Nancy Egan, and D.D. Aikens of the Inter-Library Loan Office.

Many others helped in my journey in important ways. The support of Dean James Levine of the Graduate Studies Program at John Jay has been invaluable. I also thank him for encouraging me to submit this book when I was unsure of its length; you were right, Jim!

As always, my mentor, Dean Ruby Malone, supports and energizes me through the best and worst of times. Dean Witherspoon has been generous-hearted and full of valuable suggestions. Other friends and colleagues responded to my call for help along the way. Much appreciation to Drs. D. Jones-Brown, Z. Henriques, C. Alford, K. Kinshasa, J. Domingo, N. Sokoloff, M. Aldridge, and Professors John Russell and Horace Banbury. Ken Chen was a terrific and generous resource in providing technical assistance, and Sima Vosough of the 57th Street Video Store was most helpful in my search for films for the studies.

It is difficult to find appropriate words to thank the two people who most nurture me. My sister, Deta Clarke, a proud supporter of my work, shares my many frustrations and celebrates my successes—deepest thanks. Carmen Marshall, whom I have called friend since girlhood, sharpens my ideas in our long philosophical talks, for which we're so famous. She provides support and the best antidote ever, uproarious laughter!

Contents

Foreword
Kwyn Bader

One of the enduring frustrations for many citizens living in America is the great disparity between our nation's promise and its behavior, between its word and its action. How does a country, whose humanistic ideals inspire great expressions of liberty and aspiration, dehumanize so many of its own with historic regularity? Nowhere is this national paradox more visually apparent than in our movies, reels of celluloid wonderment tapping into the shared subconscious of the culture, with central characters, viscerally representing us all, traversing an obstacle course of the spirit on their way towards change and higher consciousness. American movies are wanted everywhere in the world—to the extent that industries in once great filmmaking countries like Italy can no longer support such an enterprise, their citizens preferring Cameron to Bertolucci. Even those who are enemies of the U.S. obviously admire the spectacle of our cinema. The design of the violence directed on New York in September 2001, so obviously the stuff of the summer blockbuster, reflects that its perpetrators may hate America, but they sure as hell connect with American movies.

The problem is, that despite all its technical and creative wizardry, the Hollywood industry I work in has made only small advances in its development of non-white characters. Thank God for Denzel Washington, who is a phenomenon of talent, able to cultivate part after part with Robert Duvall– and Robert De Niro–like levels to huge mainstream box office success. But try to get a black cast movie off the ground when it's not a laugh-a-minute comedy and doesn't have Washington. Even if the screenplay is well crafted and fits in a tried and true commercial genre— let's say, even if the most prominent black filmmaker in the world is on board to produce it for you. Just try it. I'm doing it right now.

"We don't know how to market that."

It's not pretty. And while the depictions of any multi-level, fully-dimensional characters (the understanding of which expands our sense of the American and human experience) are few in movies at large (which is why the actors who play those few characters usually get nominated for Oscars), when it comes to black women, these depictions are virtually non-existent. Dr. Norma Manatu's writing seeks, through its comparison of depictions of black women by black and white male directors, to demonstrate the extent to which American films have failed a significant segment of the country's female population, forbidding its members parts in films that might present them, for good or for bad, as fully realized beings with universally accessible stories and experiences.

As a screenwriter and director I have the unique opportunity to believe daily in that which isn't and that which hasn't been, since it is the spirit of the unrealized that I let run about in my imagination. It is an innately hopeful state of being. So there's never been a film with a four-eyed neurotic bi-racial antihero in a French New Wave–inspired American film with a multi-racial cast that's only concerned with each other's differences when it comes to attitudes on sex in love. There's one running around in my mind. I'll write it. Direct it. It might be five years in gestation, but during that time the movie I feel sustains me. When I do make it and it finds its way onto some big screens and then remains out in the world, re-running on cable somewhere, it's butter on the toast. Though insecure, off-balance, and often lacking in sustaining capital, it is, I admit, in its nourishing escapism, a charmed existence.

But any woman or man who doesn't live the life of a mad-brained filmmaker can view only what has already been made, and for that matter, only what has been distributed on a mass level. She or he does not have the irrational comforts of the films that could be, but must watch the movie that really is playing in the local cineplex, searching for someone in the action to relate to and live through. And the films that have been made with black female actresses in American cinema generally depict characters which conscious, multi-dimensional black women cannot find themselves in, which instead offer incomplete projections that neither they nor anyone else can fully relate to. Most people accept that this is just the way things are, or they don't pay attention, or they may criticize without offering any constructive advice, or they may concentrate on inspiring exceptions to the rule.

Dr. Manatu, however, exhibits the courage to stare the monster in the face, and in a comprehensive study, to look at the history and current state of affairs, with the foreknowledge that what she's going to see cannot make her feel good. She's gone ahead and done hard, dirty investigative work needed for critical understanding of race and American cinema. *African American Women and Sexuality in the Cinema* offers the type of evolved, challenging, and direct thought that must be engaged in by cineastes, movie viewers, actors and filmmakers (and even, by some miracle, industry executives) if we are to share more intelligent, aware, and meaningful cinema. I hope that her words find an interested audience in you, the reader, and I offer best wishes that the sentiments expressed here may find their way, either now or eventually, into the national dialogue on film.

Kwyn Bader is the writer and director of the film Loving Jezebel *(2000).*

Preface

I confess that each and every time I am confronted with media images, no matter the storyline or plotline, no matter how glorious the cinematography, music score, or costume, I search the visual landscape for images of subjects representative of me—every time! If I locate such a subject, I next work to see how she or he is situated within the story; what activity she or he is engaged in, for I have grown keenly aware that media "presence" is not necessarily representative of, nor uplifting to, the self-image of a given social group. Indeed, more often than not, the opposite is generally the case where it concerns depictions of underrepresented groups. What role does the subject occupy? Is that subject's presence central to the plot? It is against this backdrop that I view films, particularly those containing images of black female subjects.

My first such film came in the form of the infamous *Imitation of Life* (1934), starring Louise Beavers and Fredi Washington (original version). Though Beavers' character, Aunt Delilah, was dark-skinned—hallelujah—she bore little resemblance to me or my experiences. This rather round, plump black female character was depicted as purposefully and unusually accommodating to her white mistress and the daughter of the mistress. In fact, her adoration of both was in sharp contrast to her attitude toward her own daughter. I felt uneasy (or was it embarrassed?) about her "eager-to-please" disposition, for it struck me that these depictions fed into the "blacks are just so happy to serve whites" ideology, an

1

ideology quite common back then. What I found even more disturbing was the portrayal of this black female character as accepting of the powerlessness that threatened to determine the course of her life and that of her own child. You may recall that the black female character was depicted not only as fiercely loyal to the mistress-daughter pair; she was also depicted as choosing to give up her right to partnership in a business which her own created recipe had made possible, and which had resulted in her white mistress' economic prosperity. Despite the mistress' offer to share the wealth with the Beavers character, audiences were assaulted by images of this black female who was shown to be more desirous of remaining in service to her mistress than she was of claiming her independence and freedom. I left the theatre wondering how could I love a medium that so poorly treated this black woman, a woman who could have been my own mother.

If I had been disturbed by black women's characterizations in films shown in the 1930s, I would be downright appalled by degrading images of black women in films of the 1970s. The Blaxploitation era of this decade brought with it the "Supermama/Macho-Goddess" genre of films (*Coffy*, 1973; *Foxy Brown*, 1974), many of which exploited black

Claudette Colbert (right) stars as Laura and Louise Beavers as Delilah in Universal's *Imitation of Life* (1934). Here, Delilah prepares a meal for Laura.

women's sexuality. Drug-taking, street-walking prostitutes were ubiquitous in many of these films. What were presented as their opposites fared little better, for the "macho-goddesses" were not your average women; these were fictionalized superwomen who tackled with exceptional ease endless ludicrous situations that would have killed the average ten women.

According to Bogle (1989), the Supermama/Macho-Goddess was a cross between the militant "mammy" and the oversexed Jezebel. Many in this subgroup were characterized by their portrayals as sex objects. Many, in fact, were fused with raw sexuality; were portrayed as on-the-ready for sex; and were frequently shown to use men as sexual play things (Bogle, 1989, p. 251). This new filmic development saw a shift in characterizations of black female subjects, which now placed them at the other end of their denigrating film role continuum: black women had graduated from "mammy martyrdom" to "oversexed degenerates."

The mid-1980s finally brought fresh hope: a new emerging black film culture was in its inchoate stage, promising black filmmakers control of their own images. Unlike the independently-made "race movies" of 1917–1949, blacks would write, cast, direct, and produce mainstream representations of themselves, thus rescuing black culture from media degradation. Spike Lee, an independent black male filmmaker who later became the godfather of this new commercially-driven black film culture, was to be the much overdue savior of that filmic culture, and by extension, black female subjects.

The much anticipated new black aesthetic came in the form of Lee's independent turned mainstream film *She's Gotta Have It* (1986), and viewers learned fast and unequivocally just what that "it" was. Save for who now controlled the images—the very ones mainstream filmmakers had earlier created—not much else had changed. Black female subjects were still being sexualized to the point of the obscene. Needless to say, *She's Gotta Have It* was a raving success. It set the stage for a cadre of other black male filmmakers who carried on in like fashion, and viewers watched as film after film in the mid-1980s to the early 2000s dragged black women through the mud.

What you are about to read questions whether the emergence of black male filmmakers has altered the negative image of black female sexuality in contemporary American films of the 1980s to the early 2000s. The book centers on one major aspect of black women's depictions—sexuality. The study's main focus is on four dimensions related to black women's sexuality as articulated in filmic narratives purporting to mirror black cultural life: the diversity of their roles and relationships with

Pam Grier stars as Foxy Brown and Peter Brown is Steve Elias in Warner Bros.' *Foxy Brown* **(1974).**

men; the sexual attitudes of the black female characters; their attitudes towards men; and the nonverbal and verbal sexual behaviors of the black female characters.

Media critics continue to argue that descriptions of black cultural life in the general media far too often present blacks in deviant or comedic roles, the latter employing gags and physical antics to showcase black cultural life (Bogle, 1989; Fine, 1995; Inniss & Feagin, 1995). Indeed, the popularity of blacks in comedic roles suggests that aligning black issues with the verisimilitude inherent in dramatic roles is neither popular nor profitable. Inniss & Feagin (1995), in fact, suggest that, in film, "black life and black issues are not taken seriously" (p. 707); instead, blacks are generally presented as comical.

This book, therefore, does not include films that feature black women who are comedic, such as *Made in America* or *Sister Act*, nor works that feature a black male actor or character who plays the role of a black female within the world of the film, such as *The Crying Game*. Rather, the book focuses on those films where the black female character has a well-developed role (a main character; a co-star; a strong supporting character; or a character otherwise significant to the outcome of the plot) as a black American in the dominant filmmaking culture and in the emerging commercial black film culture. It is a study which sets black male filmmakers' visions of black female sexuality against those of white male filmmakers because, given their different histories, one supposes there might be racially-based differences in the sexual sensibilities and visions of these two groups of men. A comparison of black male– versus white male–produced works is also undertaken because too few films are written and directed by women, black or white, to provide a basis for comparing female with male visions of black female sexuality. While the sixteen films located for comparison include works based on novels (as in the case of the film *Devil in a Blue Dress*), such adaptation requires that both the novelist and screenwriter belong to the same race, or that the novelist be the screenwriter also; otherwise, an interpretation of an interpretation might result, as was the case in the film *The Color Purple*, which was based on a novel written by a black female, but directed by white males. Cinematic offerings not situated in the U.S. and those that do not feature black American female characters are excluded from the study. Finally, only those works from the mid-1980s to the early 2000s are included in the study, since not until then did the contemporary American film industry see the beginnings of black-controlled commercial films.

Although the book is delimited in this fashion, the central question framing the study—have black male filmmakers altered the sexual image of black women in films?—invites a comparative inquiry. One of the claims offered for the proliferation of negative images of black female sexuality was that the images had been out of the control of black filmmakers (Leab, 1975; Reid, 1988). As late as the 1980s, conventional wisdom had it that films from an Afrocentric perspective would yield more positive depictions of black women. In order to accurately assess any differences in portrayals, a comparison of black versus white male-produced works was needed. The research question, therefore, precluded a broader inclusion of other films, ones with more depth and richness of diverse black female imagery.

Such films as *The Color Purple* and *Sounder* would have been a useful addition to a study on black women in American film. As delineated above, however, questions of timing and control determined those works that could be included in the study. I, too, mourn the loss of films like *Sounder* for the study. The minimal role diversification for black women is representative of the skewed, all too-common "oversexed" Jezebel stereotype in films of the mid-1980s to the present. As you read, you will get a sense of the frustration black feminist writers express over persistence of the sexual image, as exemplified in contemporary American films. You will also sense their concern, and mine, about the social implications of the primacy of the sexual narrative about black female characters on screen.

This book offers a different approach to the chronicling of black women's role in contemporary American films by providing a comparative examination of one major aspect of their experiences—sexuality. It employs a content analysis instrument developed for the purpose of analyzing sixteen contemporary films of the present for black and white male filmmakers' version of black female sexuality. To date, no other study has examined this issue from this perspective, though various media critics have raised serious questions regarding the negative portrayals. Many have pointed out that the highlighting of this one aspect of black women's experiences on screen—the sexual—is problematic because other aspects are suppressed. Such imagistic disparity (it is alleged) has profound effects on social attitudes toward actual black women in U.S. culture.

Considerable concern over the permanence of the negative role and the enormous amount of critical discourse by black feminists devoted to the social implications of the negative depictions of black women laid the groundwork for this book. Accordingly, the book provides a comparison of sixteen films from the mid-1980s to the present to determine whether the image of black female sexuality is similar or different when the filmmaker is black or white, and if so, how? I share with the reader different perspectives on film's socializing influence and its interactions with gender and race, interactions that hint at the exclusion of black women but actually exclude them. I also examine how love and romance, as compared to sex, are depicted in films based on social prescriptive, and how such depictions marginalize black women. The findings will be confirming and contradictory all at once, and the reader will be left to wonder how the next generation of films will treat black women and their sexuality.

1

Introduction and Overview

As a group, black women have not fared well in the media, specifically in the television and film industries. Indeed, the 21st century began where the 20th century left off, with minimal role diversification in the visual depictions of black women in films. The media's persistence in presenting black women in substandard roles of the oversexed jezebel, the prostitute, the superwoman, and the aggressive, intimidating bitch has been frustrating to critics and black female audiences alike—black women who have made valuable contributions to society, yet fail to see themselves accurately depicted on screen (St. Jean & Feagin, 1998).

As recently as 1995, one missed opportunity to present a varied depiction of black women's experiences outside of the sexual can be found in the film, *Waiting to Exhale* (1995). Here were four black women, all linked in an important friendship, who could have been portrayed in more complex ways. Could have been—because instead of presenting these women with more depth and intelligence, the film depicted all four women primarily as interested in their own sexuality. When the women were not depicted as seducers of men, they were shown to be preoccupied with getting a man. The narrowness in the representations of these women was such that hooks (1996) was moved to note the following: "so simplistic and denigrating to black women [is the film] that we should be outraged to be told that it is 'for us'" (p. E19).

Save for the critically acclaimed and commercially successful film

9

Sounder (1972), starring Cicely Tyson and Paul Winfield, few film roles-
for black women are devoid of the comedic or the sexual, or feature black
female characters as sensitive and intelligent (Leab, 1975; Bogle, 1989).
Few showcase the diversity, complexity, and dimensionality that make
up black women's cultural life. Even fewer have come close to portraying black female characters as dignified and believable, as was the case
of Tyson's depiction in the film *Sounder*. Bogle (1989) notes that Tyson
was what one critic called "the first great black heroine on screen.... She
is visually extraordinary" (pp. 249-250). Tyson's role represented a black
woman infused with sensitivity, vulnerability, and strength—qualities
lacking in most roles black women are allowed on screen today. What
was extraordinary about *Sounder* was the human problems the characters
confronted (the father's struggle to keep food on his family's table; the
mother's valiant struggle to nurture her three children, keep her family
intact, and save their land during the father's sentence of a year in jail for
having stolen meat for his family). Nearly thirty years later, viewers still
await black female characters who are presented in commercially-suc-
cessful films as "believable human beings" (Leab, 1975, p. 260), with similar depth and quality as that found in *Sounder*.

Interestingly enough, despite the dearth of intelligent character roles
black female subjects are allowed, many nonminorities appear to be at a
loss to comprehend the frustration black women viewers frequently
express over the substandard roles (Bobo, 1995). With so few dramatic
roles featuring black female subjects outside of the sexual, I often find
myself squirming at the images presented on screen. To maintain focus,
I frequently resort to critically attending to each image viewed. Though
the works may be "entertaining," I rarely experience joy in viewing such
scenes; certainly, I am not purged! After enough visual assault, I am forced
to embark on a temporary boycott of films altogether. Even all-white
cinematic offerings manage to offend my sensibilities by their absence of
black subjects (male or female), and equally important, by the role diversity allowed members of the dominant group.

At some point during my boycott, many nonminorities are perplexed
by my stance, preferring, instead, to offer various ways in which I might
approach the viewing of films. I have no doubt that these detractors are
well-meaning. Still, one wonders if many nonminorities' failure to recognize the pathetic state of affairs for black women on screen, their failure to see Hollywood's perennial fixation on black female sexuality, is not
reflective of persons for whom diversity in filmic roles is being fulfilled.
Has their place in the peri-center of the dominant cultural fare, with a
balance of images and icons of themselves, blinded them to the reality

of black women's repeated on-screen reminders of their place in a medium infused with racial and sexual images? Perhaps, as Hall (1980) reminds us, different groups of people from different social circumstances actually do perceive the same media messages differently. For while failing to note a distinction between rhetoric and reality, a good many nonminorities point to the very films that so assault black women as "evidence" that these women do have full representation in the media. Many, in fact, point to Oprah, Halle Berry, and other such celebrities as manifestations of equality among "women" both in film and in the culture at large.

I dare say most black women are the first to embrace these celebrities as their own. Nonetheless, an increase in black female celebrities, like the increase in the substandard roles, is not representative of black women in general. Neither the roles nor black female celebrities recognize the full dimensions of black women's experiences. Each merely obscures what is by now a common, but limited view of black women's cultural identity in America: the defining symbols of "the sexual," and "the superwoman" (Collins, 1990). The dearth of varied roles for black women in commercially successful films and the increase in roles absent the "sexual" inform this comparative inquiry.

An equally compelling rationale for my concern regarding film's focus on black female sexuality is the consequence of aligning these women primarily to the "sexual." The danger of such misrepresentations lurks ever present. For, judging from filmic portrayals of black women over the last decade and a half, two important metamessages can be deduced about these women: black women are "superwomen," near fictive characters who do the impossible; and black women do not fall in love. For example, when presented as professionals, these women are aggressive and amazonian, real and unreal all at once (St. Jean & Feagin, 1998). When presented as involved in male-female relationships, black women have sex; they do not make love. They are shown as women who do not value romance and so are coded as far from being romantic figures (Iverem, 1997); their approach to men, instead, is often presented as crass. Whether in television or in films, especially films of the last two decades, images of black women too often fall within the category of the "other" object, replete with negative sexuality. That category is created, defined, and disseminated by image-makers through the film medium, a medium quite capable of compelling verisimilitude (Gianetti, 1972; Metz, 1974; Boyum, 1985). If, therefore, I was to better understand how and why black women's roles are constructed as chiefly sexual, why these women are not represented as romantic characters, I had to examine a diverse set of American films by black and white filmmakers.

It should be realized that imagistic disparities in filmic representations of black female subjects are not merely harmless entertainment. Film's generic treatment of black women extends well beyond seeming entertainment. Although films may be entertaining, and many are, they also provide viewers with ideas (Leab, 1975; Jowett & Linton, 1980). The debate about whether films really do influence viewers' perception founders against the evidence that for large numbers of viewers, films are the "primary sources of information about society and human behavior..." (Sklar, 1975, p. 316). Films are storytelling mechanisms, designed not just to entertain, but to circulate ideas about our culture and its people, as reflected within the larger society. As Leab (1975) points out, "[Films] are entertainment, but they are also symbols, and behind every shadow on the big screen is the struggle to impose definitions upon what is and what should be" (p. 263). What, then, is the filmic story shown about black women? More specifically, what stories and ideas do contemporary cinematic narratives circulate about black female sexuality? And what does the literature have to say about these narratives shown of black women, as articulated by contemporary black and white male filmmakers?

The Literature on Black Women in American Films

For as long as blacks have appeared in American films, criticisms have been directed at the film industry about their negative portrayals. These critiques have typically arisen from black organizations, such as the National Association for the Advancement of Colored People, which, in 1915, 1951, and 1990 respectively, delivered scathing attacks on the industry.

Generally, critics have traditionally argued that negative portrayals of blacks in film engender alienation of them from the dominant culture and limit the dimensions of the lives of blacks. These charges, however, have chiefly concerned depictions of the black male character (Reddick, 1944; Cruse, 1967; Noble, 1970; Murray, 1973; Leab, 1975; Bogle, 1989). What is remarkable about these charges is that after more than a half century later, the criticisms still mirror the very ones directed at the industry today.

Where scholarly examination of black women's filmic treatment is concerned, up until the 1980s, the major works on blacks in films have also focused primarily on images of the black male character (Mapp, 1972; Bogle, 1973/1989; Leab, 1975). Each references black women's characterizations, but these discussions are scant by comparison.

Scholarship on "women" in film has been even more negligible in its examination of the treatment of black women. The four seminal works which comprise the major scholarship on women in American films include *Popcorn Venus* (Rosen, 1973), *From Reverence to Rape* (Haskell, 1973, 1987), *Women and their Sexuality in the New Film* (Mellen, 1973), and *Visual and other Pleasures* (Mulvey, 1989). However, save for Haskell's brief mention of blacks, in the section where she chastises Hollywood for its negative portrayal of "women" (p. 370), no representations of black women are examined by these writers. The major writers on women in film since the 1970s have tended to imply that since black women fall within the category of "women," their representation need not be singled out for separate study. Thus, black women's on-screen representation as a major area of scholarly examination remained negligible in these studies.

Recent writers, primarily those from a sociological or historical perspective, have noted that the different histories of black and white women in American culture have resulted in different constructions of their sexuality (Simson, 1983; Young, 1993; Roberts, 1994; Freydberg, 1995). Roberts (1994), for example, explains that in the 1700s–1800s, "The white world drew the black woman's body as excessive and flagrantly sexual, quite different from the emerging ideology of purity and modesty which defined the white woman's body" (p. 5). Other writers intimate that the subsuming of black women's representation under the rubric "women," obscures the double jeopardy of race and gender faced by black women (Simson, 1983; Giddings, 1984; King, 1988).

Several researchers, however, have finally begun to give serious attention to black women's treatment in film, including the essay collection *Black Women in America* (Hines, 1993). Exceptions to the negligence in scholarship concerning black women's representations have been primarily those generally found in the works of black feminist writers, such as Wallace (1990, 1992), hooks (1992, 1996), Jones (1992, 1993), Kennedy (1992), Painter (1992), Baker Jr. (1993), Guerrero (1993), and Iverem (1997). These writers argue that an explosion of sexual images of black women in contemporary American films has been offered to American viewers, which is reminiscent of the sexist Blaxploitation works of the 1970s.

Up until the 1970s, that imagery was the product of a film industry controlled by white males. In fact, prior to the decade of the mid-1980s, the belief was that because black filmmakers were mere hirelings of mainstream studios or directors, the white-controlled images of blacks were gross distortions. Further, the cinematic content was viewed as interpretations of disparate voices (black and white). Complete control of the films by blacks, it was thought, would alter the images (Leab, 1975; Reid, 1988). Leab (1975) elaborates on control of the films' content before the decade of the eighties:

> Direction ... was usually in the hands of whites.... Production and distribution were almost exclusively controlled by whites. And concerned as they were with making a profit, they gave little thought to changing the movie image of the black or of furthering his knowledge of film production [pp. 187–188].

Not until the mid-1980s did the film industry see the beginnings of black male-controlled commercial films (Tate, 1986), during which time popular works by black male filmmakers began to attain widespread distribution. And it was here that popularity of the images became a point of contention for black feminist writers. Contemporary films by black male filmmakers, feminists argue, do not portray black women more positively than those of their white counterparts. Writer bell hooks (1992), for example, notes that Spike Lee's work "mirrors the cinematic construction of white womanhood as object, replacing her body as text on which to write male desire with the black female body" (p. 126). She contends that this process is merely "transference without transformation" (p. 126).

For black feminists, the imagistic disparity in representations of black women is problematic on two counts. First, the transference process hooks (1992) speaks of is seen as routinely reflected in films of both black and white male filmmakers; and second, the disparity is thought to distort the image of black women, culturally. In a hard-hitting critique of the content of black and white male-produced works, Guerrero (1993) asserts that:

> ...when it has come to representation of Black romance or sexuality on the screen, Hollywood has almost entirely avoided or repressed the former and to this day, has depicted the latter in the most distorted and perverse terms and images, from the romantically sanitized star vehicle of Sidney Poitier to the black woman's routine construction as the sign of the whore... [p. 238].

As black feminists see it, such habitual construction poses inherent problems because, unlike the case for other groups of women, it is feared that the negative sexual image could likely come to define black women culturally (Jones, 1993). While acknowledging that white women, too, are portrayed on screen as sex objects, black feminists intimate that white women are afforded a much broader range of characterizations. In sharp contrast, black women are habitually coded and positioned in films of the 1980s to the present within the "sign of the whore" (Jones, 1992; Guerrero, 1993), much as they were coded in those of the 1970s.

Concern over the potential of the images to impact how black women are perceived in the culture by both black and white audiences typifies the writings of most black feminists. Jones (1992) contends that the sexual roles of the last two decades assign an "accusatory space" to black women (p. 96), while Wallace (1992) decries the sexual roles for their masculinist representations. Another author, hooks (1995), is disturbed by films' failure to challenge sexist constructions of the black female body (p. 27). Kennedy (1992) points out that, in particular, Spike Lee's works are treated as a "hand-held mirror by the collective body from which to view black bodies" (p. 110). And with everyone viewing, she argues, the black community gets its sense of its shape, texture, age, and gender from its unflattering on-screen portrayals. That is, the medium offers up images that speak for the black community and define black identity. These charged critiques regarding the portrayals make clear the concern over whether black audiences, in particular, will come to identify with the negative characterizations.

We need then not just to look at the potential impact of the negative images on dominant group members' attitude toward blacks generally, but to understand why the moving image appears to have such appeal for blacks. In particular, Kennedy's (1992) above observation regarding blacks' perceived sense of self as defined by their on-screen portrayals indicates that blacks generally may be especially susceptible to the lure of media images. The danger, of course, is that in the process, they may be learning to view themselves through the eyes of creators of the images. Such filtering may be especially the case for untutored black viewers who could likely come to accept negative images of themselves and their own group.

And indeed, one can infer from the evidence that black audiences are drawn to electronic media, particularly film (Kennedy, 1992; Wallace, 1992; Parks, 1995). Parks (1995) notes that blacks get a good deal of their "cultural sustenance from films because the medium is a particularly important part of the aesthetic and informational lives of blacks" (p. 14). Parks explains:

> They interact with the immediacy of oral and visual meaning with an enthusiasm that continues to surprise distributors and theatre owners, who live outside of the black culture [p. 14].

Parks' observation suggests that blacks respond to films in a way that is not fully understood nor shared by whites, and some writers have argued that this is the case because black culture is more heavily weighted toward visual and oral traditions (Bobo, 1992; Hall, 1992; Young & Young, 1993; Parks, 1995). If so, then who constructs the on-screen images blacks view of themselves may well play a role in how blacks receive those images. That is, black filmmakers who share the visual and oral traditions of their black audiences may produce works perceived to be more powerful and authentic by these audiences than white-produced films. If that is the case, then it is all the more important to examine black-produced films for the images of black women they present. Moreover, since according to Mulvey (1989) and others, it is the male "gaze" that dominates in films that feature women's sexuality, it is especially important to examine the works of black male filmmakers for their representation of black female sexuality. As Jones (1993) so aptly puts it:

> Failure ... to address the demoralization of black [women's] characterization through the manipulation of sexuality leaves open not only the danger of recycling the same dysfunctions in black films, ... but also the likelihood of critics to define [black women] based on these relationships [p. 256].

Jones' point is a salient one, but she merely hints here at a possible similarity of the sexual imagery in black and white male-produced works. She is far more direct in stating her conclusion about the depiction of black women in films generally. The roles assigned to black women in film, she argues, "...represent the ambiguity between and the narrowness of ... two categories ... that of the bitch and that of the 'ho'" (1992, p. 96).

Cultural Ideology of the "Other"

Though black women now appear in film in greater numbers and with greater frequency, such appearances are excessively limited to portrayals of the amoral Jezebel, superwoman (Collins, 1990), prostitute, and bitch. Films such as *New Jack City, She's Gotta Have It, The Bodyguard*, and others are blatant examples of the permanence of the sexual imagery of black women. This imagistic disparity involves a complex range of cultural beliefs played out in fictionalized narratives, which the dominant culture creates and propagates. As I will illustrate in the next chapter, the form of the film medium helps drive the image. But "form" alone cannot account for profusion of the profligate imagery. To explain issues regarding Hollywood's stereotypical coding of black women's roles as expressed through their sexual behaviors necessarily requires discussion surrounding popular beliefs about these women and their sexual proclivities. Merely providing a descriptive account of how their behaviors are constructed does not tell us how film is complicit in restraining positive images of black female sexuality. Cashmore (1997) suggests that a close look at history will help uncover its "ligatures with the present" (p. 28). Apart from revealing who constructs the sexual images, mapping the historical terrain of representations helps elucidate why the on-screen images of black women are constructed as deviating from prescribed social norms.

Repetitive transmission of negative and false visual images of black female sexuality has its roots firmly fixed in a very old, cultural tradition—belief in the oversexed black female Jezebel (Collins, 1990). Historically, Jezebel was linked not only to immorality, but to "sin" (Lockyer, 1967), an idea so inimical to American Christian values that the sinful "Jezebel" was viewed as an abomination unto the Almighty. In fact, the "oversexed Jezebel" symbol dates back to biblical times (Lockyer, 1967; Vaz, 1995), and, in Western culture, has long been associated with black women (Roberts, 1994; Freydberg, 1995). Collins (1990) argues that "jezebel's function was to relegate all black women to the category of sexually aggressive women..." (p. 177). And indeed, belief in their unrestrained sexuality can be seen in how, during the 1700s and 1800s, Europeans habitually depicted, in books and other forms of literature, African women (and men) as naked and as possessing unusually large sexual organs (Roberts, 1994). Historically, whites' view of images of the naked body has been a "sexual" one (Simson, 1983); thus, applying their definition to images of the black female body laid the foundation for belief in black women as amoral. Depictions of their supposed sexual nakedness and exaggerated sexual organs then came to serve as public markings of black women's sinfulness. In turn society came to expect black women to depart from cultural norms of female modesty and virtue. Consequently, black women's bodies—their very essence—became linked to the profane. Such linkage conjured up in the white imagination images of black women as possessing animalistic sexual tendencies.

According to Jordan (1968), the perception had to do with the belief that black women were closely related in both nature and character to the orangutan, a popular notion said to have been created and written about by Thomas Jefferson. Jefferson asserted that the black woman had mated with the orangutan at some unspecified time in history, which rendered her a female animal. This was one distinct quality in black women's essence. But the first difference had to do with the perceived absence of femininity and beauty in black women. As Jefferson saw it, this absence was fixed in nature because the aspect of the Negro's color was in its reality. The reality of that difference is outlined by Jefferson when he asks the following:

> ...Is it [the difference] not the foundation of a greater or less share of beauty in the two races? Are not the fine mixture of red [the Indian] and white, the expression of every passion by greater or less suffusions of colour in the one, preferable to that eternal monotony, which reigns in the countenances of that immovable veil of black which covers all the emotions of the other race? Add to these, flowing hair, a more elegant symmetry of form, and their own judgment in favour of the whites, declared by their own preference of them, as uniformly as is the preference of the Oran-ootan [sic] for the black woman over those of his own species. The circumstances of superior beauty is thought worthy of attention in the propagation of our horses, dogs, and other domestic animals; why not in that of man [Jordan, 1968, p. 458]?

According to Jefferson's beliefs, white women represented real beauty; black women, on the other hand, possessed no physical beauty. Even the red woman (the Indian) was accorded a "greater ... share of beauty" over the black woman. Parenthetically, such attitudes might help explain why, even today in the beauty selection process, both minority and majority groups generally prefer other "ethnic" women's perceived beauty characteristics over those of black women (Bond & Cash, 1992; Taylor, 1993). Jefferson's philosophy apparently referred to black women specifically, for according to Jordan (1968), "the passage had reference not to Negro men, not to Negroes in general, but in implicit yet highly specific fashion to Negro women" (p. 464). They might not have had flowing hair nor elegant symmetry of form, but black women were sexual animals to be exploited, for had they not had relations with orangutans?

Though there was no evidence, scientific or otherwise, to support the perplexing orangutan claim, there was clear evidence of what was deemed virtuous, feminine and beautiful. Embedded in the idea of virtue was the white woman, whose female form by comparison was infused with ideas of femininity and beauty. White men held up to society as proof of her femininity white skin color, "flowing hair," "symmetry of form," and moral chasteness, sharp perceived contrasts to black women. Arguably, having been raised in such rhetorical tradition, it was inevitable that dominant group members would come to believe the latter differed from white women in both sensibilities and character. Depictions of the contra-distinction between these two subgroups of women led to an asymmetry among women. In turn, the asymmetry created an ideology of "otherness," presumably rooted in America's two-valued, either-or, ori-entation. Based on polar opposites, this world-view is evidenced in our routine "right-wrong, good-bad, black-white" mental processing (Hayakawa et al., 1990, p. 129; Lorde, 1984, p. 114). Having aligned white women to ideas of delicacy and sexual purity, the application of "other-ness" assigned to black women was well on its way to becoming complete: the white female form would come to represent universally the "femi-nine" as well as the cultural standardized ideal of beauty; black women's bodies, on the other hand, would come to be viewed as symbols of sex-ual excess, unattractiveness, and immorality—as the deviant sexual "other."

Such dichotomous characterizations had a far-reaching impact on both sets of women, which is what makes the same-gender female dual-ism so interesting. A paradoxical effect of the split, felt even today, is the implied sexual freedom women of the dominant group can more easily express without much public condemnation compared to black women (Wilson & Russell, 1997). Because the white female form represents the "feminine" and all that the feminine implies, beauty, gentility, and vir-ginity (Christian, 1985), membership in the dominant group automati-cally grants white women credibility as women of virtue. So that on the individual level, those who engage in serial sexual exploits of whatever kind, for example, can always refashion themselves back into symbols of virtue and the "feminine." This is because—and this point is of extreme importance—on the aggregate level, group membership allows for per-ceived sexual virtue. No matter how sexually debased a particular woman of this group behaves, with a bit of effort, she can reinvent herself once again; group membership generally assures this.

Perceptions of black women's reputed socio-sexual experience, on the other hand, have had quite a different effect. On the aggregate level, this subgroup has inherited the dubious distinction of being perceived and labeled as symbols of sexual wantonness which, on the individual level, mark each black woman. So that no matter how virtuous the black woman, no matter how feminine, she is more likely than not to be viewed as hypersexed because black women's virtue has had no place in the "fem-inine" mythos of U.S. culture. From the onset, then, the "other" ideology has covertly provided a space for the sexual expression of the one group of women held up as virtuous; conversely, it has overtly placed a wide net of sexual imputation onto the group of women least capable of deflect-ing attention away from their lurid public imaging. For to successfully offer counterexamples to any negative imaging requires having control of the information flow within a given culture.

Thus, while analysis of the effect of same-gender dualism on black women is of vital concern, we need to understand not just the role of the racial-gender split in the life and arts of the dominant group in relation to blackness; we need also to consider how control of the dominant mode of communication was employed to advance the same-gender split. Morrison (1992) illustrates how white writers used black presence in their works to improve their cultural image by representing blacks as "other" (p. xi). Absent an oppositional gaze through which to counter the devaluation of blacks generally, "blackness" symbolically split into polarized selves; transformed into signs of the "sexual," the "savage," and the "beast"; while "whiteness" remained pure, undifferentiated, whole, and universal. Portrayal of such binary opposites was a striking revelation of what Hall (1997) and Feagin & Vera (1995) contend is whites' view of themselves versus how they see "others." And such appears to have been the case. For how blacks in general and black women in particular were defined and socially constructed in relation to whiteness nearly always pointed to an opposite of the positive. Gilman (1985) argues that, for whites, evidence of black women's sexual deviance (unlike the white female's) was rooted in the black female's protruded buttocks. Hooks (1992), too, makes a similar claim, asserting that the black woman's "...protruding butt [was] seen as an indication of a heightened sexuality" (p. 65). This protruding icon-of-sexual-deviant ideology closely mirrored Jefferson's orangutan ideas, promoting a public perception of black women as possessing animalistic sexual tendencies (Jordan, 1968; Omolade, 1983; Palmer, 1983; Roberts, 1994). As has been seen, the thinking was steeped in popular assumptions held regarding black women's presumed "would-be" departure from society's moral and sexual codes of behavior—the very behaviors now shown in films featuring black women. Intemperance in attitude, hence, helped fuel the negative stereotypes accrued around the black female form. Such beliefs in turn established not just a racial hierarchy, but a female hierarchy among black and white women as well, setting the stage for the practice of female polarization both culturally and in the arts. Freydberg (1995) notes that repeated negative images of the black female body continued to appear in white literature well into the 20th century, successfully permeating the collective mind-set. Undergirded by the culture's two-valued orientation, the then-dominant mode of communication, literature, promulgated an "us-them" mentality, achieved through much of its pictorials. So that even to the illiterate eye, print's lurid visuals easily conveyed the message of a hierarchical social construction of womanhood, black women graphically depicted as sexual deviants.

In light of the dual construction both in the popular mind-set and in the literary arts, the black Jezebel mythos has had a staying power to rival no other. Popularized since the inception of slavery, lack of proportionality in their negative depictions served as a kind of metaphoric rape of black women, achieved through the persistent debasement of this subgroup. And this was the case even as images of their white counterparts uplifted that subgroup of women. Having been fed on a diet rich in stereotypes, many in this latter group distanced themselves, becoming indifferent to the socially constructed female dualism as played out in the culture. Consequently, collective oblivion brought the process of female polarization closer to legitimacy. As it was then, so it is today. Routine negative images of black female sexuality in what can be termed a divisive film culture keep many oblivious regarding how female polarization is still operational in the cultural psyche. And indeed, Frankenberg (1993) concludes from her research on white women that whiteness is still "difficult for white people to name.... Those who are securely housed within its borders usually do not examine it" (pp. 228–229).

From the onset, then, the deviant "other" ideology served to fuel the negative stereotype of black women as "oversexed," which, in U.S. culture, has lasted up to the present day with little questioning from audiences. That the promiscuous Jezebel stereotype effectively shifted from the literary arts (Anderson, 1997, Freydberg, 1995) to its cinematic equivalent was to be expected. Although the "mammy" image enjoyed a long spate in U.S. literary arts, for example, quantitatively, that image cannot now match the explosion of sexual images of black womanhood offered in contemporary American film. Bogle (1989) argues that stereotypes about blacks generally

> ...were merely filmic reproductions of black stereotypes that had existed since the days of slavery and were already popularized in American life and arts. The movies, which catered to public tastes, borrowed profusely from all the other popular art forms [p. 4].

When film became one of the popular forms of mass mediated message systems and began to represent black characters, the medium "...simply adopted the old familiar stereotypes, often further distorting them beyond recognition" (Bogle, 1989, p. 4). Such visual distortion was particularly directed toward black women, as evidenced in the film *Birth of a Nation* (1915). Bogle (1989) observes that to represent black women characters, the film used white performers with blackened faces to divide black women into color categories; thus, establishing three major images for black women: the "Tragic Mulatto" was "cinnamon-colored," unlike the "Mammy" and "Aunt Jemima" types, both of whom were depicted as middle-aged and so dark-skinned that it was "preposterous even to suggest that [they] be [considered] sex object[s]" (p. 14). As a result, they were "de-sexed," unlike the tragic mulatto, who was a girl of mixed blood. Her divided racial inheritance, however, led to an unhappy life (Christian, 1985; Bogle, 1989); still, she was graced with much "sex appeal."

Putting aside for the moment the way in which *Birth of a Nation* categorized black women, a look at the function of blackface in the film is revealing. For whites in blackface served two major purposes. Diawara (1993) argues that a primary reason a mostly white cast was featured in the film was to protect the purity of white womanhood on the set. This fear, of course, centered around widely held beliefs about the black male's insatiable appetite for white women's bodies. A second, perhaps more sinister reason is furnished by Modleski (1991). She notes that from its inception, it has been the tendency of film to cast white people in blackface in order to suggest that "blackness may be so monstrous it can only be signified but not directly represented" (p. 118). The importance of Modleski's observation lies in her explanation of the way in which blackface collapses blackness into allegorical "otherness." To deal with blacks directly requires a verisimilitude which, of necessity, must acknowledge the full humanity of blacks. But such a depiction would only serve to negate the very ideology the dominant group had promoted—the "threat" of black monstrosity. If presented in humane terms, blackness could not, then, signify "otherness"; thus, the use of blackface.

It becomes clear that the purpose of blackface in *Birth of a Nation* was a means of maintaining and supporting the negative associations accrued around blackness; its function, then, was to signify the black female form, the tragic mulatto image being the most palatable to white viewers. She was not white, but neither was she quite black! Here again, Jefferson's "greater ... share of beauty" ideology surfaces. Bogle (1989) argues that prior to the 1970s, "every sexy black woman who appeared ... in movies was to be a "cinnamon-colored gal" with Caucasian features" (p. 15). He contends, however, that these women were too often cast as whores and as women at odds with society. Mapp (1972) echoes a similar view. He argues that the black female as "hot mamas" is as old as the motion picture medium itself. Not only a bad girl, she was capable of bringing "white males to manhood" (pp. 228–229). In fact, save for the "Mammy" and "Aunt Jemima" images, the "tragic mulatto" was the only image of black women found on screen prior to the 1970s. Bogle (1989) asserts that being closest both in color and features to the white beauty ideal, the tragic mulatto generally had a chance at lead roles. Dark-skinned actresses, however, were "considered for no [filmic] role but that of a mammy or an Aunt Jemima," a practice which continued well into the 1960s (p. 15).

Then, with the movie boom of the 1970s (Leab, 1975), especially Melvin Van Peebles' defiant and successful film, *Sweet Sweetback's Baadasssss Song* (1971) which portrayed black women as overtly "sexual" (Bowser, 1981), the film medium appears to have recognized the economic potential in portraying black female characters as excessively oversexed. It might even be that, given its visual and rapid mode of communication, the medium adventitiously discovered itself a potential vehicle for the advance of negative imagery of black female sexuality. The bonus here would be that voice needn't have been accorded a given stereotypical message; one moving image acted as surrogate for a thousand words! Hence, what once operated primarily in folklore and in literature now took on heightened meaning because the imagery was particularly well suited to the medium's explicit and magnified imaging. The marriage of myth and the moving image established a symbiotic union, successfully recreating the lurid mythological narrative; the "oversexed" stereotype had found a new home in this vivid message system, film, which freely dispensed the myth.

That filmic images helped promote a climate of misrecognition of black women by explicitly, vividly and repeatedly carrying forward the "other" ideology of black women's sexuality helps explain the stereotype's staying power today. Combine film's explicitness with its unlimited potential for metaphor and allegory, one that surpasses that of other media (Gianetti 1972; Boyum, 1985), and the persuasiveness of the image becomes better understood. Kracauer (1947) proffers that while other media generate information about the social attitudes of a culture, film exceeds these media in its inclusiveness because its narrative and visuals reflect the deep structure of the "collective unconscious" of a culture.

Wolfenstein & Leites (1950) point to the concept of "day-dreams" to explain film's role in the "collective unconscious" of a society. They intimate that just as "day-dreams" contain "clues" to the underlying "fears, wishes and dreams" of the individual (p. 11), so, too, films can act on a deeper psychological level to symbolize the hidden fears and desires of the collective unconscious. For if "...people share a common culture, they are likely to have certain day-dreams in common" (p. 13). But it is here that a culture's collective beliefs and attitudes can have devastating effects on social "others," for such "day-dreams" often can close the gap between myth and reality, thereby crystalizing a given stereotype. This is especially the case when cultural members are deprived of a mechanism through which to challenge the merits of a given stereotype, a point to which I will return shortly.

Not only do members of the dominant culture within a society share certain daydreams; cultural members are also directed into conforming to that culture's beliefs. Direction is typically achieved through a culture's dominant mode of communication. Further, that culture determines how other cultural subgroups will be defined (Bem, 1993), because it is the dominant culture which controls the flow of social information within a given society (Postman, 1979; Meyrowitz, 1985). More and more in U.S. culture, definitions of cultural subgroups have come to be disseminated chiefly through electronic media, film being one of the dominant modes of communication. Considering film's capacity to reach a wide, general audience, on-screen repetition of negative stereotypes of black female sexuality has given it room to grow and be preserved within the collective body. Over time, hence, filmic content helped shape viewers' conceptions of reality (Gerbner, 1986; Signorielli, 1989) by vividly exposing audiences to a limited model of black women's socio-sexual experiences. The stereotype's shift from print to film also worked to decontextualize black women's "other" status, removing it from its historical roots and placing it in the here and now. This transference process has gone unquestioned by the general populace for generations, circulating throughout the culture, first orally, then through literature, and finally through film. But collective oblivion, combined with the reality that the medium's images are far more extreme than in real life, have called into question how audiences might receive such images. Indeed, where it concerns audience response, the transference process gives rise to one of many inherent contradictions.

Generally, film has claimed to reflect social reality, the suggestion being that whatever images it portrays are reflective of subjects' actual lived experiences. Upon closer inspection, however, such a claim becomes specious. For film cannot, on the one hand, claim that it merely reflects social reality, but on the other hand, claim that it has no effect on viewers' perception of reality. If film is a reflection of social reality, presumably its images are faithful portrayals of the social experiences of the various subgroups it claims to represent. The message its images convey, therefore, must be viewed by audiences as at least containing some measure of truth; otherwise, what reality are the images reflective of? It is true that film cannot determine how viewers will respond; yet, we know viewers do interpret images in some way (Hall, 1980; Bobo, 1992, 1995). The question is, what parts of filmic narratives should audiences accept as valid and what parts should they reject? Indeed, where in filmic narratives is the mechanism that will help viewers decide which images of impersonal social "others" are true reflections and which are false? Nowhere has the industry admitted to presenting a false reality; only that it reflects reality. The assumption, then, must be that its reflection accurately mirrors the social experiences of cultural others.

Where images of black female sexuality are concerned, it is precisely because film purports to mirror black women's socio-sexual experiences that the images offered take on social significance. Even taking into account popular folklore of the past, film has provided perhaps the most explicit and vivid conceptions of the image of black women as "oversexed." Writers, in fact, suggest that film plays a significant role in how viewers perceive and come to understand black women culturally (hooks, 1992, 1995; Hall, 1988; Jones, 1993). If this is the case, ignorance of black women's lives combined with their persistent negative stereotyping is particularly troubling. For it must be understood that relegating black women's roles almost exclusively to the "sexual" clearly has inherent problems. The skewed presentation of black women's on-screen characterization raises questions of "What is the meaning associated with black women and their sexual experiences as presented in film?" "How do members of society understand black women based on their filmic representation?" and "What is the potential impact based on how black women are coded on the big screen?"

These questions arise from film's ability to simultaneously reach a mass audience, giving it a noticeable influence on mass-beliefs about diverse subgroups (Friedman, 1991). And the fact that most Americans still live and socialize among people of their own group (Tobin, 1987; Entman, 1994), while simultaneously, they are immersed in vivid cinematic representations of their own and others' cultures helps close, exponentially, any "credibility" gap between cultural sexual stereotypes about black women and the filmic images offered. With few personal experiences with which to compare the mediated image, viewers are left with no other options but to accept, as valid representations, the images presented. Any argument, therefore, that film has no effect on viewers' perception of reality is weakened by the medium's very claim that it is a reflection of reality. Audiences do not receive images in a vacuum (White, 1983); there must be some residual impact.

A major reason film has been effective in perpetuating the "black-woman-as-sexual-other" ideology, then, is that its vivid images are presented as reflecting the truth. And because the act of viewing a film generally affords little time in which to examine the truth or falsity of a negative image, in-depth analysis of the stereotype's origin is not encouraged. Certainly, Hollywood has shown little interest in countering the negative image! There is only presentation of the profligate image housing the stereotype. In a sense, it is as if the very existence of the image makes the stereotype real. As I will illustrate in Chapter 2, such is the nature of film; the immediacy of the medium adds credibility to the negative stereotype.

Where do filmmakers fit into this process? Apart from being creators of their works, filmmakers are, themselves, products of and contributors to the cultures to which they belong. Presumably, they, too, also share in those cultural ideology and attitudes as reflected in film. Still, black male filmmakers differ from white male filmmakers in one major respect. Unlike the latter, black male filmmakers share a history of sexual oppression with black women which, according to Gilman (1985), has defined the black female body as an "icon for deviant sexuality." Indeed, so powerful has been this belief that it remains firmly fixed within U.S. culture, even today. St. Jean & Feagin (1998) note that "[m]yths about wanton black women abound in this society" (p. 101), where black women are still perceived as sexual gratifiers (Jordan, 1968; Gutman, 1976; Simson, 1983; hooks, 1992, 1995). Thus, whether as in the 1700s or as today, whether educated or untutored, black women have been unable to rid themselves of the deviant sexual stereotype.

Nor has the black male been spared of his own set of negative sexual stereotypes (Jordan, 1968; Leab, 1975; Bogle, 1989; Diawara, 1993). He, too, has been accused of being "oversexed and savage ... as [he] lusts for white [women's] flesh" (Bogle, 1989, p. 13). Historically, in fact, black men have been viewed as symbols of rape, charged with plotting to commit sexual assaults on women of the dominant group, what Cash (1941) calls the "Southern rape complex." According to Cash (1941), during Reconstruction, slaveholders imagined bands of dehumanized black men bent on raping white women for the purpose of revenge. Cash notes that "what the Southerners felt was that any assertion of any kind on the part of the Negro constituted in a perfectly real manner, an attack on the Southern woman..." (p. 115). Though Lerner (1972) argues "there were no records of the rape and violation of white women..." (p. 180) by hordes of black men, the belief persisted well into the 20th century. Black men's shared history of racial and sexual oppression with black women, thus, indicates that black male filmmakers should hold more positive views of black women's sexuality. Their depictions, therefore, would be expected to be more sensitively portrayed.

From their vantage point, white filmmakers, on the other hand, might be expected to hold more negative ideas of black female sexuality.

The literature on the black woman's sexual history in U.S. culture suggests that both her blackness and female form have evoked and embodied all of the hidden sexual fantasies and desires that have captured white men's imagination since the beginning of slavery (Stampp, 1956; Jordan, 1968; Gilman, 1985; hooks, 1981, 1995).

According to Stampp (1956), during slavery, slaveholders' easy sexual access to black women extended to their neighbors and to their young sons who were eager for initiation into the mysteries of sex (p. 355). Given that white men had almost institutionalized sexual access to black women with little fear of actual reprisals, black female slaves generally had little or no power of refusal (Brownmiller, 1975; St. Jean & Feagin, 1998). Despite such widespread violation, black women were then accused of sexual promiscuity (Brownmiller, 1975; Omolade, 1983; Collins, 1990). Gutman (1976) indicates that the stereotype owes not a little to historian Phillip A. Bruce (*The Plantation Negro as a Freeman*, 1889). Bruce asserted that black women were "openly licentious," "morally obtuse," and worse than black men because as women, it was their responsibility to shape the institution of marriage, which Bruce saw as the safeguard against promiscuity. Even the sexually-potent black male stereotype was based on black women's promiscuous reputation. Bruce's thinking, according to Gutman (1976), was that to satisfy such hot-natured women, the black male had to be especially potent. The "wantonness of the women of his own race," for Bruce, explained the black male's proclivity to rape (p. 536). Beyond these claims, Omolade (1983) observes that when European men first encountered the African, these men viewed the African woman's "expression of sensuality through public rites ... and dances as evidence of the absence of any sexual codes of behavior..." (p. 351).

Together, these historical beliefs have fueled the sexual stereotype of black women as symbols of sexual excess. Given the symbol's long history in American culture, handed down from generation to generation and, within the dominant culture, from father to son, presumably, most white males are at least aware of the stereotype. Considering their intergenerational cultural training, therefore, white male filmmakers' portrayals of black female sexuality would be expected to be represented in more sexually-explicit ways.

Though black feminist writers claim there is no difference in portrayals, this study should reveal how the portrayals compare in the films of black and white male filmmakers. I am not concerned with any one filmmaker's vision of black female sexuality; my interest, rather, is with what the films as a group reveal about perceptions of black female sexuality, and whether black male filmmakers represent black women more positively than do their white male counterparts. In both studies, therefore, no two films share the same filmmaker.

The question remains, might black and white male filmmakers' works, when taken together, reflect certain cultural attitudes about black women? How are black women represented sexually in the popular films of black male filmmakers? How are they represented sexually in the popular films of white male filmmakers? And how does the representation of black female sexuality as articulated by both sets of male filmmakers compare? These questions prompt other important questions. To what extent do representations of black female sexuality in the films found available for this study deviate from expected sexual codes of behaviors for women in general? To what extent are these representations perpetuated by black and white male filmmakers? And how do the representations impact black women culturally? These questions frame the remainder of the book.

Black Women at the Margins of Film Study

The relevant literature on black women's representation in film evidences a notable lack of systematic study in the investigation of black female sexuality. What predominates in this scarce realm of scholarship are textual analyses which tend to be sociological (Painter, 1992), historical (Roberts, 1994; Freydberg, 1995), or interpretive (hooks, 1981, 1992, 1996). It is to their credit that these attempts have provided valuable insight into Hollywood's construction of black women and their sexuality, which, in turn, helps shed light on those filmic structures that can limit inclusion of underrepresented groups. Still, there remains a need for a specific and systematic area of inquiry regarding black women's cinematic portrayals that has not as yet been addressed by media scholars: Do black and white filmmakers differ in their representations of black female sexuality, and if so, how?

Generally, black feminist literature on the filmic treatment of black women's sexuality suggests that films featuring black female characters contain certain sexual elements that are routinely applied to black female characters. Hooks (1992), for example, asserts that black female characters are depicted as "sexual outside the context of marriage"; are portrayed as more "sexually free" and "sexually ready"; are depicted as being "on the make"; and are coded to be synonymous with "prostitution," "accessibility," and "availability" (pp.62–69). Other writers contend that black female characters are portrayed as "initiating sexual encounters" (Jones, 1993, p. 253), and are more likely to be shown "unclothed, in bed, and in the midst of coitus" (Painter, 1992, p. 210). I redress the lack in systematic study by engaging in a comparative content analysis inquiry of ten popular American films from—1986–1995 and six films from 1997–2001 to discover whether the claims of black feminist writers are supported by the evidence.

The method of inquiry used in the study is a quantitative (but nonstatistical) content analysis of films by black and white male filmmakers, five each per set of filmmakers for one time period and three each per set of filmmakers for the other (See Appendix A). Employing a content analysis inquiry allows for the teasing out and categorizing of units of a character's behaviors found in films. Nafziger & White (1963) note that:

> A character, or person, or class of persons is sometimes used as a coding unit in content analysis. All relevant information about the character is sifted out of the article or story [or film] and classified [p. 189].

Berelson (1952) suggests that a content analysis provides a highly objective and scientific method for describing the content of a communication behavior. Thus, a content analysis schedule also allows researchers control of the variables, thereby assuring a high degree of reliable conclusions. Holsti (1969) explains that if, in the operational definition, the researcher specifies those variables which determine whether a given unit of behavior falls within the category defined:

> A good operational definition satisfies two requirements: it is a valid representation of the analyst's concepts, and it is sufficiently precise that it guides coders to produce reliable judgments [p. 95].

If the claims of black feminists that certain sexual elements routinely applied to black female characters are to have any value, this method of inquiry seems the most useful.

Hence, the study of the content of ten films from one time period and six films from another by black and white male filmmakers was analyzed with respect to the representation of the sexuality of the major female characters using an instrument developed for this purpose (the *Sexual Behavioral Film Analysis* Scale—SBFA). The black female characters' sexual behaviors were initially coded on fourteen (14) items, each consisting of a set of subitems on the film analysis instrument. These items were then clustered into eight (8) categories for the analysis of the black filmmakers' and white filmmakers' films. The eight categories were further collapsed into four (4) categories to simplify the comparison of the sexual representations in the two sets of films, and to highlight major dimensions of the female characters' sexual characterization. These four categories address the diversity of the black female characters' roles and relationships (both with men and with others), as represented in the films; the sexual attitudes of the black female characters; the nonverbal and verbal sexual behaviors of the black female characters; and the attitudes of the male characters toward the black females.

While similarities were found among the above four (4) categories, notable differences were also found which fell into four (4) distinct areas: role diversity of the females; their sexual aggressiveness as initiators of the "pick-up" and of the sex act; their interest in men as persons versus their sexual interest; and their display of anger/hostility toward the males. The major findings in these latter four (4) categories, with respect to the films as a whole and to differences between the films of black and white male filmmakers, will be discussed in Chapter 5.

Chapter Outline

Before delineating the upcoming chapters, I wish briefly to clarify my use of certain terms. I use the terms "sexual image" and "images of black female sexuality" to mean a filmmaker's visual portrayal of sexual behaviors (implied or explicit) related (directly or indirectly) to the sensual rather than the cerebral, which generally attract men to women. Sexual behaviors are divided here into nonverbal and verbal behaviors. Nonverbal behaviors are observable acts, revealed through expressive action, such as touching, kissing, making eye contact, engaging in sexual intercourse, and so forth. The terms "black women" and "black American women" are used interchangeably. Each is used herein to mean any female character identifiable by phenotype, such as color and facial features culturally interpreted as Negroid; cultural behaviors whose meanings are interpreted according to values and norms established by the in-group; and/or cultural signifiers of shared experiences. The term "filmmakers" denotes the writer of the screenplay and the director of the film, both of whom must be of the same race in order to avoid cultural misinterpretations.

Chapter 2, "The Form of the Film Medium: Visual Images and Viewer Perception," examines the form of the visual medium, and explores the process by which the film medium influences viewers. I further briefly situate the different theories of "media effects" within their assigned eras, showing how changes in both the technology and in society altered research on the effects of media on public perception. Chapter 3, "Love and Romance: Cultural Prescriptive for 'Appropriate' Sexual Behaviors for Men and Women," explores how love is portrayed in film based on different expectations of sexual behaviors for males and females. I next illustrate how black women's sexual behaviors on screen are coded such that the behaviors are akin to those generally applied to males in U.S. culture. I also show how film perpetuates cultural attitudes held about black women in its formulaic construction of black womanhood, and illustrate how such constructions limit the roles black actresses can occupy on screen. Chapter 4, "Cultural Impact of Film's Imaging on Black Women," explores how film's stigmatization of black women affects these women's marital status by contributing to black males' dismissive attitude toward black women. I then show how such attitudes can adversely impact the black family. Chapter 5, "Similar, but Different," reports the findings of both studies by providing a discussion of the similarities and differences evidenced in the films of black and white male filmmakers. Chapter 6 considers "Implications of the Incongruity in Black Filmmakers' Depictions of the Black Female's Nonsexual Rolse." I also illustrate how the images can adversely impact young black girls, and I speculate about why deviation in the images is made more explicit by black male filmmakers. Chapter 7 is the Conclusion section wherein I discuss what in the culture needs to change to perhaps alter the (mis)representation. Additionally, I provide recommendations for further study in this section. Appendix A is a list of the sixteen films coded in the two studies, and Appendix B reproduces the scale rating the importance of sexual contact behaviors in the films.

2

The Form of the Film Medium: Visual Images and Viewer Perception

The relationship between media and conceptions of cultural reality has long been an area of concern to most media theorists. Scholars such as McLuhan (1964, 1969), Innis (1977), Postman (1979, 1985), and Meyrowitz (1985) intimate that rather than being neutral tools, media create environments for social interactions, changing not just the speed of transmission and the volume of messages, but the very nature of the messages. This is because the "medium [itself] is the message" (McLuhan, 1964, p. 24). In other words, regardless of the surface "content" of a given message, the form of each message system creates its own messages, which then shape both the culture and individuals within that culture (McLuhan, 1964, pp. 23–35). Thus, the structure of any communication medium is a determinant of the content that medium produces, which in turn controls the scale and form of human interaction. Indeed, any change in the dominant medium of communication influences not just the culture to which it belongs, but produces a change at every other institutional level of that culture. Thus, for example, a culture dominated by "time-biased" medium—print—will emphasize tradition, religion, and

32

hierarchical organizations. In contrast, a culture dominated by "space-biased" media, TV and film, emphasizes expansion, politics, centralized governments, and bureaucratic organizations (Innis, 1977). Accordingly, print and electronic media are associated with different types of cultures, each producing its own form of social interactions. Postman (1979) argues that each medium, from speech, to print, to electronic, is contextual. Each creates a different view of the world for a particular culture; each carries an epistemological bias to tell cultural members where truth lies, how to find it, and what is worth knowing about and studying (pp. 16–29). It is from these perspectives that film as a dominant means of communication in U.S. culture takes on social significance. For almost from its inception, the medium has been a "potent message system" (Gerbner, 1967) through which most Americans socially construct meaning.

Through the film vehicle, ideas about culturally-accepted values, beliefs, and behaviors are transmitted. Most media researchers have explored the socializing nature of film as it represents cultural ideas, myths, and fantasies (Kracauer, 1947; Wolfenstein & Leites, 1950; Rosen, 1973; Tudor, 1974; Sklar, 1975; Jowett & Linton, 1980). It has been found, for example, that people formulate ideas about diverse cultural subgroups with whom they have no direct contact primarily from mediated sources (Bandura, 1986: Friedman, 1991; Entman, 1994). Whatever the source, whatever the idea, media information is transmitted chiefly through visual images (McLuhan, 1964; Boorstin, 1977). Representations of black women, it is alleged, are typically transmitted in the form of unflattering filmic images.

But the film industry has long engaged in disclaimers regarding perpetuation of its negative content regarding any one social group. Still, that black women's cinematic coding as the "mammy" dominated the screen up through the 1960s (Anderson, 1997; Bogle, 1989; Modleski, 1991) cannot be denied. What is also undeniable is that the "mammy's" dominance on screen abated at the end of the 1960s only to be replaced in the 1970s by the appearance of the dominant "oversexed" black female predator. Metamorphosed from "mammy" to "oversexed," the image has permeated U.S. culture for nearly thirty years, becoming what is by now a tradition (hooks, 1992; Painter, 1992). Similarly, as discussed in Chapter 1, the images have historically reflected some form of negative symbolic ideology (hooks, 1992; Young, 1993; Roberts, 1994; Freydberg, 1995), whether that of the culture (Mellen, 1973; Mulvey, 1989), the individual filmmaker, or both (Haskell, 1973, 1987; Rosen, 1973).

Determining which factor accounts for the negative imaging, however, is a complicated business. But if, as has been suggested, popular films express the ideology of society in general more than they do the ideology of ethnic subgroups, it may be that black and white male filmmakers offer quite similar representations of black female sexuality. For it has been suggested that habitual exposure to multiple media, each generating similar images, provides some indication of how an image can so infiltrate a culture that even black filmmakers sustain it in their work (Bogle, 1973/1989; hooks, 1992). If the artist's membership in a particular racial group, however, plays a larger role in shaping his work than does the dominant ideology of the society at large, black and white male filmmakers may portray black women quite differently. A close look at the representation of black women in black and white male filmmakers' works can help us see if there is a distinction.

The likelihood of any one filmmaker admitting to portrayals of unflattering sexual images of any woman, let alone black women, is slim. And considering that we now live in a climate of political correctness, anti-black female stereotypes are rarely expressed verbally and in public. They tend, instead, to be vividly and overtly shown in living color, via the celluloid reel in the form of visual images. In this way, the dominant and negative symbolic ideology of black women can potentially be propagated and culturally maintained (hooks, 1981, 1996; St. Jean & Feagin, 1998). The film medium, in fact, acts as an effective tool in driving the negative ideology about black women within the larger culture (Hall, 1995). But just how does this ideology operate in film?

One primary way to maintain any ideology is through the process of repetition; for if a thing is repeated long enough, it tends to assume a life of its own. As I argued in an earlier section, repetition has been key to preserving the cultural stereotype of the "oversexed black Jezebel." Repetition, it seems, lies at the heart of influencing learning, particularly that gleaned from the media (Leab, 1975; Gerbner, 1986). And perhaps nowhere else is repetition more potent in influencing viewers' conception of reality than in the moving image, film.

In his research on the role of television in influencing viewers' constructions of reality, Gerbner (1986) contends that "...the repetitious patterns of mass-produced ... images form the mainstream of a common symbolic environment" (p. 20). Applying Gerbner's (1967) "mainstreaming" theory to film, Jowett & Linton (1980) describe this "mainstreaming" process as a visual public "consensus" (p. 75) whereby film transfers individual perspectives into "broad public perspectives" (Gerbner, 1967). The process is achieved by providing audiences with a constant supply of tried-and-true story-formulas, images and characters (Jowett & Linton, 1980, pp. 74–75). Public consensus is also achieved by reinforcing the beliefs, attitudes, and values of the dominant ideology of American society, what Linton (1978) refers to as "dramas of reassurances" (Jowett & Linton, 1980, p. 109). Presumably such dramas work to satisfy dominant group members' curiosity about who various social "others" are. For film "...ha[s] made a significant contribution to the collective vision we all have of things about which we know very little" (Jowett & Linton, 1980, p. 75). But these dramas may also work to reinforce any jingoistic attitudes dominant group members may hold toward cultural "others." Whatever the case, film's mainstreaming process is further accentuated by the creation of an inaccessible "reality," transporting viewers outside of their own cultural experiences into those of a wider cross-section of the culture. So that where members of the dominant group lack direct exposure to cultural "others," film's dramas of reassurance provide the former with explanations and definitions of the latter.

While the extent to which film influences behavior is still not entirely clear, it is known that film has contributed to the overall cultural perspective viewers have of society and of social "others" (Gerbner, 1967). Because of this, the processes involved in directing viewers to perceive film's visually defined exhibition of impersonal subjects' social experiences have become a point of contention for many underrepresented groups (hooks, 1992; Sethi, 1998; Manatu-Rupert, 2000). Indeed, these processes have served to give film its status of what has been called a "...'massive' socializing force on a national scale" (Jowett & Linton, 1980, p. 73).

Significantly, film's socializing influence chiefly depends on its dramas of reassurance because such dramas resonate with the dominant beliefs of U.S. culture (Jowett & Linton, 1980, p. 109). As we have seen, it is generally thought that members of the mainstream cultural group are likely to share in the beliefs, attitudes, and dreams of that particular culture (Wolfenstein & Leites, 1950; Jowett & Linton, 1980). It is also the case that many, if not most, members of marginalized groups likewise share, at least on a subconscious level, the beliefs, attitudes, and dreams of the dominant culture (Frazier, 1957; hooks, 1992, 1995; Yamato, 1998). So that even negative ideas projected in the media about underrepresented groups are likely to be believed by certain members of those very groups.

Gerbner (1986) uses his "cultivation" theory to explain that it is the "cumulative" effect of media images, acquired from infancy, that "cultivates" people's attitudes and ideas about social reality (p. 20). Leab (1975) argues that though film is limited in its power to permanently influence viewers, "constant repetition that emphasizes certain stereotypes—as is the case with the black presence on screen—is overpowering. And this reinforcement has residual effects even when the stereotypes have begun to change" (p. 263). Thus, despite the diverse make-up of the American population, for example, film still captures and holds the imagination of cultural members at large because film is a "logical extension and recombination of existing elements in the folk-popular culture continuum" (Jowett & Linton, 1980, p. 70). Moreover, because film is a "mass cultur[al] product ... designed to please the average taste of an undifferentiated audience..." (p. 17), film is said to have a socializing influence on cultural beliefs and attitudes.

Film's influence, however, tends to be generally more subtle and less explicit in its transmission of specific behaviors than, say, that accomplished in schools or in the family. These latter sources "formally" instruct individuals into proper and acceptable behaviors which then serve the interests of the culture to which they belong. But according to social learning theorist Albert Bandura (1977), at the same time, "both children and adults acquire attitudes [and] emotional response ... through film and televised modeling" (p. 39), allowing people to "...acquire large integrated patterns of behavior without having to form them gradually by tedious trial and error" (p. 12). This may explain why viewers who lack direct exposure to different social groups are particularly susceptible to media images' definitions of impersonal social others.

Such modeling suggests that the role of observational learning is vital to the social transmission process (Bandura, 1977, 1986). Indeed, the suggestion has been made that observational learning may be a driving force in preserving cultural ideas and attitudes about cultural subgroups (Mellen, 1973; Hall, 1995; Yamato, 1998), a process appearing so natural and universal that it is rarely seen as based on role-modeling. Yet, it is here, through this process of role-modeling, that film can eclipse the "formal" sources of instruction, often extending learning well beyond the direct experiences of individuals. In a subtle manner, viewers frequently are influenced to view events and different social groups in an excessively simplistic and fragmented manner.

Film, however, does not in itself have an "unlimited capacity to directly affect [viewers'] behavior..." as it has "influence through a complex set of cultural ... factors" (White, 1983, p. 281). If, for example, we still lived in a predominantly print-oriented culture with print's insistence on logically-ordered assertions (Ong, 1981) and its tendency toward contemplative thinking, viewers might then be educated to distinguish between misleading images and authentic ones. Any negative social attitudes reflected in film about, say, women and their sexuality, might then be refuted as a matter of course.

But it is evident that we now live in a visual culture, where McLuhan (1964), among others, points out that the visual image has supplanted print's place at the center of the culture, thus shifting print to the periphery. In other words, contemplative thinking is being replaced by visual imageries, which themselves are exempt from reflection because of the fragmented, symbolic, and persuasive nature of the moving image (Boorstin, 1977). Thus, when one looks at film, one is met with a set of ideograms in the form of simplistic, context-free images, where questions of the truth or falsity of an image generally do not apply (Postman, 1979).

Herein lies black women's dilemma. For how does one refute a visual image? Indeed, how does anyone refute repetitive, rapid-fire images of behaviors deemed "immoral" in a society, with little or no time in which to do so? Whatever it may communicate, film is a medium of communication, but it is a one-way form of communication. Postman (1979) notes that there is no refuting the images because media images are not propositional. One either likes the images or one does not. Likewise, filmic images are not refutable because, being "affect-centered" (Postman, 1979), the images are more heavily weighted toward emotional responses. Film's ability to simulate reality makes it an effective tool in provoking strong feelings and attitudes, particularly attitudes regarding cultural myths about social "others."

Even less obvious is the speed with which viewers are bombarded with massive amounts of pre-selected visual information. During their unfolding, for example, filmic images do not generally invite critical discourse, if only because the speed of the medium takes social events and social groups out of their context and sequence (McLuhan, 1964; Boorstin, 1977; Meyrowitz, 1985), often for the sake of dramatic effect (Atkins, 1992; Gray, 1995; Cashmore, 1997).Unlike print's imaging which provides readers of texts with time in which to reflect and muse about the actuality of a given character's world, the speed with which visual information is made accessible to viewers is a point on which McLuhan (1964), Meyrowitz (1985) and others have commented. McLuhan (1964) explains that film, in particular, has the power to "convey a great deal of information" (p. 252) because it takes viewers out of the world of sequence and linear connections into one of configuration and images (p. 27). Film's visual form operates quite differently from print. The moving image takes preference over substantive information (Boorstin, 1977) because people and events are often presented within a collage of ahistorical and disparate images, pieced together to provide a framework within which to explain who impersonal "others" really are. And it is by way of such visual configurations that viewers often come to believe they actually "know" impersonal "others" and how those "others" live.

But it is not merely the mode of the film medium which contributes to preserving cultural beliefs and attitudes; it is also repeated exposure to the images. Over time, filmic images produce an altered worldview through a process of "modification of [people's] previous orientation..." (Gerbner, 1986, p. 26). Directed to respond to vast amounts of simplistic images, offered at a fast-paced tempo, compressed into a two-hour period, viewers likely come to receive the world presented there as "objective." In combination, the form of the film medium and repetition of the images are powerful seducers; the mode in which visual information is made accessible to viewers often reduces serious social issues to entertainment, and thus, misinformation.

Though critics suggest that film is no more effective in influencing viewers today (Schudson, 1984; Johnson, 1995) than were comics of their day, or even books for that matter, it is important to note that the form of the moving imaging adds multi-dimensionality and meaning to its imaging (Stacey, 1994; Meyrowitz, 1985; Postman, 1979). Filmic images tend to give the appearance of actively "mirroring" the lived experiences of human beings. Whereas print's imaging (images in comic books, for instance) tends toward deflation of characters into an abstract and cardboard-like world, film's moving imaging tends toward simulation of human action. Essentially, film's form temporarily closes off the mental space normally employed in "creating" viewers' own "visual" interpretation of subjects and subjects' actions. Viewers' active use of their imaginings, hence, is held in temporary abeyance. Combine abeyance of imagination with suspension of disbelief and the predefined visual images often act as credible sources for many.

Significantly, while words and visual images constantly compete for control of viewers' perceptual field, the primacy of the moving image supersedes that which is heard. Being "attention-centered" (Postman, 1979), the moving image becomes a reservoir of cultural information because visual images contain a great deal more information than a speaker can produce at any one time. It was Postman (1979) who suggested that in our visual culture, "knowing" has come to mean having pictures rather than words in our heads, by which he means that it is the visual images which inform what we come to know, what and whom we value, and what behaviors are socially in vogue. Indeed, one need only look at the ways in which our young people imitate video and film's social scenes in the form of dress, speech, and new styles of conduct to conclude that filmic images serve both to influence and reflect social attitudes (Robinson, 1967).

Media "Effects" Theory

But for nearly as long as film has been in existence, debates have raged concerning its influence on the public: is film a tool which shapes cultural attitudes or is the medium merely a mirror that reflects cultural practices? Research on the "effects" of media on viewers' perception of reality has had a long but conflicting history. Beginning in the 1920s–1930s and leading up to the 1950s, research sought to determine whether film had any effect on viewers' behaviors, particularly those of children, and if so, to what extent? (Klapper, 1960; Atkin, 1979). The results were mixed. During the 1920s and 1930s, mass media were conceived of as a hypodermic needle–like machinery, one that could directly inject information and attitudes into viewers. A primary concern during this period was that children might model their anti-social behaviors after those found in filmic images, which, incidentally, is not unlike the concerns of many media groups and parents today.

To address the concern, Blumer and Hauser (1933) conducted a series of research projects, *The Payne Fund* studies (1928–1933), one set of which was designed to determine the effects of movies on children. The researchers concluded that, indeed, movies were influential in providing children with patterns of conduct to emulate (Stanley, 2003). As a result, belief in the "direct effects" theory lasted well into the 1950s. Then, in the 1950s, several studies concerned with various types of public policy issues, including media's effect on voter selection (Atkin, 1979), eventually debunked the "direct effects" theory. Studies of this period suggested that mass media were an ineffective and unpredictable tool in the study of their influence on public attitude because there were far too many uncontrollable variables to draw any useful conclusions about the media's effectiveness (Janis & Feshbach, 1953; Klapper, 1960). As a consequence, research on media effects was dismissed as a serious form of inquiry (Atkin, 1979).

But in the 1970s, several social and technological changes brought about renewed interest in mass media's effects on the attitudes of viewers. As television became more accessible to a broader audience (McLuhan, 1964; Meyrowitz, 1985), the pervasive use of television sets in most American homes began to weaken traditional social ties (Meyrowitz, 1985). At the same time, the dominant technology in the workforce began to change, moving the culture from the industrial age to an electronic one. This shift in the workforce brought with it the need for improved career and job opportunities, resulting in more and more Americans becoming geographically and socially mobile. Such mobility profoundly impacted people's traditional mode of communicating. Where before people relied on other people for social information, they were now becoming more and more reliant on mediated images for such information (Atkin, 1979; Schultz & Barnes, 1995).

These societal changes were now viewed by media researchers as increasing the potential for media to influence the public's construction of social reality. As a result, changes in the social realm were largely instrumental in the development of the current view: namely, that the media can be effective in influencing the public under certain circumstances (Atkin, 1979; Schultz & Barnes, 1995). While a socially isolated and untutored consumer was generally thought to be more susceptible to media's influence (Robinson, 1976), it is still unclear exactly what the nature of these circumstances involves. What is a generally accepted belief, however, is that some people are influenced by some media, some of the time (Jowett & Linton, 1980, p. 74). Perhaps the most persuasive argument that film, in particular, is a powerful socializing influence in U.S. culture may lie in film's central place as a primary source of cultural information for many viewers within the overall media marketplace (Sklar, 1975; Jowett & Linton, 1980). Indeed, that the film industry continues to regulate the content of its images further suggests strong evidence of its socializing influence. For if film is mere entertainment and has no effect on viewers' perceptions, why then monitor its imagistic content?

Apart from its ability to influence cultural ideas and attitudes, film might be appealing to audiences, too, because it presents a complete narrative which comes to closure at the film's end. However, Postman (1979) reminds us that visual media are "image-centered, affect-centered, and attention-centered," so that, although human speech is heard, "it is the pictures that always contain the most important meanings" (p. 58). Following Postman's observation, visual images may have a persuasiveness beyond any language in a given film. If this is the case, the images could potentially provide insight into a culture's social attitudes regarding sex-roles and women's sexual place in society. We will return to this issue in Chapter 3. For now, we want to look at how the ideology of black women as symbols of "sexual excess" operates in film.

The Intersection of Film and Culture

It has been said that film does not create reality; film merely reflects reality as expressed in the culture (Schudson, 1984; Johnson, 1995). Film may even circulate ideas about power and status relationships as reflected within the larger society. That is, filmic images may tell viewers who is valued in society and who is not, but so subtle is this metamessage, that it is almost imperceptible to the average untutored viewer of film. Permit me to recount an incident which may help illustrate this subtlety. While conducting research for this study, I visited numerous video outlets in New York City in search of films featuring black women as central characters. One such outlet became my second home where a kind worker walked me through aisles and aisles of films. We were having trouble locating white male–produced films featuring black women in central roles. Over a period of several days, this helper suddenly remarked that though he is a film connoisseur, he hadn't realized the extent to which black women as central characters were absent in films by white filmmakers. One can only wonder what the average viewer thinks about the status of black women in mainstream films, or even if viewers think about black women's on-screen status at all. What many viewers may not realize, but what I see as vitally important, is that in film (as in television), there is a general system in place—a tacit "rule," if you will—which assigns different concepts to different groups of women, as reflected in their different roles. As I will argue, the concept varies depending on the group to which the woman belongs.

On the one hand, roles for white women in American films have traditionally been comprised of a wide range of characterizations, allowing white women a full diversification of images (hooks, 1992; Zook, 1996; Iverem, 1997). White actresses occupy roles that include romantic heroines, socio-political heroines, action heroines, bored housewives, sexual psychopaths, adventure seekers—roles that go on and on, ad infinitum. In other words, the roles white actresses occupy can be dramatic, comedic, sinister, and so on. Moreover, a given white actress can portray multifaceted roles, allowing full expression of the self, while still maintaining credibility in each venue. Hence, the same actress who portrays a wanton, or psychopathic, or sinister woman in one film can and often is allowed to portray a sympathetic wife or mother in other films; for white women are not necessarily locked into a given type role. Actresses Glenn Close, Demi Moore, Jane Fonda, and a host of other such white actresses serve as examples. Concepts of purity and morality are routinely applied to white women in film, as evidenced by the preponderance of role diversification assigned them. This point is especially important, if only because such diversity in roles, fueled by the unspoken "rule," allows for diversity in perceptions of white women within the culture.

For example, white women's filmic portrayals have provided a broad range of representations, allowing audiences to view the private emotions of white female characters. These cinematic presentations, in turn, have evoked a range of emotions in viewers. Viewers have cried for and cried with white female characters; they have rooted for and against; sympathized and empathized with; hated and loathed; laughed at and laughed with; condemned and embraced characters featuring white women—the list is endless. What often occurs in this process is that audiences are socialized to "see" themselves in white women's filmic characterizations because the portrayals are depicted as universal. Viewers' ability to view different situations from white women's perspectives is then heightened, for the portrayals put a human face onto white women's social selves, which works to endear them to audiences. Here, white womanhood may become especially desirable to black males in particular, since "role-diversity" adds appealing qualities not just to white women's persona, but to their cultural experiences as well. Public perceptions of this subgroup hence become linked with qualities typical of the average person, for the perception is seamlessly connected to white women's humanity.

The issue of black women's filmic roles, on the other hand, is troublesome. Not only are they locked into the sexual roles, roles we will later see that are pilloried, and that result in punitive measures for violators within films (and in the culture, by extension), but the narrowness of the role gives viewers little else with which to link black women culturally (Manatu-Rupert, 2000). Whatever the differences between black and white women, there is the capacity to feel related to the other and that other's experiences. Yet, viewers are not given the opportunity to imagine and be sensitive to the interior lives of black women; instead, viewers' empathic potential toward black women, what Weil (1951) would call "attentive love," is aborted by filmic constructions of persistent negative sexual images of this subgroup. Unlike white female characters, roles for black women are not framed in universal terms. Roles are also not linked to black women's humanity. Descriptions of black women's essence offered through media images "ghettoize" these women's lives (Staples & Jones, 1985; Bogle, 1988). In fact, there is a growing body of evidence which suggests, if not corroborates, that the roles for black women in films (as in television) are akin to gross caricatures of these women's everyday lives (Bogle, 1988; Bobo, 1992, St. Jean & Feagin, 1998). Such coding assures black women's exclusion from participation in the verisimilitude housed in serious dramatic roles. There are, for example, no black ingenues; no black romantic heroines; no black socio-political heroines; no black action heroines (unless one counts as significant roles such as Tina Turner's *Mad Max Beyond Thunderdome*, 1985, or Grace Jones' *A View to a Kill*, 1985, where these women play "exotics" or "amazons"); no black dramatic heroines; no bored black housewives seeking adventure—in short,

Grace Jones stars as May Day, amazon-like villain, in MGM/UA Entertainment Company's *A View to a Kill* (1985).

there are no multi-faceted roles routinely available to black women in American films with which to counterbalance their "sexual" images.

What remains are sexual roles (and comedic roles, but do we dare venture into that realm?), roles that have dominated black female characters in films (Iverem, 1997), at least since the early 1970s. As a result, audiences are not socialized to cry for or cry with black female characters; they are not socialized to feel for or feel with; to root for or cheer on black female characters in films situated in the here and now. One danger is that audiences are being socialized to misrecognize, indeed, to disaffirm actual black women based on black female subjects' consistent negative imaging.

There is also another sense in which black women as "other" operate in film. When the black female body is not sexualized on screen, a related difference occupying equal significance for understanding their limited cinematic-coding lies in the industry's seeming comfort level with positioning this subgroup in films set in some earlier historical time (Wilson & Russell, 1997). It cannot be overlooked that, absent portrayals representative of debased sexuality, black female subjects are often presented as foreign "other," as in films such as *Mad Max Beyond Thunderdome* (1985) and *Quest for Fire* (1981); or they are coded as other-worldly, as in *The Scarlet Letter* (1995), *The Matrix* (1999), where they appear as "mystical

Tina Turner stars as the charismatic ruler of Bartertown in Warner Bros.' *Mad Max Beyond Thunderdone* (1985).

Whoopi Goldberg stars as housekeeper Clara Mayfield in Warner Bros.' *Clara's Heart* (1988). Scene shows her comforting David Hart (Neil Patrick Harris).

sources" who "live for others" (Helford, 2002, p. 89); or else, they are portrayed as "all-knowing" and in the service of whites, as in *Clara's Heart* (1988) and *Ghost* (1990), where black women are then coded as "more masculine than feminine" (Modleski, 1991, p. 132) and/or are "defeminized" to the point of the absurd.

Who can forget Whoopi Goldberg's ridiculous attempt at donning feminine clothing in the film *Ghost*? Upon exiting the bank scene, she was coded as so uncomfortable in her femininity that she waddled awkwardly down the street, much like a caricature of a caricature. Hooks (1981) argues that "images of black women that are shown as positive usually are those that depict the black woman as a long-suffering, religious, maternal figure, whose most enduring characteristic is her self-sacrificing self-denial for those she loves" (p. 66). And, indeed, Goldberg is never more at "home" than when she is frumpily dressed and assumes the role of maternal figure to the couple in *Ghost*. Modleski (1991) goes one step further to argue that "the black woman is seen either as too literally a woman (reduced to her biology and her biological functions) or in more crucial ways not really a woman at all" (p 133). I take Modleski to mean that in film, black women are usually reduced to the sexual or to the ambivalent maternal category. The sexual coding is unequivocal;

Whoopi Goldberg stars as psychic Oda Mae Brown whose psychic powers assist Sam Wheat (Patrick Swayze) in rescuing his girlfriend (Demi Moore) and solving his murder in Paramount's *Ghost* (1990).

the maternal coding, however, is conflictive. Is the black woman a maternal human or maternal "other?" This latter coding naturally begs the question, given that the filmic maternal characters such as many of those portrayed by the star vehicle, Goldberg, are typically coded as possessing powers not of this world.

These two major extremes of black women's on-screen coding have serious implications. For one thing, same-sex female polarization perpetuates exaggerated and false distinctions between black and white women which threaten to color all social exchanges between them. Moreover, because the depictions are presented as comedic and in many cases "endearing," audiences generally may completely miss how such images work to foster the "otherness" of black women culturally. Rarely are audiences directed to take black female characters seriously; rarely do audiences get to see black female characters presented as real people with diverse and real human problems, situated in real time. This lack in representations is deleterious to actual black women: confronted with only one major role situated in "real" time, audiences are left with little option, but to link black women to the "sexual." Quite apart from film's form which drives the image, viewers have little choice, precisely because black and white audiences still do not socially interact with each other (Entman, 1994; Farley, 1993) and so do not know or understand each other.

Essentially, Americans, black and white, still live in a segregated world (Tobin, 1987). Over three decades ago, the *Kerner Report* (*National Advisory Commission on Civil Disorder*, 1968) concluded that America was moving toward two separate and unequal societies, one black and the other white. More than thirty years later, America has seen few inroads in its interpersonal race relations. Admittedly, legal and even institutional gains have been made to a degree, but with regard to our interpersonal social intercourse, with regard to how each group relates to and feels about the other, those areas remain largely in their infancy. On the aggregate, we are civil to each other (thank heavens!). And for the most part, we seem to get along, primarily because a good majority of black and white Americans now work together (Wilson & Russell, 1997; Bell & Nkomo, 2001). Many shop in the same stores, ride the same trains, and attend the same schools. In fact, according to Rhines (1996), with so few black-owned movie theatres, "most Blacks see movies—even Black films— in suburban theatres, not in the inner cities where they live" (p. 7). Still, there is an illusion of harmony between the two groups. One might even go so far to say that blacks and whites live in a harmony of illusion. The illusion is largely evidenced in some of our entertainment media offerings (sports events, game shows, commercials, and the like). But the stark reality is that, for the most part, the two groups do not know each other as individual people, nor even as individual groups. And from most accounts, many may not want to get to know how the other group lives (Wilson & Russell, 1997; St. Jean & Feagin, 1998).

Certainly, television and films point to our segregated way of life. Apart from the sports arena, America's cultural fare is primarily a divided world: we have "black-oriented" television programs and "white-oriented" television programs, particularly in situation comedies (Farley, 1993; Gray, 1995; Inniss & Feagin, 1995), where black men are perpetually shown as court jesters, and black women, as fused with exaggerated hypersexuality. Signs of our segregated society also show up blatantly in films: there are "black-oriented" films and "white-oriented" films (George, 1994), where again, black women show up primarily as extreme sexual characters. Meanwhile, female characters belonging to the dominant group are allowed a diversity of filmic roles which counterbalance their sexual portrayals. Is it any wonder audiences likely link black women to overt "sexuality"?

Kennedy (1992) argues that, "our [black women's] bodies are shot through with meaning, riddled with definitions and qualities not of our own choosing" (p. 110). My own view is that as portrayed in film, black women's seeming lack of interest in "romantic" male-female relationships, their interest in all things "sexual," generally goes unquestioned. Audiences, especially white audiences, may not "see" themselves or their experiences reflected in black women's filmic imaging. The images beckon with importunity; audiences, hence, may feel alienated from black women as persons. Black women may further be alienated from the dominant culture because the absence of counterexamples in their filmic roles helps define black women as "sexually-immoral," a condition akin to that which is sinful. The lack of a diversity in cinematic roles for black women contrasted with their repeated images as "sexual" may even foster the impression that it is in black women's nature to deviate from culturally prescribed sexual behaviors for women in general; hence, they are responsible for how they are perceived in the culture.

I am not asserting that there are no differences between black and white women. Nor am I arguing against diverse filmic roles for white female characters. I am arguing for cinematic depictions that present a view of American society in which women from different cultural subgroups are recognized as different, but portrayed as equally valued. From my perspective, in our daily relating as social human beings, same-sex female differences ought not be treated any more differently than male-female differences; yet, female polarization in film is an all too-common occurrence. Films have failed to provide American audiences with images of black women in diverse roles, situated within black and white communities, dealing with ordinary problems. The medium, in fact, has no trouble depicting black women in substandard roles representing loose sexuality and prostitution (Iverem, 1997); yet, it seems to have little trouble in "...down-play[ing] ... the role of white women [engaged] in prostitution within white communities" (St. Jean & Feagin, 1998, p. 114).

As it stands presently in film (as in television), its depiction of the difference between black and white women is treated differently, which makes a difference in how each is perceived. Of course, the difference in how both groups of women are constructed may not always be perceived as conflictive nor felt as offensive to audiences. For example, based on *Variety's* List of "Top 250 films of 1997–2001" and its "All-Time Box-Office Rentals Champions" (1994 and 1995) which ranks films by number of video rentals, viewers may not have been offended by the images in the films analyzed in this study. If such is the case, then ticket purchases and rentals strongly suggest that the larger the viewership for the films found for this study, the more influential were they as sources of information (thus rendering them important sources for analysis in both studies).

One wonders why audiences were not seemingly outraged by the images in the films analyzed in the studies. Why, if the ticket purchases and video rentals are any indication, were audiences not filled with righteous indignation? In fact, why were audiences seemingly not offended by the negative sexual images in these mainstream films, films which were not pornographically-rated? These questions may be only the tip of the iceberg, but they are necessary questions in the search for understanding and humane visions of change.

Film's significant role in contributing to stereotypes about diverse social groups becomes evident in how it positions subgroups within a given film. How women are portrayed in film resonates with viewers because they likely connect members of the group not merely to the category in which that group is shown, but to the behaviors that accompany the category. If characters' role-behaviors become stagnant, the behaviors then work to define the given character. In turn, characters' nonverbal behaviors likely work to define subjects who represent the roles they are assigned.

Thus far, I have merely hinted at the relationship between nonverbal behaviors and meaning, and their centrality on screen. Nonverbal behaviors become of importance, for as a visual medium, film's dramatic format depends on such behaviors. While words are also important on screen, nonverbal behaviors or acts drive the story along because this visual medium tends toward dramatic performance. In fact, film lends itself to action genres—melodramas, suspense, horror, and so on (and this point may be especially true of American films, where action films seem to favor those that emphasize character study). To the extent that the film medium relies on the nonverbal behaviors of characters, meaning, then, lies primarily in characters' behaviors. Under nonverbal communication theory, decoders of a message are said to receive 65 percent of the meaning of the message from senders' nonverbal cues (Birdwhistle, 1970). Nonverbal cues include body movements, use of touch, facial expressions, eye-contact, vocal tone, environment, and so on, all of which are vital in film's dramatic formatting.

If, as communication researchers indicate, receivers who attend to body and vocalic cues (tone of voice) interpret meanings of senders' messages more accurately than those who attend to the verbal (Ekman, 2001; Dimitreius & Mazzarella, 1999; Burgoon et al., 1989; Harrison, 1974; Ekman et al., 1969), viewers may be attending to portrayals of the nonverbal sexual behaviors of black women in cinematic offerings more than to their verbal behaviors. That is, how characters are coded to behave or act in a given film may be more important than what they are coded to say; for often, there is nothing so powerful as that which is not spoken. Hence, when negative role-behaviors assigned to one subgroup (as in the case of black women) take on permanence, such objectification problematizes the group as negative and deviant "other." The dominant defining characteristic of black women as "sexual other" may, in fact, become seared in viewers' minds.

As can be seen, perpetuation of the negative imagery of black female sexuality involves a complex set of social systems and beliefs that works together to preserve the image. The practice of locking black women into one primary role, the sexual, clearly suggests that, in film, certain roles are assigned to certain subgroups. Images are arranged to suit the given role and then offered up to audiences in a package of "difference," wrapped in an illusion of harmony. The form of the medium (the speed with which ideas are transmitted through visual images) contributes to the illusion because the medium limits critical inquiry of its offerings. The images then appear normal and universal, as if ordained by the Almighty. Beliefs about the immorality of black women are thus preserved, prompting Roberts (1994) to remind us that, culturally speaking, blackness is still "loaded with sexuality" (p. 5).

These are subtle, nearly imperceptible, yet multifaceted systems of operation presented in film as homogeneous, for aren't white women also portrayed as sex objects? If not mindful, viewers could come to accept the routine visual representations of black female sexuality offered in film as normative behavior for black women generally. Indeed, given film's persuasive quality, it may be difficult for audiences to separate black women from the roles they represent. In the next chapter, I will examine how love and romance are constructed in films based on cultural expectations of sexual behaviors for males and females in American culture, and how black women's sexual construction is presented as deviating from culturally prescribed norms of the "feminine."

3

Love and Romance: Cultural Prescriptive for "Appropriate" Sexual Behaviors for Men and Women

A basic value strongly held in American culture is women's attitude and behaviors regarding love as compared to sex (Bem, 1993; Haste, 1993; Lerner, 1989; Lorber, 1994; Person, 1988). Almost from birth and in different ways, attitudes about love are inculcated into both sexes, where cultural imprints of the "feminine" and the "masculine" are fostered and encouraged. Indeed, during pregnancy, if the sex of a child is made known to parents, they begin to "genderize" the child, even prior to its birth (Lorber, 1994). We can witness this gendered processing in those social markers used to indicate whether the child is a boy or girl: type and color of clothing, type of toys, adornments (ribbons, earrings, etc.) or lack thereof, and so forth. A major part of this gendered processing involves the traditional cultural archetypes of the "feminine" and the "masculine," where men are socially constructed as instrumentalists: independent, dominant, rational, adventurous, and aggressive; women as relational: passive, dependent, emotional, intuitive, and irrational. Lerner (1989) argues that women are told their sex is "passive-dependent—that it is men who take charge and make change happen in the real world" (p. 223). Following this suggestion, white women come to be perceived by society and to perceive themselves as passive-dependents, which adversely impacts their social experiences. But if the issue of "passive-dependence" has been restrictive for women of the dominant group, issues of "sexual-aggressor" and "dominant-matriarch" have been virtual nightmares for black women.

Allow me one last musing before we proceed into discussions of "appropriate" sexual behaviors for men and women. I had just ended a talk on images of black women in film, wherein I had alluded to the absence of black women as romantic figures on screen, when a member of the audience raised her hand. She wanted to know why would black women want to go back into the patriarchal ideology of the feminine when "women" were working so hard to escape it? After I took a deep, calming breath, I responded with what I hoped came close to sounding rational. That question, in fact, helped spark the idea for this book. For the question fails to note one of the major systems of oppression for black women in U.S. culture—class discrimination—which film vividly carries forward in much of its imaging. This form of discrimination is insidious because it is under this practice that the "feminine" is invisibly but securely housed. In turn, social and economic rewards are deeply embedded within the feminine concept. And where it concerns black women, from most accounts, class discrimination has its roots firmly fixed in 19th century sensibilities.

Unlike white women, black women have never had the benefit of being on the proverbial pedestal and allowed to be "feminine." Excluded from the world of the "feminine," black women have long been confined to the world of work and sexuality (hooks, 1981; Davis, 1983; Beale, 1995; Gaines, 1997). Beale (1995) aptly captures this phenomenon in her article, "Double Jeopardy: To Be Black and Female." She observes that during the 1800s, black women were perceived as far from delicate beauties who needed care and protection. Notes Beale: "Most black girls were forced to deal with poverty, violence, and a hostile outside world from childhood on" even as white women of the upper and middle class ranks were "raised in genteel refined circumstances" (p. 157). Given that white women were invested in the "cult of true womanhood," "[t]he sexually denigrated [black] woman ... [was] used as the yardstick against which ... true womanhood was measured" (Collins, 1990, p. 176). Being considered as not belonging to that "cult," rather as natural deviants, allowed perceptions of indelicacy, infragility, and unfemininity to be assigned to black women. Over time, such beliefs became an easy lure for white society, which almost consciously came to treat black women as "non-women." While these cultural attitudes generally appear invisible to the dominant culture, the mind-numbing attitudes are operational and felt by most, if not all, black women, even today.

Considering their long history of same-gender exclusion, then, black women would hardly know whether they want to stay on the "feminine" pedestal or if they wish to get off. Indeed, given their continued gender devaluation, many black women may intuitively sense but be unsure of just exactly what all the "feminine" entails. What is clear is that escaping the "feminine," first and foremost, involves a question of choice—and the operative word here is "choice." For until black women as a group are allowed access and participation in the "feminine," until they are allowed the choice of accepting or rejecting it, they can hardly join in a fight to escape that to which they have not been privy.

If we grant that black women could cavalierly dismiss their historical exclusion from the "feminine"—if they then were to unite with women of the dominant group in their struggle to escape the "feminine"—black women would almost certainly be consumed with ideas of what might have been, had their inherent right to experience the feminine not been repudiated. Much like a dream deferred, thoughts of the "what if" would be almost too overpowering to bear. Perhaps it is a function of the human condition that that which is deemed culturally valuable, but is denied, generally becomes the thing most sought after. For in a merciful twist of fate, this idea is not unlike white women's long-held yearning to become equal with men. In fact, the idea is closely related to white women's deep desire and subsequent fight to become integral players in the public sphere, where they might gain opportunities to freely, equally, and fully express themselves as individual human beings. And it is this point that is so crucial in understanding black women's reluctance to embrace mainstream feminist ideology. As has been pointed out by hooks (1981), McIntosh (1998) and others, that ideology fails to see the nexus of race, color, class, and gender, the latter variable being the major focus of dominant feminists. Yet, such an ideology offers black women no clear way through which to articulate their quadruple social oppression. In the final analysis, there is little point in debating that black women have been denied participation in the "feminine," a major result of which has been that on both the cultural level and in film, black women's very presence virtually speaks of wantonness. Unsavory on-screen images insist on presenting this subgroup as lacking in virtue such that romance is rarely, if ever, treated as a natural outgrowth of their male-female relationships.

From a larger sociological perspective, where it concerns love and romance, the archetypal social construct of the "feminine" and the "masculine" gives rise to assumptions and expectations about different behaviors for women and men. It is generally agreed that men and women value romantic love differently (deBeauvoir, 1974; Person, 1988; Lerner, 1989; Keen, 1991; Borisoff and Hahn, 1992; Ivy & Backlund, 2000); thus, their behaviors and expectations in matters of romantic love tend to fall within the "masculine" and the "feminine" mode of operation. Romance is generally characterized by intimacy, sentiment, emotions, and expressions of tenderness and gentleness, where the act of "falling in love" can take place (deRougement, 1956; Everson, 1979; Person, 1988; Keen, 1991). Person (1988) observes that women are more inclined toward the "mutuality implicit in love," whereas men tend to separate sex from love (p. 265).

A primary reason for these differences in approach to love is the different cultural imperatives urged upon both sexes (Person, 1988: Lerner, 1989; Keen, 1991; Bem, 1993). Different socialization inclines both sexes toward different pursuits in love: women are expected to establish their "femininity" through love; men, to establish their "masculinity" through achievement. That is, cultural socialization functions as a dominant factor in predisposing women to define themselves in terms of romance, men in terms of work, a point which becomes a harsh indictment in Harriett Lerner's *The Dance of Intimacy* (1989). Arguing against the essentialist determinant implicit in the socialization of the genders, Lerner points to differential advantages inherent in the male construct: "a man's job [is] to make something of himself in the world; a woman's job [is] to find herself a successful man" (p. 5). Here, each sex utilizes love in oppositional ways because each is motivated in large part by their "feminine" and "masculine" directives: she must be "good" and patient while she waits for that successful man who will transform her into a "love object"; he must seek after work and adventure, much of his adventure "interspersed with encounters with women who supply spice and sex" (Person, 1988, p. 276). Understandably, certain males might support a stance which emphasizes their advantaged gender distinction. Yet, to entirely overlook the contradictions inherent in the gender construct, especially given the precarious social condition of their womenfolk, is a mistake.

Within the "masculine" sexual construct, for example, the adventure-seeking male is encouraged to exploit what is culturally expected to be the "feminine-good girl." For while the "feminine" directive expects women to delay sex until after marriage, the "masculine" directive encourages sex prior to marriage. Such duality suggests that someone's daughter necessarily must fulfill his "masculine" urges. His quest for sexual encounters necessarily may force the male to coerce, indeed, to deceive many "good girls" into becoming unwitting sexualized participants. Thus, for example, in his attempt to secure sex, the adventure-seeking male might profess everlasting love for, or at least deep interest in, what he knows is the relational female, even while he may have no intention of fulfilling such a promise. Edwards (1998) finds that the relational role into which women are socialized—what he refers to as the "communal" gender role—is a more salient predictor of positive interpretation of an ambiguous message than is biological sex, which also plays an important role. When considered alongside findings which reveal that in their intimate relationships, men and women not merely interpret verbal and non-verbal messages differently (Tannon, 1990), but also listen in different ways (Borisoff & Hahn, 1992), the meanings a woman attributes to a seemingly ardent suitor's messages may be based not so much on his messages; rather, on her relational expectations. In turn, her expectations may lead to misinterpretation of his relational intent. Built into the ethos of the masculine/feminine construct is a major flaw of cross-purposeful expectations. Different gender expectations may propel many "good girls" into deviating from the cultural sexual prescriptive for the "feminine," one often carrying social consequences (Haskell, 1995; McLean, 1995). In fact, by its very nature, the gender construct condemns certain women into "whores," women who must satiate the "masculine urge." Thus, conforming to the "appropriate" sexual rule for the "feminine" generally means many women are caught in an untenable situation. Men's adventure-seeking directive takes preference over women's "good girl" directive.

Cultural messages of this kind are still so pervasive that even today, according to Lerner (1989), despite the gains of the women's movement, many parents, nonetheless, may expect more restrictive sexual behaviors from their daughters than from their sons. For "boys will be boys" is still a widely accepted sentiment (Lerner, 1989, p. 7). Indeed, Keen (1991) notes that the "male identity revolves around the penis in a way that female identity does not revolve around the vagina" (p. 71). He argues that this is because there are differences in the imagination of men and women. Men "imagine sex directly and intimacy indirectly, while women imagine intimacy directly and sex indirectly" (p. 78). Culturally, these differences appear to be an accepted way of life to the point that the societal directive still expects "appropriate" sexual behaviors from women while it tolerates unseemly sexual behaviors from men.

These cultural expectations serve to encourage, if not dictate, how women, not men, should behave in matters of love. If they want to be valued and reap the rewards of the "feminine," women must work doubly hard to be "good girls." The implicit message in the dual processing of valuation of women is the cultural metamessage that "good girls" or what Haste (1993) refers to as "nice girls" are those women whose behavior is sexually passive, or at least modest. Notes Haste (1993): "Nice girls [don't] ... express sexual interest, or wear provocative clothes. The underlying assumption [is] that women [are] supposed to operate the sexual constraints, and [are] rather delicate creatures who need protection from the unpleasant manifestations of sexuality" (p. 277). Here, Haste's description of the "nice girl" model mirrors definition of the "feminine" construct, one associated with qualities black women are believed not to possess.

Social rewards await those who remain within the borders of "appropriate" sexual behaviors. Women perceived as sexually modest are accorded society's highest honor reserved for the "feminine"—social respect and consideration, and defense of honor (Christian, 1985). A second major reward centers around securing a husband who can provide access to "economic security and social status" (Lerner, 1989, p. 6). This metamessage, incidentally, is consonant with men's cultural directive of "provider," allowing him to prove his masculinity by providing handsomely for his wife and children (St. Jean & Feagin, 1998). "Bad girls," on the other hand, are viewed as those women who actively seek out sexual encounters, behaviors which have social and personal consequences (Haste, 1993; Haskell, 1995; McLean, 1995). And it is these very images of female polarization that can be found in our cultural products, specifically within the film medium.

Film as Reinforcer of the Cultural Directive for Women's Sexuality

Representations of male-female cultural stereotypes are pervasive in most U.S. films. DeRougement (1956) observes that in American culture, two qualities distinct to romantic love are housed in our cultural fare: love is equivalent to marriage, and "love overcomes all obstacles, as is shown everyday in films ..." (p. 292). The pervasiveness of love stories in film has been documented by scholars such as Rosen (1973), Ivy & Backlund (2000), Everson (1979), and Haskell (1987). And as in the culture, women's attitudes and behaviors regarding passionate love as opposed to sexual pleasure have been values historically depicted in most American films featuring women—white women's virtue emerging as a traditional site of battle on screen.

The post-war era saw "women" routinely portrayed in film primarily as "love objects" (Rosen, 1973; Haskell, 1987). Though specific to romance novels, Radway's (1984) study found that the feminine lust for romantic love is evidenced in central plots that revolve around a beautiful woman who can melt the cold and aloof heart of the sometimes tortured hero. The man with whom she is smitten is distinguished by his masculine characteristics—independence, withdrawn comportment, instrumentality, and authority. Person (1988) observes that generally, "women have a tendency to eroticize relationships with men in authority ... which is congruent with our society's prevailing romantic fantasies (fantasies which seem relatively untouched by the changing roles of women in the workplace)" (p. 258). To "catch" the male, the woman must appear to be both accessible and forbidden all at once, which allows enough "structured separation that the imaginative work of falling in love can take place" (Person, 1988, p. 264).

These plots culled from the romance novels are applicable to those of film in that they each mirror the social prescriptive which directs women to seek out romance as a major part of their identity (Person, 1988; Haste, 1993) in favor of sexual autonomy. But a number of scholars views post-war filmic stories of romance as perpetuating the myth of the "happily-ever-after" of marriage (deBeauvoir, 1974; Everson, 1979; Haskell, 1987) because the myth restricts women's social reality by depicting a distorted image of gender roles. DeBeauvoir (1974) characterizes romantic love as a rationalization for female subordination and dependency, in part because women are depicted as finding their identity through romantic relationships. Haskell (1987) intimates that through the dialectic of gender differences, film reinforces women's inferiority status. She refers to this status as the "Great Lie," an idea so embedded in social institutions, in social groups, and in the individual psyche that, in film, women's ambitions, intelligence, and sexuality are suppressed, while the pursuit of romantic love is amplified and promoted. In the meanwhile, men's achievements and sexual freedom are promoted, while their interest in romance is downplayed. Note that "most romantic ... movies are aimed at women—young and old ... [while] males ... learn about romance (as such) from unromantic sources such as *Playboy* [and] locker room talk ... [These] images ... tend to lead men to focus on sex and women to focus on being swept away in a romantic rush" (Ivy & Backlund, 2000, pp. 297–298).

Indeed, Everson's (1979) study on images of romantic love in Hollywood films in the post-war period finds that for women, love is portrayed not only as a lasting value, but as a changeable one. He notes that love is sometimes expressed "openly ... and with a great deal of sentiment." At other times, the emotions are concealed, but are no less honest (p. 10). Implicit in the works of these researchers is the notion that romantic love primarily accentuates sentiment and emotion, attributes clearly not associated with, nor expected of, black women. While deRougement (1956) concludes that U.S. culture has become addicted to heavy dosages of "romantic drug," chiefly through film, nothing of black women is discussed. Indeed, the reader of the above books would have to conclude that black women do not experience "love" as conceived by these authors, for nowhere do readers find any references made to black women's romantic experiences. Likewise, based on the dialectic of same-gender female differences referred to in film's visual silence, the viewer of the vast majority of love stories in U.S. films must arrive at the same conclusion: black women experience sex, but not love. Viewers, in fact, must conclude that black women do not experience or value intimacy, tenderness, and gentleness in their male-female relationships, qualities widely accepted as key components in fueling romantic love. As portrayed, all that black women seem to require is raw sexual pleasure. The omission points directly to Guerrero's (1993) argument regarding black women's filmic coding—"sign of the whore"—a point reiterated by Iverem (1997), who also observes that where romance in film is concerned, no "romantic sensibilities are developed for most black women on screen." Instead, viewers are met with images of "loose sexuality..." (p. G4). Because on-screen romantic heroines have traditionally been limited to women of the dominant group, hereafter, when the word "women" is discussed in this section, it refers to white women; black women will be so identified.

Traditionally, the cinematic heroine, like the romance novel heroine, has been depicted as genteel, intelligent, virginal, and beautiful, conditions representative of female respectability. She may even be incorrigible, but rarely does she veer afar from the genteel lady that she inherently is. The advantage to such constructions is that they allow the hero to lure the heroine away from her casual dalliance with independence to a focus on romance and marriage—indicators of her rightful social status. Radway (1984) notes that although the romantic heroine was often portrayed as spirited and independent, she was ultimately portrayed as losing herself emotionally in romance by surrendering her sexual autonomy to the hero and to marriage. "Love," as it were, tamed the independent female, who then emerged as "love object." But according to Rosen (1973), the sex-symbols and bombshells of the 1960s and 1970s replaced the filmic love objects of the post-war era. Perhaps to undermine the social gains of independence and achievements garnered by women during this period, denigrating filmic images of sex-objects, whores, mistresses, and sexually repressed women emerged in films (Rosen, 1973). This filmic trend has continued to one degree or another since then, creating a conflictive phenomenon for women where it concerns the cultural prescriptive for women's sexual behaviors.

In spite of women's depictions as sex-objects, the cultural expectations of the "feminine" also remain simultaneous with the "sex object." In other words, women's behaviors regarding romantic love are still a basic cultural value in film, even while women-as-sex-objects are simultaneously advanced. Thus, although film is a "rich field for the mining of female stereotypes" (Haskell, 1987, p. 28), specifically the sex object, at the same time, its visual images communicate powerful metamessages regarding expectations for sex-roles concerning the "feminine" (Rosen, 1973; Basow, 1980; Haskell, 1995; McLean, 1995). These metamessages, according to Rosen (1973), keep women in check by portraying disastrous consequences for women who seek liberation in their sexuality, and rewards for women who pursue romantic love and marriage. Haskell (1995) makes a not unrelated point. She notes that women are discouraged from expressing their sexual autonomy by on-screen depictions of extreme poverty for those who pursue such liberation. Women who conform to romantic love, on the other hand, are rewarded with hearth and home (Rosen, 1973), social respectability, and protection from destitution and public condemnation (Haskell, 1995; McLean, 1995).

The heroine, Vivian, in the film *Pretty Woman* (1990), serves as an example of a woman who, though a street prostitute on the verge of destitution, gains financial freedom and is made "respectable" by her implied marriage to the male protagonist. But as if to support the foregoing arguments regarding female polarization on screen, Vivian, it should be noted, is viewed not as the street whore that she is. Rather, she is described as "independent and carefree," a characterization which is consonant with the inherited status of women belonging to the dominant group, and which, incidentally, is often unlike that assigned to women of color in similar scenarios. Great effort was devoted to humanizing this street walker's construction, from softening her "street" behaviors to referring to her as "Ms. Vivian." Presumably, the pseudo-respect granted Vivian in her role as whore is a foreshadowing of the "real" respect she will enjoy when she is finally rescued from degradation and made into a madonna by the hero, Edward.

Yet, while Vivian apparently gains social respect, the predictable result is that she does so, not through her own agency; rather, through that of the male. The implied cultural metamessage in this and other such

Julia Roberts stars as prostitute Vivian Ward, who falls in love with tycoon Edward Lewis (Richard Gere) in *Pretty Woman*, Touchstone Pictures (1990).

films is that without male protection, sexually free women are destined to a life of poverty. In fact, the film suggests that a woman's whole *raison d'etre* is to "catch" a man who will transform her into a madonna, or else she risks a life as a destitute whore. Whether madonna or whore, film's relentless meta-message indicates that the shift from one to the other can be made possible only through male agency. The huge popularity of *Pretty Woman*, for example, suggests that audiences, especially women, buy into the madonna-whore concept, which is precisely what Mellen (1973) and Haskell (1995) decry. Mellen (1973) argues that the film medium socializes women into responding to one of the most entrenched icons in American culture—the madonna symbol.

Indeed, within the cultural context, embracing the madonna concept eventually may become problematic for some women. The romance many expect to flourish in their marriages will likely evaporate because male fantasy tends to separate wives into madonnas; mistresses into whores (Mellen, 1973). This is yet another contradiction embedded in the different oppressive socialization of women and men's sexuality. The cultural liberal tolerances for men's sexuality encourage a dual, parallel, but opposite valuation of women, generally. Person (1988) contends that there are two very different images of women constructed through male fantasy: women as temptress, seductress and femme fatale; and women as nurturer, comforter, earth mother, eternal mother (p. 278). This oppositional cultural view of womanhood most probably works to impoverish the choices of actual women; hence, the role of wife in many instances may rob women of the free expression of their sexuality. If the male brings to the marriage bed a dual imaging of womanhood, he is likely to view his wife as a "sexless" madonna. The predictable outcome is that he may then turn to a mistress or two in order to satiate his sexual desire, a desire driven in part by his masculine socialization. Should enough men engage in such practices on the aggregate level, female polarization then flourishes.

In part, this is why, since the 1970s, film's major role in advancing female dualism has been of great concern. Mellen (1973) points out that the "pure" woman in film versus the "loose" presents a closed world of the sexual lives of women in the culture; "loose women" forfeit the protection granted "domesticated" women, since the former choose to remain unmarried (pp. 25-26). Haskell (1995) echoes a similar view. She suggests that so destitute are depictions of the lives of sexually-free women in film that the metamessage serves as a warning to actual women in the culture at large. And indeed, that the condition of actual women in the culture can be inferred from women's dual cinematic coding speaks to film's strong potential for persuasiveness in its role as reinforcer of both the "feminine" and "sex-object" images. Film's push-pull dual processing creates not just a sexual tension, where each message—that of the sex-object and of the good girl—vies for dominance in film's depictions of the "feminine"; but the process is used as an invisible/visible same-gender female tool, a point to which I will return in a later chapter. What is important to note is that however it is used, the on-screen sexual tension mirrors that created by the cultural madonna/whore model, one which splits women into female polar opposites (Mellen, 1973; Person, 1988; Modleski, 1991; Haste, 1993; McLean, 1995), "loose" women portrayed not merely as the cause of male sexual transgression, but also as deserving of social punishment.

It is ironic, then, that while the message in film vilifies sexually-liberated women, simultaneously, film also actively sets women up as sex objects, reflecting, perhaps, ambivalence on the part of male filmmakers, who generally construct the images (Mulvey, 1989). Haskell (1987) argues that the first principle of film aesthetics is the conception of women as "idol, art object, icon, and visual entity..." (p. 125). In essence, women on screen are expected to be "good girls," despite the fact that, simultaneously, they are purposefully conceived of and positioned as sex objects.

Having been coded as sex objects, women are then shown to be penalized by the projection of a destitute future for those who choose a sexually-liberated lifestyle. Yet, despite these dire warnings, woman as "visual entity" predominates in film. Just why this is the case is addressed by Haste (1993), who notes that woman-as-sex-object is a means through which expressions of male fantasy can play themselves out in the media.

This idea is not original to Haste, however. A number of writers have already argued that "women-as-sex-object" is a function of men's fantasies. Mulvey (1989) refers to the act of men watching women as the "male gaze." She contends that film projects the fantasy of the male gaze onto male viewers, so that "the gaze of the [male] spectator and that of the male characters are ... neatly combined without breaking narrative verisimilitude" (p. 19). Here, both male spectator and male characters control the film fantasy because a woman is positioned and coded to be "spectacle." Men, on the other hand, emerge as "bearer[s] of the look..." (p. 20).

Butler (1990) broadens the male fantasy discussion to include explanations of how men and women come to be configured as sexual beings. She asserts that the body as sexually perceived is fantasmatic and, thus, sexual differences between men and women are imaginary ones. She goes on to say that "perhaps this construct called 'sex' is as culturally constructed as gender; ... perhaps it was always already gender, with the consequence that the distinction between sex and gender turns out to be no distinction at all" (p. 7). Because men have traditionally constructed images of women in film (Mulvey, 1989), Butler's speculation suggests that how women are coded on screen is a reflection of the filmmaker's fantasy regarding what women are like sexually versus what men are like. If we recall Keen's (1991) argument that men imagine sex directly, then male filmmakers can organize women into any number of sexual categories because, as Freud (1962) argues, sexual aims are multiple. Freud (1962) separates sexual objects from sexual aims, explaining that the former are the ones with whom we have sex; the latter are the multiple things we do to achieve sexual pleasure. Viewed from this perspective, multiplicity appears to heighten men's sexual fantasies, allowing for endless expressions of woman-as-sex-object.

One trouble with cinematic expressions of male fantasy is that such symbolic characterizations can potentially become the yardstick through which men in the culture measure women generally. In fact, Jowett & Linton (1980) contend that "movies can serve as a kind of collective unconscious, inspiring, creating tensions, and almost causing a 'standardization' of fantasy" (p. 100). Though the authors use "fantasy" in its generic term, the point is appropriate for discussion here because fantasies of any kind are subject to becoming "standardized." Indeed, it can be argued that men's on-screen sexual fantasies have created a standardized mixed message where it concerns concepts of womanhood: the conflicting filmic conceptions of the good/girl-bad/girl persona which often act as signifiers through which assumptions about women's sexuality are then played out in the culture (DeLauretis, 1984; Mulvey, 1989).

From a contemporary viewpoint, film becomes a powerful site of conflict for women. How to live as sexually free women while still maintaining social respectability becomes a challenge, since living such a life invites accusations of moral looseness (Mellen, 1973; McLean, 1995); fear of poverty restricts others from living as free women (Haskell, 1995); for others still, sexual liberation signals "the old maid" syndrome, which mothers in particular fear to the point that many solicit perfect strangers in attempts to get their daughters to the altar before the biological "clock runs out" entirely. And do we dare discuss homophobia! For if all else fails, suspicion of lesbianism for the "unattached" female lurks just beneath the surface (Rich, 1980), waiting to be given voice. This latter condition may be especially the case for unattached black females, where their single status is generally viewed with deep suspicion (Lorde, 1984). And indeed, in the film *The Best Man* (1999), the unattached black female character, Jordan, is virtually accused of suspected lesbianism by the males.

It is safe to say that the film medium acts as a powerful visual tool through which images of the "good girl" and the "bad girl," already a cultural mainstay, are reinforced. Indeed, the medium seems to function as a kind of regulator of women's sexual behaviors. But such functioning raises the question, which women? It has already been shown that, in film, by far the vast majority of romantic heroines are white women, a point that cannot be debated (Rosen, 1973; Mellen, 1973; Haskell, 1987). Hence, that the filmic-cultural prescriptive for "appropriate" sexual behaviors is directed toward white women is implicit in white women's overwhelming presence as romantic figures on screen, even as they also appear as sex objects. Nor can it be overlooked that the film medium also functions as a mechanism to maintain a hierarchical division among women. Black women's absence on screen as romantic heroines, juxtaposed with their habitual presence as sex objects, more than suggests such a division.

Images of black women as sex objects appear to have a socially prescribed function different from that prescribed for women of the dominant group. We have already seen how, in films, dramatic and romantic roles are absent for black women. Thus, it can legitimately be said that black women's presence in film offers no counter-balancing images to which the cultural directive for women's "appropriate" sexual behaviors is designed to speak. From film's point of view, there are no "feminine" black women to keep in check with regard to societal "rewards" versus "consequences," unlike the case for white women. Rather, sexual images of black women appear to be constructed as a means of reinforcing black women's "other" sexual status.

In this age of black women's relatively high media visibility, film has not presented rewards for black women who conform to society's prescriptive of "appropriate" sexual behaviors for women. Nor has film depicted "disastrous consequences" for black women who fall outside of society's mainstream codes of "appropriate" sexual behaviors. That is, in film, no rewards nor consequences are highlighted that would distinguish "negative" from "appropriate" sexual behaviors on black women's part. The sameness, in fact, is breathtaking! Whether black women's sexual behaviors conform to or deviate from the cultural prototype of the "feminine-good girl," these women, nonetheless, receive the same treatment: Black women are coded as those particular kind of "other" sinful, immoral, low-class, unlady-like type women. Too frequent is film's failure to apply to black women's male-female relationships expressions of warmth, gentleness, and tenderness, sentiments understood in Western culture as signals indicative of "romantic love." One indirect result is that "rewards" of social respectability are often denied actual black women. Then too, the "successful husband" theory Lerner (1989) alludes to does not generally function for black women in film. And given actual black women's low rate of marriage in the culture (Cherlin, 1996; Mitchell, 1993; Besharov, 2002) relative to the desire of many for such unions, it is safe to infer that such lack may well be a byproduct of public and filmic perpetuation of their undesirability as "feminine" women. Certainly, public perception has not acted as a site of reward for the majority of black women who do conform to the cultural directive to be "feminine-good girls" by society recognizing and acknowledging black women as such. Nor has film offered an oppositional gaze through which stereotypes of black women as hypersexed would be contested and, so, disaffirmed.

One of the most memorable films of the 1990s, *Boomerang* (1992), memorable for its cast of over-sexed black female characters, offers no consequences or rewards for that matter to its cast of sexually "deviant" black female characters. Who can forget the restaurant scene in which Grace Jones' character boldly propositions Eddie Murphy's character for sex; where, upon his refusal, she loudly screams, "Pussy, pussy, pussy"? Or Robin Givens' performance in the same film as the aggressively insensitive sexualized character who is as anxious for sex as any man, and who uses men for sex?

Another big budget film of the 1990s, *A Rage in Harlem* (1991), also saw Givens' character not only as highly sexually-charged, but also as cruelly so. She is depicted as using Forrest Whittaker's character for sex to get what she wants. Whittaker's character is presented as an innocent, sincere in his interest for the Givens character. But while he brings honesty and caring to their relationship, she is merely exploiting him. Where, based on the filmic caution for "women," are the "good girl"/"bad girl" reinforcements in these films which are supposed to function as "feminine" regulators for black audiences much the way they work for white audiences? Viewers did not witness the feminine reinforcement at work in these films, unless one views Halle Berry's portrayal of the seemingly caring friend in *Boomerang* as an example of the "feminine" symbol as against the "oversexed" Givens character.

Berry's character is depicted as sweet, thoughtful, and socially conscious, a characterization which, to the film's credit, dispels the usual demeaning stereotypes of black life, generally. But even here, her characterization as "romantic" is ambivalent. She is portrayed as "innocently" seducing and moving in with the "boyfriend" of her female boss, even while she is friendly with and still works for the boss. Yet, when Murphy's character, Marcus, returns to the boss, Berry's character, Angela, is outraged and hurt. But there is a disconnect in her depiction, for from the onset, Angela knows Marcus is still smitten with the boss. Angela, in fact, is shown as the party who encourages the start of a sexual relationship between herself and Marcus. A few lines from the film will suffice to illustrate that Marcus is quite unsure of his feelings for Angela. As they begin to kiss, Marcus asks:

> MARCUS: What are we doing?
> ANGELA: We're kissing (as she continues the kiss).
> MARCUS: We're friends!
> ANGELA: So? Friends can kiss (as she actively encourages the seduction).

Thus when, upon Marcus' return to his first "love," Angela expresses outrage, viewers cannot be entirely sympathetic to her cause. She was not portrayed as conducting herself in a manner consistent with that of a "romantic" figure. Their coming together began with and was founded on the "sexual." A formal date might have been a good starting point from which to get to know each other; a starting point from which to give the other time in which to allow the "imaginative" act of falling in love to occur, but not so the black woman's construction! In the end,

Angela is shown to triumph over her boss by winning the Marcus character. Yet, even here, the message of triumph is tenuous. In spite of her seeming victory, Angela is heard chastising Marcus for ogling another woman as they make their way down the street, presumably to embark on their new life together—this, moments after they have newly reconciled! No clear-cut rewards here! Why is this the case?

The black woman's debased sexuality, long amplified on the big screen, comes to the forefront in these films as normative behaviors for black women, generally. These women are not "love objects," and, given their persistent filmic coding as "over-sexed," they cannot be perceived as objects of love. Remember Person's (1988) reminder that women establish their "femininity" through love; that women must simultaneously appear to be both accessible and forbidden in order to allow the process of "falling in love" to take place? How, as presently coded on screen, could black women be seen as feminine love objects? In film, these women are not shown as characters who give themselves time in which to fall in love. Nor are they depicted as allowing men they encounter time or separation such that the imaginative act of "falling in love" can take place; theirs, instead, is a depiction of sexual aggressors whose imagination revolves solely around the sexual. Like the social construct of the "masculine," black women are depicted as not only separating sex from love; romantic love is rarely a concern for them. Rather, much like the social construct of the "masculine" where his male identity revolves around his penis, black women are portrayed as women whose gender identity revolves around their vaginas. They are primarily depicted as sexual predators, on the ready to pick up and seduce men. Constructed as initiators of sexual encounters, theirs is a representation of female characters who are actively sexual, aggressively sexual, and on the quest for sexual adventure. Accordingly, their gendered status as "feminine" women becomes suspect.

Bem (1993) argues that those who deviate from their mutually exclusive gender identities are typically defined by the culture as "pathological" (p. 195). Is this the message film wants audiences to glean from black women's filmic construct? If not, why are there no routine counterexamples of black women on screen? Certainly, there are enough black women in the culture who represent the ideal of the "feminine," such that their experiences can also be reflected in black women's on-screen coding. Why is it, then, that in filmic narratives, black women's diverse cultural experiences continue to be held in permanent abeyance? Why is the focus on deviant sexuality? Black female characters' sexual behaviors on screen are suggestive of deviance, since the behaviors are reminiscent of "masculine" sexuality, a clear deviation from the "feminine" construct. Such role reversal on a persistent basis is, according to Bem (1993), "defeminizing for women" who have been socialized to be "yielding" in affairs of the heart versus "assertive," the latter being the case for men's socialization. Culturally, in matters of romance, the male is "...supposed to be the dominant in ... initiating the date ... to guiding the sexual activity" (p. 163). But black women's filmic coding as habitual initiators of sexual excess, juxtaposed with routine counterbalancing images of white women, creates a female dualism. And while such polarization manifests itself vividly on the filmic level, it is on the cultural level that this polarization is simultaneously operational and felt.

Black Women as Cinematic "Other"

In the history of filmmaking, never has there been a period when the black female subject has enjoyed a prolonged spate of positive portrayals on screen. From the onset, black women's cinematic representation has been an ambiguous one. They have spanned the gamut of "otherness," simultaneously moving from "mammy," to "Aunt Jemima," to "Sapphire," to "tragic mulatto." With each such portraiture, the meta-massage conveyed has been that these women fall outside the borders of true womanhood. Now, in our era, black women have moved to yet another category of "otherness" on-screen—that of "oversexed jezebel." The comfort level with which this de facto imagery is received by viewers weighs heavily on the black community, which has long envisioned a day when the film industry would come to view and so depict black women as integral members of society.

Within the black community, two subgroups of women are simultaneously impacted by film's negative imagery: black women as social subjects; and black women who represent black female subjects on-screen. Regarding the former, it is still unclear to what degree the negative imagery has adversely impacted this subgroup socially, since rarely have black women been viewed as a group worthy of serious study. What is clear is that as more baby-boomers within this subgroup of women come of age, there is more and more dissatisfaction among them regarding their ambiguous filmic and social status (Bobo, 1995; St. Jean & Feagin, 1998). While it is true that, historically, black women's cultural construction as negative "other" adversely impacted the vast majority of black women, as of the 1970s, their growing numbers in the middle-class ranks have steadily increased. Notwithstanding this, their on-screen representations continue to be inaccurately reflective of this change. The medium's failure

to correctly interpret black women's diverse life experiences and circumstances, for instance, stands in stark contrast with the educational and
career achievements of many (St. Jean & Feagin, 1998). Treated as social
pariahs, their inclusion in the daily social practices of femininity and
respectability remains dormant.

Now, it may be that old habits die hard! For prior to the decade of
the 1970s, on the aggregate, black women were forced into ambiguous
gender roles by the unequal socio-economic structure, resulting in their
being viewed as aggressively tough women. Back then, denial of equal
treatment in the feminine sphere forced most black women to assume
functions and roles typically expected of males of their group—males
who themselves were rendered impoverished in their attempts to lessen
the burden on women of their group (Manatu et al., in press). It may be
that, because of systematic economic oppression, the survival mechanisms
employed by many poor black women, especially (menial work, sole
responsibility for child care, self-reliance for personal safety and support,
ill-attempts in the search for love, etc.), resulted in their borrowing
pseudo-roles and mannerisms culturally perceived as those prescribed for
males. It may even be that after having been successfully constructed as
"feminine inferiors," black women's forced masculine roles likely reinforced that construction for some.

But as of the 1970s, changes in the social circumstances of a good
many black women have steadily been becoming the norm. Despite this,
constructions of black women as a debased and subordinate monolithic
group continue to be presented to viewers on the big screen. Indeed, when
it has come to depictions of these women's lived lives, film has tended to
present them in the most self-offensive manner, thereby perpetuating
cultural alienation of them. Perhaps even more revealing is that, familiarity notwithstanding, many black males appear to also feel alienated
from black women. Such is likely the case if only because as constructed,
black women's filmic behaviors generally compete with those of their
male counterparts.

Cultural alienation strongly suggests a relationship between black
women's (mis)representation on screen and the culture's misunderstand-
ing of them. Literature on the relationship between film and culture
informs us that film is one primary window through which most Americans view themselves and each other (Sklar, 1975; Jowett & Linton,
1980; Lorber, 1994). This link between film and culture further suggests
that the medium is one major avenue the dominant group looks to as a
signal to help direct it in how to view and to treat black women. But the
fallout from mass perceptual distortion evoked by this "potent message

system" resonates with many actual black women; the link brings into focus a troubling sense felt by most black females in U.S. culture—that perceptual awareness of them is that of alien and social deviants.

When, for example, some nonminorities assume black women will have answers to a nonminority's racial discomfiture (Wilson & Russell, 1997), such supposition says something about how the former views the "other." One of the ways this becomes clear is seen in the nonminority's different approach to one belonging to their own race, but who is of an unfamiliar ethnic group. The impulse is not automatically to seek out members of that ethnic group who will offer ways in which the former might deal with that same-racial, but unfamiliar ethnic other. Perhaps the most telling point is that some nonminorities often turn to black women primarily for counsel regarding what is generally viewed as sordid matters. They fail to see the implication embedded in such solicitation: that black women will have answers because there is something about the essence of black womanhood which makes them especially knowledgeable in matters of the profane. These assumptions are not just insulting; they do little to advance mutual respect or trust.

Of course, if one were to ask nonminorities their perception of black women, most responses might well belie actual feelings. This is not to suggest that nonminorities, generally, are cognizant of having negative attitudes toward black women. As we are all aware, people generally attend and are sensitive to those things and people who are of importance in their lives. No, attitudes are not so much conscious (McIntosh, 1998) as they are evinced unconsciously (Bem, 1993)! Many know black women through work or school; many even have pseudo-relationships with black women, believing in an abstract sort of way that people generally have certain common concerns. But throughout U.S. history, black women have understood something which appears to perplex many nonminorities: that to be equal means not just to engage in quasi-relationships; to be truly equal means creating a meaningful space in which to understand each other's world.

But as we have seen, those two worlds as played out on screen are presented as alien. In fact, as in the film world, the cultural attitude toward black women is that of native-to-foreigner, indicating a lack of understanding of these women. Despite that black women have been a part of the social fabric of American culture for nearly as long as the culture has been in existence, their cultural and media treatment stands in striking contrast with that history. A divisive film culture, especially, speaks volumes about their "otherness," helping to promote social indifference toward and exclusion of them from mainstream American culture.

Yet, these social responses adversely impact this subgroup of women, many of whom (it is argued) may have difficulty developing a positive self-image as a result (hooks, 1981; Wilson & Russell, 1997). Black women, as it turns out, are no different from other women in their use of film as a mechanism through which to learn how they are viewed in relation to others (St. Jean & Feagin, 1998).

Film's sexual exploitation of black women, in particular, poses a threat to their self-perception by limiting their freedom of expression and by forcing many actual black women into becoming almost paranoid self-monitors. Hooks (1981) suggests that media exploitation of black female sexuality is a "psychological weapon [used] to limit and restrain the freedom of black females" (p. 67). And indeed, fear of being perceived as "prostitutes" or "sluts," for example, forces a good many black women into over-prudish behaviors (hooks, 1995) both in dress and in manner. I dare say black women would welcome a respite from such restrictive living conditions. But in the case of film where the more unsavory and graphic images of black female sexuality are to be found, no such breathing space has yet surfaced. It should be remembered that film preceded television with the big screen's unsavory images of black women. Here, viewers were first groomed to devalue black women by presenting them in the most dreadful light; television simply carried on in like fashion. While television contributes its own share to the devaluation process, it is dubious that the small screen can compete on the same level with film's history as a mass socializing force; its more explicit vivid images; or its larger-than-life dimensions.

If it is the case that one way people learn is by seeing themselves reflected in the images they watch, how they are presented in the vast majority of films clearly poses problems for black women generally. For one thing, how do they compete with such a "potent message system" which bombards viewers on a worldwide scale with its larger-than-life lurid imaging of black women's alleged immorality? That some American films featuring unsavory images of black women are exported internationally may mean that how foreign viewers come to understand black women also may have reverberating consequences. Even prior to arriving in America, viewers have a preconceived image of what black women are like based on viewers' saturation of the cinematic lurid images. When foreign viewers finally meet a black female, their impression of her is likely to be skewed, for it has already been formed largely by media images. Viewed from this perspective, black women are likely to experience racial and gender bias not only on a domestic level, but on an international level as well.

Less obvious is the fact that with few positive roles assigned them, even black actresses are affected. Given that black female subjects are presented in mostly caricature roles, black actresses are limited in those serious roles they can represent. Being forced to represent substandard roles requires much suppression of the self-expression. It is likely, too, that black actresses must often compromise their dignity in order to maintain their professional lives. Having to watch the self encoded in negative images is no picnic either! The images present challenges in assessing how they are doing, for black actresses are viewers and performers all at once. Whether lay-persons or actresses, on the macro-level, black women as a group have not been shown in any accurate or realistic manner who they are, where they are, nor where they are headed. How, then, are they to self-actualize as fully functional women, when almost all on-screen images in one way or another present as role models dysfunctional black women?

In the case of black actresses, their self-actualization as fully functional female performers is greatly undermined by the negative images. Historically, their ability to showcase their rich and diverse talents has been severely thwarted. From Louise Beavers in the 1930s to Ruby Dee and Dorothy Dandridge in the 1950s up through to Angela Bassett, Whoopi Goldberg, Phylicia Rashad, Paula Kelly, Alfre Woodard, Shari Lee Ralph and so many other black actresses of today, talents go wasted and unchallenged; self-expression gets suppressed; and professional dreams get deferred and go unfulfilled. To appease many black actresses while at the same time create the impression that these actresses enjoy a full array of performance menu, the film medium confects nostrums of caricature roles with ever more crafty ingenuity. Humor as mask for the "sexual" symbol usually underpins such craft; "all-knowing-worldly-maternal" figure is a second element often used. As a result, no one can say blacks generally, and black actresses specifically, are not highlighted on television and in film, for more and more black faces do appear on the small and big screens. But quantity is not quality, and in either case, black actresses still experience a severe lack in serious and diverse filmic representations. Ironically, caricatures of black women as comic performers and as sexual predators both fuel and are fueled by ongoing complaints of their absence or lack of diversity on screen.

The question remains, how are black actresses to self-actualize as performers if cinematic dramas with depth and breath of characterization are denied them in most all American films? How does the soul flourish, the aesthetic urge become gratified, without a space opened for such self-expression? And who heals the wounds when these performers are made to watch while other, less talented, performers get cast in a variety of roles merely because the latter possess "the look" so prized in U.S. culture? Black actresses are either shown at their worst (oversexed and nagging bitch), or in other instances, presented in their opposite, but equally degrading role as self-sacrificing characters reminiscent of the "mammy" image. A middling of characterization has simply not been made available to black actresses. Notes actress Marla Gibbs of *The Jeffersons*: "We are more or less told who we are, rather than asked ... we sing, dance, we tell jokes—that's all we are allowed to do. We entertain" (Monroe, 1994, p. 84). Actors Tim Reed and Bill Cosby have also decried the state of affairs for blacks in the media generally. In 1992, Cosby pleaded with media executives to write the truth about the lives of blacks, or else, not write of them at all ("Cosby condemns massacre," 1992). His lament apparently fell on deaf ears. More than two years later, Cosby wearily commented that writers had not in fact listened to his impassioned speech, for there had been no changes in the degrading images presented (Randolph, 1994, p. 102).

Given their endless confining and demeaning roles, one might ask, why do black actresses (and actors) bother to perform at all? The obvious answer is that for a performer, her/his very psychic life depends on such expression of the self. Most often, denial of a diversification of roles leads to frustration, which in turn likely leads to demoralization of the self. Bogle (1989) catalogues how during her lifetime, actress Dorothy Dandridge's film roles were kept on such a narrow and confining pathway that she suffered severe emotional trauma. The psychological distress of other black actresses is also documented. More than half a century later, black actresses continue to experience the same debilitating limitations on screen.

Who speaks for today's black actresses? What are their hopes and dreams for reenacting diverse cinematic roles? How do they maintain sanity knowing they are perfectly capable of bringing to life a particular character, but will never get the chance because they do not fit some artificial model of a "look"? How might an Angela Bassett be allowed to portray a romantic character in roles such as that played by Jennifer Lopez in the *Wedding Planner*, for example? Talent notwithstanding, had Lopez not fit "the look," would she have been allowed to portray such a role? If same-gender polarization is not the sticking point, what is? Certainly, it cannot be for lack of talent! For even if Bassett had not been nominated for an Academy Award for her performance in the film *What's Love Got to Do with It*, for example, reasoned minds and eyes would have to concur that hers was a stellar performance. Surely audiences can suspend

Angela Bassett as R&B singer Tina Turner (top) with her back-up singers, The Ikettes; bottom left, Angela comforts Ike Turner (Laurence Fishburne); bottom right, Ike and Tina experience a clash of wills in Touchstone Pictures' *What's Love Got to Do with It* (1993).

their disbelief for two hours while they get lost in and are gratified by "feminine" roles featuring a black actress, even when her male suitor is of another race.

In the world of opera, for instance, audiences have historically embraced a round aging dowager in the role of a young love object without experiencing undue paroxysms. If an operatic diva's age and girth differentials are believable on stage, why not color differential in film? An actress is first and foremost a performer. That she is tall or short in stature, light-skinned or dark-skinned in color is secondary to her performance. To view it any other way does not foster equality in the arts, nor does it promote equality in American cultural life. Just as print's devaluation of black womanhood helped foster negative attitudes toward them well into the 20th century (Freydberg, 1995), so too, repeated and unsavory on-screen images of black womanhood heighten those attitudes even more today, reinforcing the devaluation process.

Indeed, despite the loud and public rhetoric of intolerance for inequality proclaimed by most institutions in U.S. culture, the media marketplace of ideas still teems with glaring same-gender female disparity—this, despite black women's achievements in education, careers, and middle-class living! To the extent that their social status has improved, one is inclined to take as a given that black women's portrayals would also be ameliorated. Yet, their representation in film stands in stark contrast with those social gains. The question is, why have the media shown such intolerance for change when the industry's own stance has been that "art follows life"? If such is the case, should not our cultural products act in concert with current cultural practices? This observation brings me to a far more rare, but important question: How might black women as positive icons become part of American cultural mythology and replace the lurid symbol? And how, by extension, might black actresses' expression of the self be realized in this process? I am not sure that in contemporary American life, these questions have been addressed on the macro-level in any serious way. In fact, I am unaware of any sustained public discourse on this most significant of issues.

In recent years, it has become somewhat of a practice that a commission is convened to examine the impact of the negative images of blacks in the media, most recently the 1993 U.S. Commission on Civil Rights. Generally, much is discussed concerning negative images of the black male and the deleterious effects of such imaging on that subgroup. But where it concerns deleterious images of the black female, those issues remain largely untapped as a source of public discourse or of scholarly research. Interestingly, despite such public hearings, little has changed in ameliorating diverse roles for black males (Gray, 1995; Inniss & Feagin, 1995), let alone those for black females. What seems to me most clear is that film's most egregious exclusion and vilification of black women, whether as lay-people or as actresses, is an issue ripe for redress.

A major social institution which helps shape public opinion and audience perception, the medium has the potential to function as a transforming agent through the affirmation of black women's triumphs. Film is a social ritualistic part of American cultural life, which Jowett & Linton (1980) argue, renders film

> more than just a successful business institution.... [For film] became an
> important factor in the actual shaping of the way in which Americans

(and those in other parts of the world) thought and how they perceived the world around them [p. 69].

So, yes, I am arguing here that film could become the vehicle through which black women's lived lives are transferred into believable filmic truths. I am also arguing for a diversification of roles for black actresses through which such transference can take place. The medium has the power to showcase the shift from where black women have been to where they are presently; it has the power to deconstruct the old myths of black women as "nonwomen," for example, by reconstructing some aesthetic which would foreground black women's present public and private "feminine" persona.

Yet, film has not elected to be a champion for change; the medium, instead, has promoted an oppressive environment for black women by presenting lurid, visual images of imaginative cultural untruths. Presently, black womanhood as a positive concept is well nigh absent in film as it is in the psyche of U.S. culture. The presentation of more black women on the big screen, even in the mostly substandard roles assigned them, confuses many viewers by giving the impression that ours is a culture wherein all women are treated as a homogeneous group. Largely because of this, in American society viewers tend to overlook the practice of social exclusion of black women from participation in the archetypal social construction of the "feminine," a major result of which has been black women's continued exclusion from rewards of the feminine: namely, social consideration and respectability on a national scale (hooks, 1981; Beale, 1995). And paralleling their social exclusion are the lurid cinematic images which present them as sinful and "unchaste" women, such that the "symbol of whore" is their defining characteristic.

Cultural/Cinematic Construct of Womanhood

Haste (1993, pp. 172-173) has identified four major images of women in U.S. cultural fare, utilized to cope with and explain women's sexuality. First is the woman as wife/Madonna who is relatively sexless, and who views sex primarily as a means of procreation. Second is the woman as waif who is childlike and, thus, nonthreatening because she is dependent. Third is the woman as witch who has autonomous sexual power, magical power, and social power. Haste (1993) contends that popular narratives attempt to defuse the witch either by destroying her or by transmuting her into a whore.

These first three images of womanhood cannot be applied to black women, the first because they are already believed to be highly sexual, the second because they are perceived to be especially strong and aggressive types. Black women, hence, could not possibly be thought of as waif-like. The third image, the witch, is a bit more problematic. Black women could almost be placed under this category, but for one significant problem: as a group, these women have no social power. Symbolically speaking, black women, like witches, possess sexual power because they are believed to be highly-sexual creatures; black women may even be perceived as having magical powers, for they are "incomprehensible" to members of the society, particularly men; but they lack real social power. Lack of social power means that, as a group, black women lack social value. This is more than suggested by social practices throughout U.S. culture which place these women on the lowest rung of most all of society's institutions, thus denying them real access to participation. Lack of social value is also evident in widely held myths concerning black women's absence of moral character, where their reputations continue to be eschewed on screen (hooks, 1981, 1995; St. Jean & Feagin, 1998). This third image of womanhood, the witch, thus, escapes black women.

The fourth and final image of womanhood Haste (1993) identifies is woman as whore, and it is under this image that black women fall because the image of whore feeds into perception of black women as sexual temptresses through the ethos of sinfulness. Haste notes that "woman as whore" is an "extremely potent media image; she allows the expression of male fantasy while being safely constrained ... [which] assuages [man's] basic anxieties about the sinfulness of sex" (p. 172). And indeed, culturally speaking, this latter media image of black women is not unlike that held under the slavery institution. After sexually exploiting the black female slaves, slaveholders assuaged their guilt about the immorality of the sex act by assigning blame to the female slaves for the men's own sexual transgressions (Stampp, 1956; Jordan, 1968; hooks, 1981; Christian, 1985). Fomented by historical events and defined by current trend, "black-women-as-whore" continue to be imputed for men's sexual desires (Jones, 1992, 1993). The major difference is that in our era, that imputation has been enlarged by film's debased narratives, its vivid imaging crystalizing the stereotype even further. Such coding not only contributes to constraining black women's gender identities in society, locking them into an immoral cultural script, but it shapes and promotes cultural (mis)perception of them as "unfeminine" types.

According to Bem (1993), the structuring of daily experiences pre-programmed by institutionalized social practices determines the kind of cultural native adults become. If we grant Bem's theory, and if for a moment we trek through the cultural terrain in which black women navigate daily life, their marginalized and oppressive positions within U.S. social structure would appear to determine—and this point is especially important—not who black women themselves become; rather, who they become in the eyes of the culture at large. I want to stress who black women become to the dominant group. For it has been the tendency of that group's institutionalized social practices to pigeon-hole black women into a debased, subordinate, and monolithic social category. Despite such exclusionary practices, as a group, black women continue to resist, contest, and disaffirm such classification. Yet, even in the face of their resistance, society feigns not to notice. Erikson (1963) long ago informed us that public acknowledgment is central to one's social identity, since the latter comes into being as a result of "cultural solidarity" (p. 412). If a positive social identity is indeed dependent on cultural acknowledgment, black women's long and continued contestation of their feminine inferiority status suggests that the society has simply chosen not to acknowledge this fact. The ongoing structuring of U.S. culture's daily social practices further suggests that its disavowal of black women as part of the "feminine" is a deliberate one.

The mere act of structuring the daily social experience of respectability such that it excludes black women ultimately renders the structure a determinant of the kind of cultural adults dominant group members become—oblivious and, so, dismissive of female-female polarization. And this point may be especially true of women of that group, many of whom seem accepting of their favored "feminine" status, while ignoring the inherent same-sex inequities embedded in the construct for most women of color. Certainly not much is heard on a national level from this favored group about female polarization within the culture, let alone in film!

Let me hasten to add that two fairly recent publications by women of the dominant group do address the issue of black women's devaluation in U.S. film. *Black Women in America* (1995) and *Feminism Without Women: Culture and Criticism in a Post-Feminist Age* (1991) indicate that a serious shift in the inclusion of black women in white feminist literature is beginning to take shape. These two works contain writings which attempt to contest black women's cinematic imaging by analyzing a number of films for their construction of black female subjects. Generally these writers use a feminist approach to analyze the ways in which racial groups are played off against each other on screen. Modleski (1991), for example, questions why in *Crossing Delancey*, a film written and directed by women, the black female body is coded as being so sexualized. And, indeed, if female filmmakers also code black women as sexual symbols, what hope have we for transformation in the negative imagery? This is why Modleski (1991) cautions that "it is urgent that white women come to understand the ways in which they themselves participate in racist structures ... of patriarchal cinema—as in *Crossing Delancey*—..." (p. 133). This shift in inclusion of black women's cinematic coding by white female writers is welcome news, indeed, and it is to their credit that analysis of black women's filmic coding is being advanced in the dominant literature.

But the reality is that the shift in the writings of women of the dominant group corresponds with that in the dominant mode of communication in U.S. culture. In an earlier discussion of the impact of film's format, I noted that we now live in an electronic culture, where visual images privilege the written word. Thus, it is not a criticism of the aforementioned works to note that the majority of America no longer read; they watch! So that while the written page may have surpassed film in contesting negative images of black womanhood, what is also needed is visual stereophonic contestation on a macro-level. If we recall Postman's (1979) argument that "knowing" now means having pictures rather than words in our heads, it is film, then, with its sustained popularity and larger-than-life imaging which has the most potential for effecting change in same-sex female polarization while ameliorating devaluation of black womanhood.

Film Meets Culture:
Devaluation of Black Women

A significant truth about human interaction is the inability to definitively interpret communicants' intended meaning. Often, respondents must rely on culturally-agreed upon manifestations of behavior as a guide to attribute meaning. Acquisition of cultural meaning is addressed by Bem (1993), who argues that social practices are transferred from the culture to individuals through an invisible process. Individuals become enculturated into believing myths and stereotypes of cultural "others" through:

> ...the tacit communication of cultural metamessages about what is important, what is of value, which differences between people ... are to be emphasized and which are to be overlooked, what dimensions are to be used in judging how similar or dissimilar people ... are in the first place ... [which] helps to make a cultural native because it nonconsciously transfers the lenses of the culture to the consciousness or the psyche of the individual [Bem, 1993, p. 140].

Bem (1993) emphasizes that transmittance of communicating cultural metamessages through social practices and acquisition of such messages are transactional. That is, both are subliminally initiated "everytime the active, pattern-seeker is exposed to a culturally significant social practice" (p. 141), such as that depicted on screen regarding cultural "others." Individuals gradually internalize the cultural scripts and become influenced to construct an image of "others" consistent with these cultural scripts.

Significantly, devaluation of black womanhood involves the process of internalized cultural scripting, invisibility undergirding the process. Invisibility, in fact, assures that such scripting will endure. One way of illustrating how the process works is to look at the way in which sexual myths regarding black males versus black females have been demystified. According to hooks (1981):

> while changes in public attitudes toward black men ha[ve] occurred, there ha[s] not been any change in negative images of black women. The myth that all black men [are] rapists had ceased to dominate the consciousness of the American public by the '70s. One explanation for the change was the growing knowledge of the way in which this myth was used by whites in power to persecute and torture black men. Once the myth was no longer accepted as absolute truth, white women who so desired could freely engage in relationships with black men and vice versa [p. 63].

Embedded in hooks' argument is the value U.S. culture places on physical versus psychological injury—yet another example of the culture's commitment to its "either-or" worldview. In the case of black males, it is now clear that from the days of slavery and beyond, they had been castrated, imprisoned, and lynched based in large part on false accusations of rape. The Scottsboro case in 1931 was a glaring example of the mendacity involved regarding alleged sexual assaults by black males. After enough such cases, the invisibility process linked to the myth began to unravel. The public saw tangible evidence of the result of the myth: severe physical brutality perpetuated against black men in the form of lynchings. Based on its valuation of physical (visible) versus psychological (invisible) injury, public perception was forced to alter itself, which helped change social attitudes toward black men as primarily rapists.

But the case of black women has been altogether a murky one. For one thing, since in a patriarchal society women are generally viewed as second-class persons, black women were at a disadvantage during slavery, for back then, they were viewed as even more "nonwomen" than they are today. For another, because they were black women, no social order existed under that institution to protect them from sexual exploitation. And shrouded in secrecy as the act was, invisibility allowed blame to be attributed to black women, who then were perceived as "initiators" of their own sexual abuse by white men. Interestingly, no laws existed to "protect" white men from black women's alleged unwanted sexual advances! To compound the situation further, their abusers were often the very men who exercised power in U.S. society; black women, therefore, had no means through which to make visible their sexual abuse. There were no physical bodies to point to as evidence of their physical and psychological scars; no legal suits which might have provided public evidence of assault, while unearthing the falsehood inherent in the myth of "black-women-as-sexual-initiators." In fact, the culture's "either-or" worldview, operating as it did even within the legal system, worked against black women. During slavery, had belief that black women also belonged to the cult of true womanhood been in place, there might have been a space within the judicial system where assaults against them might also have been treated seriously. But back then, to assault a black woman carried no legal sanctions against such acts (Lerner, 1972). Consequently, there was no "smoking gun" that made visible the psychological and physical torture visited upon black women as a result of the rapes. Most black women dared to live; their injuries, thus, were "invisible" to the outside world, which neither cared nor admitted that sexual abuse was the norm (Lerner, 1972). In short, unlike in the case of the myth of "black-men-as-rapists" where visible lynchings helped prove the duplicity inherent in such a myth, there have been no visible "test cases" through which to publicly refute the sexual stereotypes attributed to black womanhood. Public perception of black women as sluts, hence, remains firmly rooted in false myths (Lerner, 1972; hooks, 1981; 1995), invisibility fueling the devaluation process.

Physical injury aside, hooks (1981) provides an equally compelling rationale for continuation of the myth of black female sexuality. She argues that the primary reason for continued devaluation of black women is "...to discourage marriage between large numbers of [powerful] white men and black women" (p. 63). Such unions, she notes, would threaten the very foundation of white economic rule, since women (and the children of such unions) generally assume the economic and social status of the men they marry. Should enough such marriages ensue, the balance of economic rule could shift; hence, such unions are rigidly opposed. Yet, while the internalized cultural script discourages marriage between white men and black women, it silently condones interracial sex between them; but it does so "only in the context of degrading sex" (hooks, 1981, p. 65).

Hooks is here arguing from a cultural context, but her argument has considerable force for racial-gender theorizing within the film context, since film reinforces popular attitudes through its genre of realism.

Traditionally, realism has attempted to correlate to the film world with cultural ideas about the real world which audiences can at least recognize as familiar. This raises the question: what does it mean that a cultural script is approving of degrading interracial sex involving black women? We have to first consider that U.S. films "do not merely feature this or that debased black [female] image..."; the images are "correlated" into a "larger scheme" of valuation (Snead, 1997, p. 27). Given that cultural belief is that black women are essentially transgressors, sexual deviation becomes expected of them. The process is further accentuated by the verisimilitude inherent in cinematic narratives, evoking cultural meanings associated with black female sexuality, while directing viewers' gaze toward what is recognized as already having meaning. The meaning of black female subjects on screen is thus settled by resurrecting the old cultural symbol of the oversexed black jezebel, images arranged in such a way as to carry forward the narrative of debased sexuality. The resurrection then calls attention to black women's lack of feminine and moral virtue, qualities necessary to validate membership in the "cult of true womanhood." Absent such membership, debased interracial sex featuring black women can be tolerated; such tolerances reinforce the space of sexual blame assigned to black women. The interplay between film and culture invisibly renders definition of the essence of black womanhood a debased one, leading to a discourse of public degradation which appears natural to viewers.

West (1993) suggests that while interracial sex with black women is publicly opposed, such dalliances are acceptable behind closed doors because the black female body is perceived as "more intriguing and interesting" (p. 83). Here, invisibility and the culture's two-valued worldview work in concert: black women's reputed sexual passions invisibly allow for simultaneous desire and disdain of them. But disdain masks desire because the cultural script of degradation is more powerful than individual wishes. This is why, along the scale of female valuation, black women have had difficulty leveling the "feminine" playing field.

It is the case that once a false accusation is made public, it becomes nearly impossible to disprove the thing, especially in the face of a truncated version of any individual effort that can be offered. Black women's endeavors to effectively offer counterexamples to their cinematic coding remain unsuccessful for two reasons: first because, though invisible, institutional cultural practices are stronger than individual ones; second because they lack the huge capital required to produce their own narratives. Largely because of these factors, the tawdry filmic definition of black female sexuality continues to make a devastatingly eloquent statement against the virtue of this subgroup of women. In fact, hooks (1981) is adamant in her position that mass media are culpable for perpetuating the debasement of black womanhood on a national scale. And she points to acceptance of interracial marriages between black men and white women in films, such as *Guess Who's Coming to Dinner*, as an indication that the dominant group is far more accepting of those unions. The romantic versus the sexual coupling of Wesley Snipes and his white female co-star in *U.S. Marshals* (1998) appears to support hooks' above theory. Contrast that union with the interracial pairing of Halle Berry and Billy Bob Thorton in the recent film *Monster's Ball* (2001), and we note that this latter union is far from romantic! Overt sexuality, complete with the black female's coding as "sexual initiator," is once again the hallmark of the black female's on-screen union. Here, Berry's sexual coding becomes of special concern, given the rarity of black females as central or romantic characters in American films. Black-men-white-women on-screen romantic unions, by contrast, are more acceptable in U.S. films, possibly because of the psycho-gender elements involved.

The sexual prowess of black men, prominent in the decade of the 1960s and 1970s, has largely become sublimated on screen. The "buddy film" genre of the 1980s (*48 Hours, Lethal Weapon,* etc.) now appears to act as surrogate for black male sexuality (Guerrero, 1993), suggesting that black male sexuality may be perceived as so potent, it must be suppressed. Elimination of the myth of black-men-as-rapists has not dispelled this second myth: the myth of black-male-sexual-potency. Allowing black males filmic roles of the "buddy" and the "romantic" versus the "sexual" may be a twisted way of "feminizing" the black male image, since the second myth has traditionally been a source of sexual competition between black and white men. The fact that black males are now granted some degree of quasi-diversity in cinematic offerings (as seen in those roles represented by Westley Snipes, Denzel Washington, Morgan Freeman, Eddie Murphy, Larry Fishburne, Samuel L. Jackson, Danny Glover, Cuba Gooding, Will Smith, and others) might even say something about how men generally feel about men as against women. Because males monopolize most of the economic and artistic power in the film industry (Rhines, 1996; Welbon, 1992), black males' limited but more diverse film treatment (in relation to black women) might reveal that even when arch rivalry exists between them, men have the capacity to offer "kind" moments in representation of other males. What the change in black men's sexual coding does not explain is why the filmic coding of black women as "oversexed" persists. I find hooks' (1981) preceding argument for mainstream society's disapproval of romantic alliances between black women and white men quite illuminating. However, might I also suggest that because women's social value is still based on the "feminine," which includes perceived sexual virtue and a hierarchy of color valuation, a divisive film culture undergirded by the culture's "either-or" orientation invisibly assures that loving and respectful romantic unions involving black women and men of any race are suppressed?

Suppression suggests a broader sense in which the culture's two-valued orientation works to exclude black women from the "romantic." To understand this process, we must first examine the culture's structural composition. U.S. culture is divided into both a gender and racial system. But the culture's two-valued orientation, however, further subdivides the racial system into a four-tier gender system—white males, white females, black males, black females, in ranking order—a principle upon which the daily social practices of the society are simultaneously played out. In such a cultural assemblage, its either-or worldview dictates that there can be one dominant only; thus, to maintain control, dominant patriarchy must forever assert itself. It does so through creation of a hierarchical subordination of womanhood particularly, where white womanhood is demoted into an inferior rank in relation to dominant males. Simultaneously, however, white women are also granted a monopoly in the "feminine sphere." While such a monopoly places women of the dominant group into a one-up social position in relation to black womanhood, at the same time, white womanhood remains a dependent subgroup. This latter point is pivotal in the demotion process, for dependence serves as the linchpin which reaffirms dominant patriarchy's rule. Through providing economic security for and social status (Lerner, 1989) to women belonging to the "feminine," masculine identity perpetually defines and reasserts itself. Indeed, the social construction of women as dependents and men as instrumentalists points to such a conclusion. Thus, despite the gains of the women's movement, the cultural narrative of "women" as belonging primarily to the "feminine" and the "romantic" class has by no means been eradicated. And it is at this point that black women enter into the cultural narrative.

Constructed as both fourth-class racial and second-class gender persons, black womanhood must be excluded from the "feminine" in order to serve as counterpoints to white womanhood; for again, based on its "either-or" worldview, the culture can support only one dominant in any social sphere. Yet, because the "feminine" and "masculine" genders are still very much valued, revered, and expected in our social exchanges, female-female disparity argues for black women's inclusion in the domain of the "feminine." Absent their inclusion, black womanhood promises to remain locked in an ambiguous gender role, since cultural socialization, undergirded by our two-valued orientation, is still a powerful social script.

Here, I want to foreground the problem of U.S. culture's two-valued worldview and its relationship to gender dualism on-screen. Gender polarization in film becomes bound up in U.S. culture's two-valued, one-up, one-down orientation, what Snead (1997) calls "binary visual opposites." Snead argues that in film, the dominant "I" needs the "coded other" (p. 28), one implication being that preservation of the social positioning of the one-up "I" depends on the one-down "coded other." Such "marking" are vital to the "I," for absent the "coded other," the dominant "I's" sense of place is itself rendered ambiguous. The "markings," thus, become signifiers of racial coding, black females coded as "eternal, unchanging, unchangeable" (Snead, 1997, pp. 26-28). A second usefulness of the racial coding, too, is that it allows the dominant "I" to weave in and out of diverse filmic roles while suppressing those for the "coded other"; thus, invisibly reinforcing the denigration of black womanhood. Indeed, since its inception, film's stereotypes of black women have, as Snead (1997) argues, "insulate[d] themselves from historical change, or actual counterexamples in the real world. Caricatures breed more caricatures, or metamorphose into others, but remain in place" (p. 27). This is one reason black women's unchanging essence as symbol of whore surfaces into most all roles assigned them; the roles call up remembrances of past folklore beliefs of debased sexuality.

Ironically, each presentation of the one-down positioning of black female subjects on screen reaffirms dominant patriarchy through the promotion of a general suggestion of the permanence of black women's lack of femininity contrasted with that of white women. This in turn feeds dominant males' belief in their role as protectors of and providers for the "feminine." Note that constructions of black women as loud, boisterous, and highly sexually-charged surface even when they are cast as supposedly career and professional women! The implied metamessage being that despite their altered social state, they are incapable of altering their basic essence. Thus, despite that the filmic visual presence of black female subjects might be more physically attractive today, devaluation of the essence of black womanhood on screen continues in one form or another. When, therefore, media images of black women as sluts and whores are juxtaposed with diverse images of women of the dominant group, the former's one-down debased social position is invisibly preserved. The point is that the social practice of denigrating the essence of black womanhood is easily communicated through film's visuals because the myths are "nonconsciously transferred to the consciousness" of viewers (Bem, 1993) through the culture's two-valued ideology. Female polarization through the ethos of "symbolic whore" is merely another example of what Bem (1993) calls a "culturally significant social practice" (p. 141). But it is a tidy way of advancing the devaluation process, black women's feminine inferiority emphasized through film's one-up, one-down female positioning.

Female polarization on screen is reflective not just of Bem's (1993) social enculturation process, but of U.S. culture's "either-or" worldview, making it clear that film and culture both feed and are fed by the other. This is because both the metamessage of film and culture share a historical legacy of the same thought-style. Their collusion of ideas is embedded in hidden myths about black female sexuality—myths which Snead (1997) argues are a "displacement of history with a surrogate ideology of elevation or demotion along a scale of human value" (p. 27). Habitual devaluation on screen demotes black women's feminine value, effectively leading to demotion of their human value. Without an understanding of how the process works, belief in the mythos of black female hypersexuality appears nearly immutable. Black womanhood seems forever locked into a false, centuries-old myth of symbolic whore.

Discussion of the devaluation of the essence of black womanhood is not mere rhetoric. Viewers need to understand that the primary danger in devaluing black female subjects on sexual grounds is the moral component linked to black womanhood. Left unexamined, perceptual distortions of actual black women's alleged lack of moral shadings can only flourish. The implication is made more sobering when considered alongside Keen's (1991) claim that "women imagine sex indirectly, while men imagine sex directly." One conclusion to be drawn is that like men who seek out sexual adventures, black women are nonwomen who dally in sexual adventures, rendering them sexual predators. When coupled with our "either-or" worldview which acknowledges, as "appropriate," the "feminine" and "masculine" genders only, black women's filmic coding indicates they indeed occupy the space of the gendered "masculine." Expressing them on screen as characters representing a monolithic group for whom intimacy and "romantic love" are not fundamental values can mean only one thing: They are masculine women whose central interest lies in raw, impersonal sex. Presumably, being such "hot-natured" pseudowomen makes them especially desirable in matters of sex; thus, the appeal to men of all sorts—a view operational in the culture at large.

Some two decades ago, hooks (1981) illustrated the myriad of ways in which black women in U.S. culture are too frequently propositioned by any number and variety of men (pp. 51-86). In fact, even when males encounter black women who present themselves as "ladies," many are disbelieving of the virtues of black womanhood and attempt, instead, to relegate the given black woman into a debased sexual category. A primary way this is achieved is by the subtle interjection of sexual humor into an otherwise innocuous conversation, the suggestion being that black females, especially, will appreciate lurid innuendo of all kinds.

What else accounts for such mass disbelief on men's part regarding black women's virtue? Why is it that within a week of landing on American soil, for example, most every foreign male soon learns to devalue black women as "undesirable" women? Where did these strangers get the idea that they have the right to accost black women, even when these women's demeanor and attire are clearly not suggestive of persons who are involved nor interested in prostitution? Do men who represent all ethnic and racial groups inexplicably and independently come to believe black women are intrinsically symbolic of the "sexual" and not the "romantic"? These questions beg still another important question. Might it not be that film's explicit depictions have so infiltrated the collective unconscious that the residual metamessage left with viewers is that the black female body is representative of this thing we call "sex"?

If filmmakers' reluctance to cast black women as "romantic" figures is not a means of reinforcing black women's "other" status of "symbolic whore," why not simply present them in roles where they are shown to value emotions and romantic love? Consciously or unconsciously, do filmmakers fear black women's integration into construct of the "feminine"? If so, why is this the case? What would it mean to have audiences view black women as "feminine" and romantic women? And what are the personal and social costs to black women that they are shown as inveterate deviators of the "feminine"? In the next chapter, I explore some of the cultural impact of film's sexual imaging on black women, and speculate on why they are shown to appear to fall outside of the "feminine" construct.

4

Cultural Impact of Film's Imaging on Black Women

In a society where women are valued for sexual morality and physical beauty (or is it the other way round?), black women have been between the proverbial rock and a hard place. In Chapter 2, we looked at the process by which filmic images shape viewer perceptions of black women's sexuality. In Chapter 3, we learned that love and romance are denied black women because images of perceived sexual nonconformity typically applied to males are also applied to black women, thereby masculinizing the black woman. In this chapter, we will explore how negative filmic images contribute to the stigmatization of the black woman socially, connecting her behaviors, her skin color, her very being to all things undesirable.

Most black Americans of a certain generation can still recall with some whimsy the excitement many felt during the 1960s and 1970s, whenever a black actor or personality appeared on television or in films. I can still remember during the early 1970s the breathtaking palpitations racing through me as we neared the Academy Awards night. Not one, but two black women were nominated for the "best actress" award. How proud we were that Cecily Tyson of *Sounder* (1972) and Diana Ross of *Lady Sings the Blues* (1972) were graced with such an honor! For a moment, all seemed right with the world, for our one problem that evening was who to root for. That period held much promise for black women as filmic characters, and many of us believed roles for black women could only improve thereafter. How ironic, then, that black women's relatively high visibility in films since the 1970s, and especially since the 1980s, houses so few positive images through which black women in U.S. culture can recognize as representative of their lived experiences!

We noted earlier that persistent and repeated negative images of black women in film can be detrimental to the group generally, and to black women specifically. Ongoing critique continues to note that such images have deleterious social effects because the general public, blacks and whites, may associate such images with black women (Leab, 1975; Collins, 1990; Jones, 1993; Orenstein, 1994; West, 1995; hooks, 1996; Wilson & Russell, 1997; Smith, 1998; St. Jean & Feagin, 1998). This is especially the case with images that project concepts of feminine inferiority about black women. One of the troubling consequences of such negative filmic portrayals is that:

> images of femininity ... in many movies tend to promote the tastes of the dominant group. Black women often are portrayed as ... unattractive, or homely; they play roles that yet again suggest an inferiority position in the beauty hierarchy [St. Jean & Feagin, 1998, p. 86].

Issues of the beauty model necessitate traversing the historical terrain once again, for it has been suggested that beauty considerations affect black women in ways that do not generally apply to black men or to white women culturally. The concept of beauty can be summed up in one word: colorism. According to Russell, Wilson, & Hall (1993), the origins of colorism can be traced back to the Antebellum South. What was referred to as the "mulatto hypothesis"—the belief that an infusion of white blood uplifted blacks from their innate inferiority—privileged lighter-skinned black female slaves, many of whom were slaveholders' own children. As we saw earlier in Chapter 1, lighter skin as perceived by Thomas Jefferson was equated with femininity and physical beauty; hence light-skinned black female slaves were valued for their exotic beauty. Darker-skinned female slaves, on the other hand, were equated with physical strength, but were perceived as possessing no femininity nor beauty.

As a result, special advantages were bestowed onto lighter-skinned black females: many lived as free women, and, according to Russell et al. (1993), when the Civil War ended, these lighter-skinned "elites" (women and men) attempted to maintain their privileged social status by establishing their own schools and businesses, thus excluding dark-skinned blacks from the group. But by far the most restrictive code among this elite group was the prohibition of marriage to dark-skinned blacks.

Russell et al. (1993) note that this directive was especially directed to dark-skinned black women more so than to black men. While a dark-skinned black man could improve his lot by garnering enough financial stability to marry into the "elite," thereby "lightening" the skin-tone of his children, dark-skinned black women had no such option (Wade, 1996), and from most accounts, generally, a good many still do not (Bond & Cash, 1992; Robinson & Ward, 1995; Wade, 1996). Quite apart from economic restrictions, the image of the cultural construction of the "feminine" factored into dark-skinned black women's inability to improve their social lot because a woman's social value was based solely on her "marriageability"; that is, on her looks. If she was very dark-skinned, a black woman's prospects for marriage were slim, indeed. Besides representative of physical beauty, light-skin had come to be "associated with femininity, youth, and even virginity" (Wilson & Russell, 1997, p. 73).

That the "feminine" has been denied black women is one point on which Orenstein (1994) would agree. She notes that "the model of European femininity, grounded as it is in delicacy [and sexual] innocence ... has largely been unavailable to black women" (p. 159). Indeed, based on the European model of beauty, colorism, not racism, has been the driving force in the beauty and feminine concepts. We need then distinguish between colorism and racism. While one's racial make-up may or may not determine perceived beauty attributes, color bias fuels the perception, since color is more readily visible than race. That Lena Horne's racial category is "black" did not necessarily exclude her from landing plum roles in film back in the 1940s. Essentially, the darker the woman, the further from the "feminine" beauty model she is perceived to be. Thus, colorism—how light-skinned a woman appears—is a determinant of perceived femininity.

So unavailable to dark-skinned black women has been this model that even today, popular images of the "feminine" have trickled down culturally, where a black woman's skin-tone can still severely retard her marriage prospects (Bond & Cash, 1992; Robinson & Ward, 1996). Notice that I did not say retard a black woman's dating prospects because generally speaking, men, black and white, have been socialized by various means, but especially by the media, to "bed" dark-skinned black women, but not marry them. Parenthetically, while dating and sex are not necessarily synonymous, in our era, the two have tended to be treated as one. Desires to bed but not marry dark-skinned black women appear so commonplace that one is left to deduce that many men within the black community have come to associate femininity, beauty, and suitability with a light skin tone (Bond & Cash, 1992; Taylor, 1993; Hall, 1995). As curious as this phenomenon appears, so commonplace is this practice that one can observe many black men dismissing as a partner a beautiful dark-skinned young woman in favor of a far less attractive light-skinned black woman. Perhaps this observation is what led St. Jean & Feagin (1998) to note that most black males are themselves "bombarded with images of the white model of feminine beauty throughout their lives…" (p. 93), which appear to affect perceptual outcomes for most dark-skinned black women.

Within the "feminine" cultural hierarchy, standards of the beauty model are shaped by the dominant group, a group which also controls the various message systems within the culture. Through the film medium, especially, the beauty standard has bombarded white communities, reinforcing belief in themselves as models of beauty. The standard has also permeated black communities, essentially reinforcing belief in black women's "feminine" and beauty inferiority. Such cultural training has had profound implications. Though some in the black community might be reluctant to publicly admit the following, discrimination based on skin color and facial features appears rampant within that community (Robinson & Ward, 1996). Wilson & Russell (1997) argue that cultural training has fueled many black teenage boys' attraction to white girls. And, indeed, why would it not? For so pervasive are images of white feminine beauty ideal that it would require herculean will power on the part of these teens to resist such images.

Consider for a moment the theories of a number of scholars who have examined the role of a culture's media system which serves as a vehicle for the formation of children's sense of self. I noted in Chapter 2 that Bandura (1977) has argued that the media are a source of role modeling for viewers. According to him, behaviors the media portray as satisfying and socially appropriate are likely to be imitated, especially by children. Erikson's (1963) theory is similar to that of Bandura. Erikson posits that at an early age, children begin to form a sense of their own identity by identifying with others who function as role models. Often, role models are found in interpersonal relationships, but Erikson acknowledges that they may also come from popular culture and the media (pp. 241–242).

Berne (1961/1974), too, has also provided insight into the process of role modeling. His theory of Transactional Analysis views social transactions between people as games, which, he argues, are segments of larger transactions he refers to as "scripts" (pp. 116–127). According to Berne, children seek out information from different sources about what kind of persons they are and what happens to that kind of person. Based on this information, they then form scripts through which they act out and live their lives. This script formation occurs very early in childhood, and as children mature, they may revise the script a number of times; however, according to Berne, it is unusual for an individual to abandon a script entirely. In contrast to Erikson (1963), Berne does not examine media sources, though he notes that external sources such as myths contribute to this process (pp. 39–40). Still, Berne's theory can be compared to Erikson's media-as-role-model argument, for whether the script arises from the mass media or from mythical stories, the latter may also provide the basis for a script. Finally, Williams (1984) relates role modeling to expectancy-value theory. He argues that viewers are more likely to imitate behaviors portrayed by the media if they identify with the character or view the character as someone important (p. 307). These scholars all have in common the suggestion that the process by which children acquire personal identification and script formation is a function of cultural socialization; each indicates that role modeling is a powerful tool for transmitting knowledge, which in turn influences cultural learning. And this is where the work of the media enters the socialization process.

In the general media, black boys, like all boys in the U.S., are confined to a limited imaging of the feminine in a way that concentrates and focuses on white or light skin color as model. For in U.S. culture, it is popular media which take on the task of explaining to the average viewer who represents the "feminine." This is an important role the media play because what viewers understand of the feminine will help determine how viewers, especially black boys, respond to the defined model. Thus, that many black teenage boys are attracted to white girls should not be terribly surprising. Hopson & Hopson (1990) cite psychologist Arthur Dozier (1987) as noting that "...beauty, goodness and power most often have a white face..." (p. xx). Combine this with the fact that today, children spend more time learning about life through the media than they do with parents. Previously, role models were developed over time through direct parental influence; in our era, it is the media which have assumed that role (Gerbner, 1986; Kaiser Family Foundation, 1999; Federal Trade Commission Report, 2000; Villani, 2001).

The importance of the media in the lives of children and the decrease in quality family time have had a major influence on children's selection of role models. Various studies estimate that from an early age, the average child spends up to 28 hours per week watching media images (Nielson Media Research, 1993; Kaiser Family Foundation, 1999; Villani, 2001). Villani's (2001) study, for example, concludes that most children start to watch television before the age of two years old. Another recent study by the Kaiser Family Foundation (1999) reports that electronic media dominate much of children's time: children 8 years and older spend, daily, more than five times as much watching media images as they spend reading (4 hours and 6 minutes versus 44 minutes), while half of all parents have no rules regarding what their children watch on TV. Equally alarming is what the Federal Trade Commission Report (2000) shows: that the media routinely market R-rated movies to children between ages 13 and 17 years old, children who frequently are permitted to purchase tickets to such movies without parental supervision. It would be difficult to overstate that devoid of strong parental models, children are left to judge which of the images that both entice and confuse have value and which do not.

Like most other children, black children, especially black teenage boys, also spend vast amounts of time viewing media images (Cosby, 1994) which tell them subliminally that white girls are more valued than are black girls. These metamessages are communicated by the heavy presence of white girls and women in magazines, on billboards, in commercials, in television, in film, and so on. The metamessage also transmitted by these women's prominent media presence is that it is white women who are important; they are the women to seek after.

Here I want to make a personal statement. It seems to me that within the black community, there are many different types of black female beauty available to black boys and men from which to choose in pursuit of their romantic partnerships. As well, the personal and social comportment of the vast majority of black women virtually teems with propriety. Yet, in the film medium, especially, black women's physical beauty and social conduct are not shown as desirable nor valuable as that of white women. It is, perhaps, for these reasons that white women seem to appeal to so many black males. But there are so many more positive images of black female beauty and of their social behaviors that could be shown in film. Black women come in all different shapes, sizes, skin-color, heights, and so on; black women also have diverse personality types and varying emotional and behavioral quotients. If the film medium presented a valuation of the diversity of black female images; if the images presented a more inclusive model of the various types of black feminine beauty housed in the black community; and if more positive and diverse role behaviors were routinely assigned to black female subjects, black boys might begin to perceive the positive aspects of black women as also desirable.

But a large, disagreeable, and repugnant obstacle assures that such positive perceptions are held at bay for most black women, particularly dark-skinned black women. Generally, the mass media tend to showcase in more "feminine" roles white women or primarily those black female subjects whose skin color and physical features closely resemble those of the white beauty model. Colorism as distinct from racism has been the hallmark of the film medium at least since the early 1900s. Such practices harken back to Bogle's (1989) earlier observation that every sexy black woman who appeared in film after *Birth of a Nation* (1915) was to be a "cinnamon-colored" girl with Caucasian features.

Indeed, within the mass media generally, the inclination has been to feature an abundance of lighter-skinned black females in films, advertisements, videos, and the like. Same-race color bias is one indication of how female polarization, itself employed to drive the stereotype of black female hypersexuality, is ubiquitous in media offerings. When, for example, dark-skinned black females are featured in television offerings, they tend to be coded as pseudo-sublimated figures, flirtatious and sexually suggestive all at once. When featured in film and music videos, the tendency is to code them as outright hypersexed characters, since the film medium allows for more explicit imageries. In the case of television, the coding of black women as inherently "sexual" is typically presented in the guise of humorous sex-talk and/or a variety of suggestive, nonverbal sexual behaviors depicted as humorous, as in sit-coms such as *Designing Women* and *Living Single*. What often happens in this process is that viewers are kept distracted by laughter such that many tend to overlook or completely dismiss the sexual subtext. On the narrative level, humor functions to "mask" the sexual stereotype assigned to darker-skinned actresses, even as the oft times pseudo-sublimated visual images perpetuate the lurid stereotype.

Nor are humor and same-race female polarization the only elements employed by the media to drive home myths of black female hypersexuality as against sexual virtue. Same-gender female polarization is also used to differentiate between the "feminine" and "sexual" imageries. In contemporary mainstream films, female polarization is found between races (black and white) and within races, creating a hierarchy of "virtuousness." Between the family of black and white women, white women's sexual coding is usually oversublimated, where depictions of them are presented as more feminine and less sexual than are those of light-skinned black women. Thus, when a white female character in film plays opposite a light-skinned black female, the latter is usually presented as more sexual, while, predictably, an oversublimation of images is used to code the former, as seen in films such as *Jungle Fever, Mistress, The Scarlet Letter* and others. Conversely, within the family of black women, light-skinned black women are also often depicted as more feminine and less sexual than are dark-skinned black women. So that when a light-skinned

black female appears opposite a dark-skinned female, the latter is typically depicted in more sexually explicit ways—raw and gritty—than the
former, as in films such as *The Bodyguard (1992)*, *New Jack City*, *Coming
to America*, *Boomerang*, and others. The implication is that the darker the
woman, the less virtuous she is; the whiter the woman, the more virtuous she must be. Situations involving women who possess a middle range
of light-skin color are fluid; thus, such women are allowed to move up
and down the ladder of on-screen virtuousness, scenario depending. This
is because white skin color, especially, is equivalent to femininity and
virtue, whereas dark skin color is tantamount to lack of femininity and
lack of sexual virtue.

Such visual metamessages help set a cultural "tone" regarding how
women with different skin complexion are to be viewed, "which filters
down to the viewing audience, where a certain legitimacy is [then]
achieved" (Manatu-Rupert, 2000, p. 191). And while film may not have
set into motion the cultural preference for white or light skin complexion, the medium certainly works to reinforce such cultural preferences.

Let me be clear that film does not necessarily produce such preferences in viewers. Perceptual outcomes based on race and skin color have
long been salient factors in determining social worth and physical

**Robin Givens stars as career woman and temptress Jacqueline, who toys with
Marcus (Eddie Murphy) and uses him for sex in Paramount's *Boomerang*
(1992).**

attractiveness, at least since the days of slavery (Jordan 1968; Keith & Herring, 1991; Russell et al., 1993). Indeed, within the black community, a class system based on skin complexion has also been a marked position from which physical attractiveness is measured, light-skinned persons perceived as the more appealing subgroup (Neal & Wilson, 1989; Hall, 1995). This is the case even where it concerns children. Harvey (1995), for example, reports that light-skinned children are far more likely to be viewed as intelligent, hygienic, and well-behaved than are dark-skinned children.

From a larger sociological perspective, studies by Keith & Herring (1991), Bond & Cash (1992), and Taylor (1993) find that European racial features including skin color, nose, and hair texture are generally preferred among both minority and majority groups, perceptual outcomes being that higher social acceptance levels result. But if such is the case, skin color preference problematizes the situation for dark-skinned females, especially. For it has been suggested that because physical appearance plays a more salient role in women's lives than in men's, skin color has different emotional effects on black women where it concerns perceived femininity. And where dating and marriage choices are concerned (Neal & Wilson, 1989), hue bias appears to be a huge obstacle. For within the black community, light-skinned color also acts as cultural capital for women.

In and of itself, skin color preference may or may not present challenges for dark-skinned females in the mating game. But the preceding studies also suggest an equally disturbing finding. Both minority and majority groups also tend to link appropriate social conduct with persons who possess European racial or physical characteristics. Consequently, perceived symbiosis of skin complexion and behavioral expectations leads to a preference for light skin color. Sadly, this perceptual interconnection appears to be the case with many black males, unlike many black females (Wade, 1996). Poussaint (1983) argues that how blacks feel about other blacks stems from self-hatred, brought about by the high premium society places on light skin color. This contention suggests that the lower social acceptance of dark-skinned blacks may cause black males to turn from dark-skinned black women. Several scholars provide indirect support for this claim by indicating that skin color is a salient factor in black males' mating selection, light-skinned partners being the more likely choice (Wade, 1996; Robinson & Ward, 1995; Bond & Cash, 1992; Neal & Wilson, 1989). As I will later discuss, this condition adversely impacts the cultural experiences of and outcomes for most dark-skinned women. And when film's routine negative representation of black womanhood is added to the cultural mix, the social effects on this subgroup of women become further exacerbated.

I want to reiterate here once more that I do not view film as the cause of such preferences. Considering the complexities underpinning the nexus of race, skin color, and perceptual expectations and rewards, attributing causation of color preference to film is clearly not supportable. What does indirectly bolster belief in film's part in the color-preference process is its ability to perpetuate and advance such preferences by its routine positive showcasing of certain subjects and its denigration of others. To the extent that film is a mass socializing force, it is reasonable to assume that the medium reinforces this cultural "preference" through its vivid imaging.

One result of such practice is that it creates divisiveness between black and white women, even as it also fuels divisiveness and animosity among light- and dark-skinned black women. Instead of uniting in their shared struggle for gender and class equality, women, black and white, are kept distracted by their individual social positioning. Both groups fail to see how each is being used as a scapegoat for the other's social and economic subjugation. Such seeming pseudo-conflict saps energy from both camps, where unity among women is made well nigh impossible.

Where female polarization is concerned, it was always color, first and foremost, which lay at the heart of the practice. In fact, it can be said that female valuation is reducible to skin color bias, for the practice is manifested in a myriad of ways through female polarization both in the media and in the culture. This observation is suggested, for example, by differences in men's valuation within the mating game. Even if a dark-skinned male lacks enough economic resources to provide adequately for his family, he does not necessarily suffer gender devaluation because of his skin color, unlike a well-heeled dark-skinned woman, for example. Wade (1996) posits that dark-skinned men can improve perceptions of themselves by marrying a light-skinned female because men generally, unlike women, are judged by their mates' physical characteristics (p. 360). And indeed, one can find an abundance of successful black men married to women not of a dark skin tone (Mullins & Sites, 1984; Wilson & Russell, 1997). This is yet another contradiction in the different oppressive socialization of women and men where it concerns gender valuation. Women are socialized to privilege a man's ability to provide for her over his skin-tone differential. Men, on the other hand, are socialized to privilege a woman's "feminine" attributes—her skin-color and physical beauty—over her intelligence and career achievements. This is one reason dominant feminists have long argued against the restrictive socialization of the sexes (deBeauvoir, 1974; Lerner,

1989; Haste, 1993; Bem, 1994). What has generally been missing from much of these critiques is how such socialization adversely impacts black women's social experiences on a quadruple level—gender, class, race, and color—color having the most impact, since a woman's social value is largely determined by her color status. Simply put, white skin color is to femininity and beauty as dark skin color is to the sexual and the profane. Based on this formulaic social practice, black boys' and men's exposure to such persistent female dualism in media representations may help explain why so many are attracted to white or light-skinned women.

The medium's salient role in advancing concepts of female dualism is why it is so urgent that such practices within our divisive film culture be unearthed and laid bare. A little blood-letting in the pursuit of same-gender female parity is a small price to pay for transformation in the negative imaging of black female sexuality. Failure to critique the imbalance between portrayals of white and black women in film truly may limit black women as solely defined by their negative overrepresentations. Indeed, given the habitual "loose" images of black women in film, I cannot resist asking the obvious: As a result of this unrelenting on-screen stereotype, do black men identify with white women more so than with black women as suitable marital partners? If this is so, such identification might result in more interracial marriages for black men, thereby diminishing the numbers of black marital partners available to dark-skinned black women in particular. On balance, colorism is a major determinant of who receives love and who does not.

Certainly, research by a number of scholars (Mullins & Sites, 1984; Murstein, Merighi & Malloy, 1989; Neal & Wilson, 1989; Bond & Cash, 1992; Hall, 1995; Robinson & Ward, 1995) reveals that, generally, black men perceive white or light-skinned women as more desirable to pursue romantically than they do dark-skinned black women. One must ask, is it purely serendipitous that so many black males happened upon this preference? If Berne's (1961) transactional "script" formation has merit, presumably, the preferential beauty script of many black males likely was formed in early childhood. My own perspective is that given the pervasiveness of filmic images which tells black boys who is representative of the desired beauty model in U.S. culture and who is not, it is more than reasonable to deduce that a major contributor to black boys' beauty preference is the media. It is also more than reasonable to assume that the various metamessages offered through the film medium regarding which group of women is more desirable as partners than another likely resonate with black boys up through to adulthood. If left unexamined, such on-screen messages truly could help determine which group of women come to be viewed as deserving of love. It is for this and other reasons that parity in the media should be a goal, if only because black males especially could be taught to think differently about who is "valuable." Many may be conditioned to reject women of their own group in favor of women of the dominant group. Yet, despite the seeming acceptance of such unions, presumably, many in the dominant group still likely prefer that white women's "purity" be protected from black males. Methabane (2001) observes that in U.S. culture, interracial myths still nag most mixed couples. As a result, great self-confidence is needed to confront the social hostilities these couples must endure. Such responses make clear the point that racial issues still impede democratic choice for many; America has not yet dug deep enough into its racial consciousness. Accordingly, to exercise one's learned color preference may be risky business.

I am not here suggesting that interracial relationships are undesirable in and of themselves. People cannot dictate to whom they will be attracted, nor with whom they will fall in love. What I am suggesting is that romantic choices made on the basis of color bias problematizes the process of mate selection for dark-skinned black women especially. Perceptual outcomes of such choices can only serve to deny such women. It may even be that such choices are also denial of the self, which cannot be perceived as a positive. Media have perhaps "unwittingly" (and I use the word cautiously) aided and abetted young black men in choosing a path not based on true choice; selection, instead, appears to be based primarily on female polarization, itself rooted in color bias.

One of the most salient predictors of future behavior is past behavior; thus, where the "feminine" is concerned, cultural media training goes well beyond affecting the romantic choices of black teenage boys. As they age, the images influence many adult black males' mating choices as well. St. Jean & Feagin (1998) note that "some black men come to desire women in the image of the ever-present white cultural model" of the feminine (p. 93). Indirect support for the above observation is provided by research which reveals that, within the parameters of these studies, black males rate white women as more attractive and desirable to pursue than they rate black women (Murstein, Merighi, & Malloy, 1989; Bond & Cash, 1992; Taylor, 1993; Robinson & Ward, 1995). Based on these preferences, many resort to marrying white women or very light-skinned women. In fact, if the woman a black man chooses to marry is herself black, studies reveal that she must generally be as light-skinned or lighter-skinned than the black male suitor himself (Bond & Cash, 1992; Robinson & Ward, 1995). And if she is neither white nor light-skinned black, another choice is always available to many black males.

A fairly recent social phenomenon among many black males is use of the term "women of color" to refer to their choice of marriages to light-skinned women representing other ethnic groups. Typically, other minority women (Latinos, Asians, Indians, etc.) are not considered white women, but neither are they viewed as belonging to the family of black women proper; hence the term, "women of color." Not being white often places these women in the "other" category of women, where in some sense they share "otherness" with black women. And it is these women's shared "otherness" which works in many black males' favor.

For the majority of black men who choose such women as marriage partners, the term "women of color" presumably protects them from accusations of preferring white women, even as it seemingly absolves them from charges of denied group affiliation. Choosing marriage partners from other ethnic groups serves a two-fold function: it perpetuates the white/light-skin-equals-feminine-beauty ideology; and it allows for "perceived" group solidarity. In the final analysis, black males can always collapse their choice of other nonwhite women into the category "women of color." Still, this practice does not erase many black males' choice of marriage to white women overall. Generally, however, such preferences appear to be most pervasive among powerful, successful black males (Staples, 1981; Mullins & Sites, 1984; Knoll, Smith & Murr, 1991; Wilkerson, 1991; Downey, 1993). More recent research supports the earlier findings (Wilson & Russell, 1997; Besharov, 2002). Besharov (2002) notes that while interracial marriages are increasing among black women and white men (possibly because concepts of beauty are slowly changing, Besharov argues), black males more than black females are still more likely to marry outside the race, white women being the partner of choice. Based on data from 1995 (the last year for which such figures are available), Besharov (2002) finds that of the less than half of all black males who do marry, one in ten marry white women, with many more dating members of this subgroup. Kroll, Smith, & Murr (1991) report that as of the early 1990s, 156,000 or 71 percent of all interracial marriages involve black men marrying white women. Contrast these numbers with black women who marry white men—only 75,000 or 29 percent.

These numbers show that black women marry white men at a rate less than half the number at which black men marry white women. One must ask, why is this the case? Could it be that, as hooks (1981) argues, white men are encouraged to sleep with, but not marry black women? Or could it be that black women prefer to be partnered with black men? Is it possible that for those black women who do marry white men, a majority do so because black men are unavailable to them as partners? These questions are prompted by reports which reveal that within the black community, marriages are down (Besharov, 2002). Perhaps because of this black women are said to be resentful of many black males' marriage choices to women of the dominant group. To say that black men's conditioned mating preference is galling to many black women is an understatement (Downey, 1993; Wilson et al., 1997; St. Jean & Feagin, 1998). Wilson & Russell (1997) point out that as a result of large numbers of successful black men marrying white women, many black women blame white women for "stealing" their best men (p. 125).

The conditioned color preference among many black males in favor of white women may have profound implications for black women, generally. Studies indicate that black women are less likely to marry or remarry than any other group of women (Cherlin, 1996; Wilson, 1996; Besharov, 2002). And lest the reader believe black women's lack of marriage prospects stems primarily from unemployment among black males, Wilson's (1996) study shows that even when marriage market opportunities are accounted for in black women's delayed or nonentry into marriage, the drop in availability of employed black men "can account for only a proportion of the decline in marriages in the inner city, including postpartum marriages" (p. 97). What, then, helps explain this paucity? For in reviewing the data in Census Bureau Reports, Mitchell (1993) finds that by the age of thirty, three-fourths of all white women are married, while fewer than half that number of all black women get married by the same age. The situation gets even worse for black women as they get older, for by the age of forty, one in four black women has never married, while only one in ten white women has never married by the same age. What makes these figures of significance is that, according to recent statistics, in the general population, there are only seven black males for every ten black women (Mitchell, 1993), thus limiting the pool of available black men to whom black women can marry. The situation is further exacerbated when black men make themselves unavailable for marriage to large numbers of black women by marrying white women— women for whom there seems to be no shortage of men.

Statistics show that among whites, there are ten white men for every nine white women (Hanson, 1993), sharp contrasts to black women's mating situation. When black males are added to the pool of white males available to women of the dominant group, a startling cultural phenomenon surfaces. Even within the mating game, white women have choices available to them that black women cannot begin to expect. Yet, despite these multi-layered factors, black women are typically held responsible for the pathetic state of affairs with regard to their marital prospects.

In examining some of those factors that impede black women's marital status in U.S. culture, Collins (1990) points to popular images of Jezebel, the oversexed black woman, and Sapphire, the domineering black matriarch, as contributors. Collins (1990, pp. 57–90) suggests that these two images are often combined to characterize black women and to explain their single status. In this cultural portraiture, Jezebel who is sexually insatiable is similar to Sapphire in that both are unfeminine. What distinguishes the two is Sapphire's domineering and rebellious qualities. So overbearing is this black matriarch that it is an affront to the black male, who either leaves her or refuses to marry her. In either case, black women, according to this portraiture, are solely responsible for their destitute social situation. Whether oversexed or domineering, together as symbols of the biblical Jezebel and the cultural Sapphire, black women's immorality, sinfulness, and rebelliousness are believed to make them deserving of condemnation. Yet, such condemnation has far-reaching ramifications beyond the individual black woman. For it is not merely the issue of marriage or lack thereof that is troubling.

Consider the following: Stable black family-life is also impacted by these erroneous media stereotypes. Black men's cultural media conditioning may have the potential to indirectly, but severely impede continuation of intact black families. For those black women who choose to marry and have children (and not every black woman does), their choices are determined, in great part, by black men's availability. If the statistics cited above are any indication, black women's inability to form successful families with black men has serious implications for the black community at large. It is not my intention to comment here on the choice of single-motherhood, save to say that when black men make themselves unavailable to large masses of black women, these males leave the black community bereft of husbands and fathers for the children of black women. And if it were only a question of morality, that would be one thing. But the reality is that issues of monetary support and the psychological development of black children must take center stage. It is generally agreed that children in two-parent households fare far better both socially and economically than those in single-headed households (Sampson & Laub, 1994; Shihadeh & Steffensmier, 1994). But according to Jaynes & Williams (1989), the majority of black children—86 percent—will spend some time in a single-parent household, households which will be headed by poor black women. Add to this the 70 percent of all black children who were born to poor unwed black women in 1994 compared with only 25 percent of all children born to poor unwed white women (Cherlin, 1996), and we begin to get a glimpse of the full gravity of the status of poor black families in U.S. culture.

The irony is that the mate selection of masses of black men generally, adds to the pool of "love" partners for white women (one already overflowing with men), while it decreases the available pool of potential "love" mates for black women. At the same time, black men uplift, economically, a group of women who do not require uplifting, if only because on the aggregate, white women belong to the privileged group. More importantly, these men simultaneously deplete the economic prospects for black women and children, essentially contributing to the impoverished state of the black community. This phenomenon greatly affects stability within the black family. Shihadeh & Steffensmier (1994) argue that "in various ways, inequality and economic disadvantage contribute to [black] family instability" (p. 734). To illustrate this point, according to the *U.S. Commission on Civil Rights* (1990) and other sources, black women are still the most underpaid workers in the U.S. (Zolakar, 1990; Taeuber, 1996), and this fact, coupled with black men's absence in black women and children's lives, greatly contributes to severe economic distress within black families. Economic distress, in turn, has grave outcomes for black women and children, not the least of which is familial insecurity (Cherlin, 1996). What is more, such lack places a tremendous burden, economically (Shihadeh & Steffensmier, 1994) and emotionally (St. Jean & Feagin, 1998), onto black women. Given these conditions, black men's marriage choices based on female polarization and artificial beauty preference appear to be a costly proposition for the black family.

I have attempted to illustrate that a large slice of black men's color preference evolves in an indirect way from media sources, sources which define that which is "feminine" and thus, virginal, beautiful and desirable (Bem, 1993; Haste, 1993; Wilson & Russell, 1997; St. Jean & Feagin, 1998). I have also tried to show some of the long term social ramifications for black women and children brought about indirectly by film's limited definition of the "feminine." If film's definition of the feminine was merely an occasional visual presence—if that definition was not juxtaposed with repeated and opposing images of black women's feminine inferiority status—perhaps the impact of the images might not be felt as keenly as they are. But when images of white women become the cultural model of the "feminine"—when that model becomes the yardstick by which deserved romantic, economic, and social rewards are measured—the model takes on a definition that has far-reaching implications for black women, culturally.

More and more, film's insistence on showcasing images of black women as "unfemininely oversexed" and, thus, negatively different, begins to feel much like a synergistic imperative; an imperative designed, not just to inculcate each new generation with the negative stereotype, but to perpetuate that difference so as to maintain the one-up "feminine" status of one group of women as against another. To alter the negative image of black women might mean to run the risk of actually helping to reform perceptual outcomes for black women culturally. Indeed, should such a change occur, what, apart from physical differences, would distinguish black women from white women? What would distinguish black women's social and possibly economic status from those of white women? I am not so sure the medium is as noncomplicit in influencing viewers' perceptions as it wants the public to believe. For if, in fact, film does not create, but merely reflects cultural reality, why is it that the actuality of black women's changing social status is not thusly reflected in the medium? The more black women contest the negative imaging, the more the film medium seems bent on preserving that image. In fact, improvements in black women's social circumstances are simply not reflected in a realistic nor sustained way in filmic offerings. Indeed, the more black women enter the mainstream in careers, comportment, and middle-class living, the more the film medium insists on returning them to their subordinate social status by showcasing them in the traditionally debased class.

For example, in the film *The Bodyguard* (1992), the featured black female character, Rachael, is portrayed as far beyond middle-class status, complete with above-average trappings of mainstream living. Yet, she is nonetheless, constructed as "classless" and as debased and crass in response to the request of Frank, her white male co-star, that they stand back from their relationship for a time. Her sister, Nicki, fares little better. She is portrayed as throwing herself at Frank, even while she is aware of Rachael's relationship with this man. I can grant Nicki's jealousy; I might even understand it, but I fail to understand why the lead sister, Rachael, is positioned as sexually crude as she is. Were there no other alternative behaviors? A portrayal of this character as deeply disappointed might have worked, no? At this juncture, even shameless weeping might have sufficed! Instead, viewers were met with and taken aback by sexually-loaded curse words of such proportion that would have rendered a truck driver speechless (I mean no disrespect to truck drivers who I am sure are generally lovely people). Film's continued coding of black women as debased and hypersexed is indeed suspect, leading St. Jean & Feagin (1998) to argue that "...media ... effectively maintain the cultural denigration of black women, with ramifications for black [women and] families" (p. 93).

Minimally, the constellation of multiple social conditions discussed exacerbated by film's lurid imaging combines to propel black women into one of three modes of operation in the search for love and affirmation of their feminine desirability. I am keenly aware that this latter point might

Whitney Houston stars as singer and actress Rachael Marron, who prepares to seduce her bodyguard, Frank Farmer (Kevin Costner), in Warner Bros.' *The Bodyguard* (1992).

elicit objections. Still, I offer this suggestion as an example of how, for those for whom "femininity" has never ever been affirmed, such validation has profound meaning. Candidly speaking, it is not so important that one accepts this notion as it is that one respects it. And in any case, black women who choose not to adhere to the "feminine" model should have as much right to do so as those who elect to conform. For those who wish to embrace the "feminine," the absence of black men in their lives generally leaves many with the choice of celibacy, single motherhood, or interracial relationships.

For some black women as it is for some white women, celibacy is not an option, nor should it have to be. Single motherhood is also not an option for many black women, who like most single mothers themselves were raised with certain values the society at large seems certain black women lack (hooks, 1981; 1995). Marriage outside of the race is also not a personal choice for other black women who prefer to be partnered with a black male. Yet, because black women's gender status is tenuous, presented on screen as not quite that of the "feminine" and all that the feminine suggests—purity, delicacy, and beauty, actual outcomes for black women to secure romantic love become severely arrested.

Routine and repeated media images of black women as "oversexed" and as not quite "feminine" invisibly blur the distinction between personal choices available to actual black women and institutional practices that help determine perceptual outcomes for women generally. Few viewers realize that as a result of structural media practices, some women come to be viewed as deserving of romantic love with all that is implied; others, not. The policing of romantic love by the film medium, for example, helps render invisible black women's prospects for love, marriage, and a stable family life something of a gamble. I dare say there must be thousands of black women who have never been loved by a man; who will never be loved by a man; and who will go to their graves having never been loved by a man. There must be thousands of black women who will never know what it is like to share a life with the opposite sex—one that is founded on gentleness, tenderness, deep caring, and mutual respect. There must be thousands of black women for whom the concept of the "feminine" has never been fulfilled, and for whom the sense of their womanhood has never been affirmed. Largely because they are shown as not "feminine," but as "hypersexed," black women are denied full feminine expression. The combined imaging then leads to a dialectic of distrust, as a good many black males appear to have discounted black females as "desirable" or trustworthy women. Yet, increased alienation from and dismissiveness of black women by the men of their group clearly has serious ramifications. For one thing, women of most social groups are generally viewed as bearers of gentility and grace—qualities which help mollify their male counterparts. In turn, males of the group reward their womenfolk with personal and social consideration and respect. But given black women's socio-sexual reputation in U.S. culture, amplified by film's imaging, there has been little room for chivalrous protection or for basic social consideration. Even basic consideration such as the natural granting that black women might also appreciate the common courtesy of the holding of doors in stores and other public places or the halting of cars, giving free access to the crossing of streets, is often denied black women— basic consideration reserved as a matter of course for women generally. Protection of black women's "honor" poses an even more dubious proposition. Because we live in a climate where sexual offenses against women are still a common occurrence (Freeman-Longo, 1998), media images that emphasize the alleged hypersexuality of black women may even result in their not being taken seriously when they are victims of rape (Painter, 1992; Manatu-Rupert, 2000). Indeed, as constructed in the general media fare, the black woman may have come to represent a sexual "convenience."

To illustrate this point, Cleaver (1968) reminds us that before he set out to rape white women, he honed his raping skills on black women within the black community with impunity. Let me quickly add that the rape of any woman is a heinous crime, entirely unrelated to sex and is, rather, based on aggression, subjugation, and power (Freeman-Longo, 1998). The subject is here being discussed as a point of interest regarding what led Cleaver to believe he was safe in using black women as a form of target practice. For him, black women were nonwomen who had no value in U.S. society; whereas, white women were real women whom U.S. society highly values (p. 26). Such dichotomous philosophy of womanhood resonates with 19th century ideals of womanhood which, as we have seen, cast black and white women on opposite poles of female valuation in society. And it is this oppressive ideology which has further been amplified and promoted through the medium's vivid imagery.

I am not here making the claim that media images cause rape. My argument, instead, is that cinematic images that focus on black women as hypersexed are major contributors to the devaluation and denigration of black women by males generally. Clearly, filmic images have not been the only contributor to, for example, black men's dismissive attitude toward black women. Television, beauty pageants, advertisements, and a host of other cultural mechanisms have also played a part in the denigration of the essence of black womanhood. But constant cinematic images of dark-skinned black women, particularly, as on-the-ready for sex and as morally bankrupt have greatly narrowed the gap between reality and the myth. This is one reason that, where it concerns female-female dualism, black filmmakers need be circumspect in avoiding the trap of advancing "black elitism" through the visual encoding of dark versus light-skinned females as signifiers of debased sexuality. When considered alongside film's strong potential for persuasiveness (Boyum, 1985), such practices can only serve to perpetuate the influence of colorism and female gender dualism.

Negative on-screen imaging of black female sexuality has its costs. It costs the black community by contributing indirectly to black men's devaluation of black women. Such dismissiveness, in turn, leaves the black community devoid of men who can serve as role models for their children, as well as serve as providers for their families. Negative imaging also costs dark-skinned black women especially by contributing on various levels and in various indirect ways to their single status, a status which, for example, burdens these women because of their disproportionate responsibility for their children (Morash, Bynum, Koons, 1998; Henriques & Gilbert, 2000). Essentially, such imaging contributes indirectly to leaving the black community devoid of men who can serve as husbands and fathers. As importantly, negative imaging costs black women because the imaging denies them expression of their "femininity," forcing black women to find resourceful means of combatting cultural misperceptions of hypersexuality, unattractiveness, unworthiness, and undesirability.

Invisible Black Women

Given that U.S. society is still divided by the color line, concern over black women's filmic roles necessarily involves race. I would have liked nothing better than to have written a book that did not concern itself with race; alas, racial issues are ubiquitous within our pluralistic society, permeating most all public and critical discourse about "Americans" and about how each group navigates cultural life in America. To acknowledge that race matters, then (West, 1993), is to admit that we, black and white, are more often than not in the struggle toward harmony.

I want to acknowledge that all "women of color" (and men too) experience racial oppression on some level. My focus on black women is an attempt to fill out the larger picture of the cultural preoccupation with black and white issues, which have plagued America since its beginnings (Jordan, 1968; hooks, 1981; Jones, 1993), much like in the British tradition where issues of class have permeated that culture (Hall, 1992). Focus on black women is also an attempt to show how certain cultural products play to race and gender consciousness, and how such positions can have adverse perceptual outcomes for black women in particular. It is not that Latino, Asian, and Indian women are not also discriminated against filmically and culturally (Sethi, 1998). It is rather that these women do not carry with them the historical legacy black women—especially dark-skinned black women—have experienced within American culture since its inception. Though considering U.S. culture's "either-or" orientation coupled with black women's visible racial and color "otherness," perhaps it was inevitable—propitious even—that their presence would set the stage for a dual split between black and white women. Perhaps it was inevitable that whiteness would become the cultural signifier for the feminine, the virtuous, and the beautiful; blackness, the cultural signifier for the nonfeminine and all that is unholy.

Earlier in this chapter, we explored the ways in which colorism—white and light-skin coloration—separates "women" in American culture. It can legitimately be argued that, generally, other "women of color" are likely not to experience the kinds of debilitating oppression dark-skinned black women do, in part, because the skin color and facial features of other "women of color" generally come closest to the white ideal of beauty (Hall, 1995; Wade, 1996). Like white skin, light skin color tends to confer upon women some degree of inherent "goodness" not attributed to dark-skin women. Light-skinned women may, in fact, be perceived as just a bit more "feminine"; a tad more pure, delicate, and virginal (Wilson & Russell, 1997), and thus deserving of less hardship. Research by Keith & Herring (1991) reveals a relationship between skin-color bias and racial stratification. The authors conclude that "the effects of skin color are not only historical curiosities from a legacy of slavery and racism, but present-day mechanisms that influence who gets what in America" (p. 777). Where it concerns women, such may be the case because as a signifier of the "feminine," white-skin color along with its off-shoot variant, light-skin, have long been associated with virtue and beauty (Neal & Wilson, 1989; Hall, 1995; Wade, 1996). The question of dark-skinned black women, however, presents special problems because, minimally, their very visible racial and color "otherness" is a daily reminder of important dimensions of their historical exploitation in American cultural life. But as is the case with much of its legacy, American culture is far from comfortable with "remembering" the unpleasantries of its history. Thus, dark-skinned black women, especially, become invisible in the culture. And it is this invisibility which renders their ongoing personal and social experiences rife with oppression.

As in most cultures, women in U.S. culture are stratified into different social classes, some of which confer more privilege than others. In her article "White Privilege" (1998), McIntosh views "privilege" as "confer[ring] dominance because of one's race or sex" (p. 168). She argues that white women are "justly seen as oppressive" by women of color because having been "conditioned into oblivion" about white skin-privilege, whites come to view their various social and economic advantages as part of their "being human being[s]." Much of white women's "oppressiveness" operates on an "unconscious" level (pp. 166–168). Yet, what many white women may not fully appreciate is that while their stratification of "womanhood" is relegated into a subordinate class, membership within the ruling class simultaneously confers upon them a sizeable share in the social and economic power structure. Such rewards have traditionally evolved as a result of a kind of reflected glory. Access to such rewards has historically been made possible in large part through alliance with white women's fathers and husbands (Lorde, 1984; Manatu et al., in press). There is, then, a built-in privilege accrued white women as a group that is denied many women of color. For example, black women's oppressive double classification as both "women" and "black" creates a two-tier visible "otherness," making it clear that any access to social and economic rewards has not operated for black women in the way that it has for white women historically (Keith & Herring, 1991; Wade, 1996). For one thing, skin-color effects have greatly slanted how ideas of the "feminine" have been applied in U.S. culture, what Lorde (1984) argues is white women's tendency to view their oppression-as-women, as residing in their sex difference, while "ignor[ing] differences of race..." (p. 116). Consequently, the prevailing definition of "women" is still viewed in terms of white women's experiences (McIntosh, 1998). Recall the female referred to in Chapter 3 whose query regarding the need to move "women" back into the "feminine" revealed that her definition of women is rooted solely in white women's experiences. Yet such perception of the universality of white women's lives obscures the fact that, for example, black women are still the lowest wage earners in U.S. culture (Taeuber, 1996; Sklar, 1998), and, therefore, the poorest subgroup. Studies show that between 1979–1993, black women's median annual earnings were $19,820 compared with white women's median annual earnings of $22,020; black men's median annual earnings of $23,020; and white men's median annual earnings of $31,000 (Taeuber, 1996, p. 88).

Despite these figures, women of the dominant group continue to focus on "gender" as the major cause of economic and social oppression among women, dismissing the possibility that race and color are also determining factors for black women's depressed economic and social status (Keith & Herring, 1991; Manatu et al., in press). Yet, even if gender bias were to be eradicated, racial and color bias still assures black women's economic and social exclusion. Yamato (1998) argues that "racism is supported and reinforced by classism ... which feeds sexism..." (p. 152). Following this suggestion, white women's race and skin-color generally bolster their class status which, in turn, works to soften the social blow to their differential gender status. White women's gender struggle ought not be minimalized; however, the high premium placed on their skin color and their perceived right to the "feminine" combine to grant white women economic and social rewards that have appeared normative and average both culturally and in film. Indeed, it has been argued that the present interlocking social hierarchies—race, class, and sex—act as "invisible packages of unearned assets..." (McIntosh, 1998, p. 165), which have worked for women of the dominant group in unseen ways. And such has been the practice for generations, with much of white women's overall social and economic privilege going unchallenged, until recent social developments now seemingly threaten that way of life.

The decade of the 1970s saw dark-skinned black women in particular begin to experience a small shift in their status as social subordinates. Many left the domestic-type jobs and joined the mainstream workforce, first as clerical help, and more recently as professionals (U.S. Commission on Civil Rights, 1990; Wilson & Russell, 1997; St. Jean & Feagin, 1998; Bell & Nkomo, 2001). At the same time, despite their continued substandard roles, dark-skinned black actresses began to be portrayed as physically beautiful, albeit "oversexed" characters (Leab, 1975). Presumably, their modest social and economic achievements—even their changing cinematic visual presence—began to threaten the traditional social imbalance of privilege among "women," tipping the social and economic scale just enough to raise concern. I argue here that, generally, black women's attempt to challenge their social disadvantage by becoming educated in relatively large numbers (compared to black men) and by entering the mainstream workforce in equal numbers is a major cause of anxiety among the dominant group. Combine these factors with the change in black women's cinematic appearance and the confluence now seemingly challenges the "feminine" status quo.

It is reasonable to assume that many likely view such gains as a threat to their own social and economic status; these gains disrupt the practice of the culture's one-up, one-down social positioning. We need recall that not long ago, black women in U.S. culture were (and many still are) the primary suppliers of cheap labor in service to white women (hooks, 1981; Wilson & Russell, 1997; Rubin, 1998). Black women have labored as mammies and nannies for the children of white women. Black women have also labored as maids in the households of white women. And because most women still grapple with the attendant challenges of the domestic sphere, black women have also served as confidantes to many of those white women for whom they worked (Wilson & Russell, 1997).

But with continued changes in the working status of many black women, white women are now being asked to view as "social peers" a group of women whom they previously perceived and treated as subordinates. Not only must this be a difficult mind shift, much the way it is for men where it concerns equality with women, but where once white women as a group held the one-up position both socially and economically, more and more, women of the dominant group must now compete with their symbolic former maids for careers and promotions. In essence, white women are slowly being forced to compete for professional status with black women—women whom they have been socialized for all their lives to view nonconsciously as social "other." Presumably, their professional gains have begun to alter their social status (at least those in the middle class), allowing the possibility for what Marshall-Wong (2000) argues is black women's right to elegant living. Indeed, Rubin (1998) has observed that whites are generally "outraged" when blacks form their own theme houses on college campuses or move to "...the newly developing black middle class suburbs" (p. 95). What is more, black women are also challenging ideas of the "feminine." They are demonstrating daily and "in your face" that they, too, are "feminine"; they, too, are virginal, delicate, and strong all at once. Presumably, white women must respond, if only because for so long, that purview, the "feminine," was theirs and theirs alone.

These are painful challenges for white women. In discussing working-class women's (and men's) response to increased visibility of people of color in U.S. culture, Rubin (1998) notes that whites see not only "their jobs and their way of life threatened, but they feel bruised and assaulted by an environment that seems suddenly to have turned color and in which they feel like strangers..." (p. 95). Such responses are understandable, understandable because white women, like white men, have been conditioned to assume that as white persons, their very presence meant they belonged; meant they could make the various "social systems work for [them]" (McIntosh, 1998, p. 168). In a sense, then, it is as if a cruel joke is being played out on women of the dominant group.

From their perspective, one can easily see that white women, like black women, have been victimized by their distinct group-socialization, though in very different ways. White women's socialization set up certain expectations to which they have grown accustomed. Indeed, such intergenerational socialization must, by now, be at the cellular level, for historically, white skin color has provided a great many advantages, much of which was taken as a given. As McIntosh (1998) argues:

> obliviousness about white advantage ... is kept strongly inculturated in the United States so as to maintain the myth of meritocracy, the myth that democratic choice is equally available to all. Keeping most people unaware that freedom of confident action is there for just a small number of people props up those in power... [p. 169].

Ah yes, meritocracy! That specious ideology which has functioned to handicap the socialization of many women of the dominant group into an unrealistic belief that their privileged position is an earned one, if not a right. Such belief has been inculcated by the implied promise of an eternal privileged social and economic status, a status appearing as natural as breathing. And who can blame these women? For they, like blacks, have also been deceived about their inherent social rights or inherent lack thereof (in the case of black women). The difference between these two oppressed subgroups is that white women settled into their social positioning (much of which has been a comfortable one), while black women vehemently resisted theirs. It is the case that often, it is not so much what people receive as what they are denied which drives them.

Where it concerns career struggles, these two subgroups of women have indeed experienced different forms of oppression (Bell & Nkomo, 2001). The problem now faced by many women of the dominant group is that their socialization can no longer continue to automatically fulfill its promise of presumed social and economic advantage—at least, not on the large scale it did prior to the 1970s. Compounding the problem for many white women (especially poor white women) is that the privileged ideology has left many with few alternative skills. Professional, economic, and social competition between black and white women has taken what has long been perceived as meritocracy out of the world of abstraction and brought it into the domain of reality. The concept of "earned privilege," long believed to be the basis for much of white women's economic advantage over black women (McIntosh, 1998), is in the process of being debunked, prompting challenges for many women of the dominant group. Many are unprepared for the shift in social relations. Bell & Nkomo (2001) note that while gender is a common factor of struggle between black and white women in corporate America, race and class continue to be wedges between them. Having found themselves in the middle of this shift, presumably, many white women possess few psychological tools with which to traverse the minefield of social change.

From their vantage point, these are admittedly difficult times for women of the dominant group. Yet, if equality for women is what "liberated" white women wanted, if equality for women is what they fought for, they must somehow see that equality cannot be had for just a specific subgroup of women. Women of the dominant group must come to see that they have much to add to the lives of all women. Instead of fearing black women's slow and meager entry into the middle-class ranks, they can confront the challenges many now face with black women—gender and class discriminations. One way white women as a group can contribute to ameliorating the lives of all women is simply by becoming aware of the inequities embedded in the institutional structural arrangements in society, including the filmic institution. They can begin to notice how different women are treated differently on all levels in the daily social practices within the culture, and how such differential treatment impacts real lives. Such awareness necessarily promotes monitoring of one's own behaviors and responses, which can have transforming effects.

What white women should keep in mind is that black and white women are not yet fully "sisters under the skin" (Lorde, 1984). Women, black and white, cannot make such claims until full parity among women is achieved. We might at least begin by asking, what group of women continues, on a large scale, to provide domestic, health-care, and nanny "service" to which group within U.S. culture? Likewise, within filmic narratives, what group of women is routinely shown as characters in service to which group? Why, for example, is it that one never sees as a natural occurrence white women in the act of walking black babies in strollers or black senior citizens in wheelchairs throughout the society, as seen daily in the case of black women? Why is it that one never sees these phenomena depicted on screen as well, though one has little trouble viewing filmic images of black women routinely engaged in such work? Could it be that white women are socialized by both the culture and through the film medium not to work for black women, no matter how poor the white woman nor how economically viable the black woman? Wilson & Russell (1997) observe that many white women have been reluctant to work side by side with black women in pink-collar jobs. As a result, a hierarchy of work division was established within that arena to address such tensions. Even in the corporate world where, presumably, women are more educated and thus more tolerant of differences than those in pink-collar jobs, it is suggested that many white women experience discomfort with the idea of working for a black female supervisor (St. Jean & Feagin, 1998; Bell & Nkomo, 2001).

What does this say to women of the dominant group about their place in the culture versus black women's place? What does this say to them about "sisterhood"? Indeed, what is wrong with this cultural portraiture? How do white women think black women should respond to their socially-exclusive place in the culture? And what has the dominant women's movement proposed to do about such social inequity among women? Not until a comparable number of white women are socialized to perceive black women, not as "other," but as persons, can we truly say there is equality among women. Not until it becomes normative in film and in the culture for white women to also serve as nannies who can walk black babies in carriages to parks, for example, can we avow that women have achieved social parity in U.S. culture. For if mothers must work, someone necessarily must watch their children. That "someone" ought not organically be one particular group of women.

For their part, black women continue to resist their stereotype of social "other," admittedly to the distress of many. Yet, resist they must if they are to rid themselves of the various social mechanisms which threaten to diminish their every achievement. The dehumanizing legacy of a social system and its institutions, with the film medium leading the pack, has told the world in vivid terms that black women are of little value; that they are not feminine; that they are negative sexual "other." Within this resistance are deep-seated challenges for black women as well. Yamato (1998) suggests that blacks in general and black women in particular have been oppressed for so long, many have internalized the message of unworthiness; many have come to accept the message of deserved marginalization. Black women, therefore, must remain vigilant in their response to all forms of negative stereotypes, oral or imagistic, resisting each stereotype as they are confronted by such imaging.

Reversal of a Cinematic Misrecognition?

During the 1970s, along with their changing social status, an ironic phenomenon occurred in the lives of black women as they made their way to the movie theatres. The profusion of images of black female subjects in films of the 1970s paralleled actual black women's burgeoning entry into the ranks of the middle-class. This nexus of events saw a correlative shift in the expectations of black female viewers. Through film, this subgroup of viewers hoped to see their changing social status impressed upon the psyche of America. Black female viewers had a need to see positive symbolic images of the self begin to become etched in the cultural psyche; they certainly did not want their experiences discounted, nor were they content with delay! The need for affirmation of self and group resonates in the numerous complaints levied against films of the 1980s and 1990s. But among the expressed dissatisfaction, perhaps the most compelling evidence of such a desire is captured in Bobo's (1995) study of black female viewers' response to three films: *The Color Purple* (1985), *Daughters of the Dust* (1992), and *Waiting to Exhale* (1995).

In particular, the black female subjects' response to the film *Waiting to Exhale* revealed that those areas in the film which failed to reflect their lived experiences did not resonate with the black female viewers. The women resisted by purposely filtering out the lurid images. Conversely, the women responded favorably to those elements in the film which included "aspects of their lives and histories, missing from other well-known works ... depicted for the first time in a medium accessible to a large number of black females" (Bobo, 1995, p. 3). Bobo's findings suggest that though black women have different economic concerns and sexual preferences (p. 205), these female viewers are starved for films that imaginatively but accurately reflect their varied experiences. The findings further suggest that black female viewers want their lives encoded truthfully on screen; they also want to identify with other black female subjects of "like" experiences.

But the truth is that unlike other groups in U.S. films, lurid images of black women have had a permanence beyond that which is normal. Because of this, the images may have worked to undermine a cultural coming together of a community of actual black women (hooks, 1981; St. Jean & Feagin, 1998). As I have previously argued, Erikson (1963) believes one's social identity comes into being through an "accruing of the self-image one's society allows" (p. 412). If we believe, as Erikson (1963) posits, that "cultural solidarity" is central to one's sense of social identity, then film's repeated depiction of a deviant social black woman does not allow black women opportunities to view other black women of oppositional or like sensibilities. Lack of connectedness to a community of like-functioning social black women could result in in-group alienation for many.

Given the fairly high numbers of black women in corporate America, for instance, this may mean many black women operate in a space of isolation within their communities of origin. Black women who were the first to enter into certain high-profile professions, for example, may find themselves ostracized in both their work and social space. In their ten-year study of the struggles of black and white women to assimilate into the corporate culture, Bell & Nkomo (2001) report that black women continue to be a mystery to their colleagues. One explanation appears to be that the kind of social intercourse certain institutions privilege over that proportionally exercised in the black community generally may be conflictive (Wilson & Russell, 1997; Bell & Nkomo, 2001). Attempts to straddle the demands of both worlds, with an emphasis on "fitting in" with behavioral expectations of the organizational culture, can result in an imbalance of the self. When and if their "corporate behaviors" begin to spill over into their interactions within their community of origin, they may be rebuffed as too "white," and thus, shunned. A sense of isolation is likely to be one result; the difficulty of negotiating expectations of social exchange between their culture and the dominant's may be daunting, even exhausting.

This is one reason black women as a group need to have their lives become valued and normalized in the perceptual field of mainstream America. As a matter of course and to minimize their sense of social alienation, black women as a group need to see images of a community of black women with whom they can connect, if only on a visceral level. They need to see an accurate accounting of their varied experiences and diverse milieu reflected back to them. Few black women want to be viewed as individual models of the group! Such a view implies the group suffers from severe social dysfunction, but a few individual members stand apart. This attitude is not only patronizing; it sets up a divisiveness neither the group nor group members can afford. There is a further reason black women's cultural life needs to become normalized on screen: normalization could help members of the dominant group begin to have a more accurate picture of blacks in general and black women in particular. Women of the dominant group might learn they have more in common with their black female counterparts than is now believed. Such a shift in socialization holds the promise for improved relations between the two groups. But thus far, the sum of black women's on-screen representations has notably failed to create portrayals dominant group members can recognize as universal. Filmic constructions have also failed to create meaningful portrayals which black women themselves can find aesthetically gratifying. The hopes of the 1970s—that images of the "mammy" and the "buffoon" would be replaced by images which provide a rich slice of black women's lived lives—have not materialized in the works of black or white filmmakers. Yet, there is so much more to black women than has yet been narrated.

One wonders if either set of filmmakers has ever mused about what a narrative about black women absent the "sexual" might look like. Perhaps because they are men, the question has never been entertained; perhaps, too, because they are men, the sexual imagery is unintentionally skewed. Men, after all, cannot be expected to know what women are really like, or can they? In the case of black male filmmakers, especially, presumably they witnessed how women (mothers, sisters, wives, daughters, aunts, and so on) in their own familial environment functioned as persons. Are they telling viewers their womenfolk were all dysfunctional? It is difficult to conceive any of these male filmmakers wanting their women represented in such lurid and explicit ways. Most importantly, do they not see that just because their womenfolk are not objects of a given narrative simply by virtue of being black women, those women are reduced to symbols of hypersexuality, where they, too, become sex objects, and not human subjects?

On the other hand, perhaps these filmmakers take it for granted that their works are entertainment and, therefore, should be viewed purely as such. But as we have already seen, film is more than entertainment; film simultaneously imposes onto viewers definitions about what is and what ought be. Thus, although filmic narratives may be filtered through the lenses of a given filmmaker's male experience, a major part of that filmmaker's concern should be the transforming of lived facts into imaginative truths. Much the way a filmmaker routinely transforms a film subject's rage into wisdom, so too, that filmmaker can routinely provide viewers with kind and noble moments of black female subjects on screen. His goal ought not be mere entertainment; he should delight audiences while providing new insights that are revealing and satisfying. That is, after all, what good narratives ought do! And good narratives are what black female viewers want (Bobo, 1995; Rhines, 1996), indeed, deserve! Minimally, black female viewers deserve to see public markings of proportionality in their cinematic representations.

What will it take to have positive representations of black women in film become the norm? Black women have long waited for such a reversal to occur. While they waited, they labored long and hard to ensure that an accurate reversal of public perception would ensue. Many educated themselves, while conducting the self in socially appropriate ways. This in no way suggests that black women of the pre–1970s did not also have a strong sense of propriety. It is to say that their emerging knowledge of the relationship between media and cultural beliefs alerted black women of the post–1960s to media's profound influence on public perception. Over thirty years later, the negative cultural symbol of blackness has not been abated nor improved. With each cinematic viewing of the self, filmic images of blackness speak of negative "otherness." Black women's hard work has yielded little in the cultural consciousness, even as they watch images of other ethnic and racial groups gradually move toward the center of social integration. What is generally referred to as "model minority," for example, is typically assigned to other ethnic-racial groups (Sethi, 1998), with public perceptual outcomes of positivism becoming the norm. Meanwhile, public perception of "social deviant" continues to be attributed to blackness in living color on the big screen.

Such views may not be accidental! From the standpoint of the film industry, Andrew Hacker, a white political scientist, reports that his research indicates that deeply held racial fears might drive white film executives' racial ideas. According to Hacker (1993):

> There is a fear of Africa. A fear of the U.S. becoming "Africanized." That this will somehow pull us down from our European origins. From the kind of civilization that white people have built up over the centuries. As a result we are willing to integrate Hispanics, Asians. We draw the line on people of African origin.

Director Edward Zwick (2002) himself observes that "it would be naive to think that the world of movies is color blind." Yet, race is not the only challenge for black women; same-gender female polarity is also bound up in these racialized views, fostering division and animosity among subgroups of women. Few examine the source of the division; fewer still believe film plays any role in perpetuating such polarization. Yet, from the point of view of black women generally, filmic images are a symbolic attack on their feminine virtue (St. Jean & Feagin, 1998; hooks, 1996; Bobo, 1995).

But like other viewers, black female viewers want their lives reflected in realistic images that can function as a cathartic means; they also want to lose themselves temporarily in filmic truths about their experiences. If the images fail to resonate with them (much like black female viewers in Bobo's study), black female audiences are not moved to watch; they must resist the images because there is often a disconnect between their self-image and the pseudo-images presented on screen. Being forced to reject the negative images does not, however, erase the adverse impact of perceptual distortions on these women's self-image. Black women still need public reaffirmation of the self; they still need images of hope. Unlike the unsavory images, realistic narratives that truthfully reflect the self are embraced because such narratives acknowledge black women as fully functional persons. What is more, such narratives have a powerful potential to aid in transforming black women from sexualized beings to positive icons in American culture.

Films that portray black women as part of the "true cult of womanhood," for example, would affirm on both a micro- and macro-level black women's gender identity. Moreover, such portrayals have an equal potential to help black male viewers come to view black women as valued members of the "feminine," and what possibilities that perception holds! But such has not been the case. And so, black female viewers wait, while they remain hopeful for equal representation on screen as that granted other women. While they wait, they look to black male filmmakers, especially, to transform their corporal experiences into filmic truths. In the next chapter, thus, we will first analyze the content of the ten films (1986–1995) in the original study by examining the ways in which black male filmmakers in particular construct black female sexuality. Next, we will examine the more recent films (1997–2001) to determine if positive changes in depictions have occurred. In both universes of films, we will learn whether differences exist between the works of black and white male filmmakers, and if so, in what ways are the differences made manifest?

5

Similar, but Different: Films from 1986 to 1995 and 1997 to 2001

Black Female Sexuality as Depicted in the Ten Films in the First Study (1986 to 1995)

The content of the ten films in the first study, five per set of filmmakers, was analyzed for their depictions of the sexuality of their major black female characters—nine (9) in the films of black male filmmakers and seven (7) in those of white male filmmakers. That the black female characters were found to be "sexual" is not noteworthy, since by definition, the study required that they be sexual or sensual subjects. What is striking is the extent to which the females were depicted as exclusively sexual.

Results of the study generally support the criticisms of popular films' representation of black female sexuality, as articulated in the work of hooks (1992), Jones (1992, 1993), Painter (1992), Iverem (1997), and others. While in the ten films analyzed, the black female characters were often identified as having familial and career roles, none of these roles was given serious attention. Rather, the female characters were portrayed as almost exclusively interested in men. Their interest in men, moreover, was almost exclusively sexual: only three of the female characters showed any interest in men as persons (versus eight who did not) and only two had platonic relationships with men in addition to their sexual relationships. Moreover, as Iverem (1997) has argued, black female characters were rarely represented as interested in "romance": only three characters showed any romantic interest in men, and even in these cases, the "romantic" affections were not returned, or returned only with ambiguity. Depiction of the infrequency of or disinterest in dating (five of nine and four of seven, respectively) also suggests the downplaying of "romance," in favor of more direct sexual engagements. In fact, the films depicted a near absence of romantic interest by the females in favor of more explicit sexual interest. For the most part, the women were portrayed in the sexually-motivated roles of short-term lover or girlfriend, although only three were characterized outright as prostitutes, with a fourth euphemistically coded as "mistress."

Hooks' (1992) generalization that black women are usually represented as "sexual outside the context of marriage," and as "sexually free" and "sexually ready" was confirmed by this study's findings that twice as many of the female characters were depicted as having multiple sexual partners as were shown having one partner, and ten were depicted as having sex "frequently," as opposed to "occasionally," during the course of the film.

This study's findings with regard to the sexual attitudes of the black female characters also support the contention that black women are usually "assumed to be the instigators of sex" (Painter, 1992, p. 210) and are depicted as "initiating sexual encounters" (Jones, 1993, p. 253): not only did the black females in these films outnumber the males as initiators of sexual "pick-ups," but they also initiated sexual intercourse more frequently than did the men. Fourteen of the 16 female characters presented themselves throughout the films with strong sexual overtones, and the same number were represented as either aggressive or assertive during sex. A large proportion of the female characters (11 of 16) also took pleasure in seducing males, either overtly or covertly. Indeed, the representation of the black females' sexual attitudes generally in these films might be accurately summarized by Spike Lee's film title *She's Gotta Have It*.

Jones (1992) has commented fairly extensively on what she characterizes as "ambiguity" in the representation of black women—that is, their filmic characterization both as "bitch" and "ho." The findings of this study confirm such an ambiguous representation of black women—here, as both sexually eager for men and at the same time hostile to and demeaning of them. While 14 of the 16 female characters were depicted as having strong sexual interest in the males, with ten of these women having multiple sex partners, a large proportion of these females (nine of 16) simultaneously displayed anger or hostility toward the males. In fact, in their initial contact with men, 11 of the 16 females viewed the males only as potential sex-partners or sources of money, and just one female viewed a male as a potential mate and friend. Such ambiguous depictions further confirm Jones' observation of the narrowness of black women's filmic characterization.

Both the nonverbal and verbal behavior of the black female characters in the films analyzed here indicates the sexual "readiness" and aggressiveness that hooks (1992) and Painter (1992) complain of in their representation. Not only did the majority of the women wear tight, revealing clothing, including clingy dresses and sexy high heels, but they also used, as "come-on," a variety of body language, including uses of the eyes and mouth to seduce the men; nine of the 16 swayed their buttocks when they walked, and the same number eyed the males lustfully, while half of the 16 leaned forward with their chests protruded. Indeed, while 11 of the 16 kissed the males in a sexual manner, only five kissed the males lovingly. And when talking with the males, most of the women (ten of 16) bit their lower lips coyly, and five licked their lips with their tongues.

Painter (1992) has argued that black women are routinely shown in film "...unclothed, in bed, and in the midst of coitus" (p. 210), which is supported by the depictions of the black women's display of their nude or partially naked bodies both in and out of bed. Nine females were nude exclusively for sex, six were nude to seduce the men, and eight were explicitly depicted during the sex act. Moreover, Guerrero's (1993) contention that black women are represented in film in the "most distorted and perverse terms and images" (p. 238) is confirmed by this study's findings that nine times as many women were depicted as using crass and degraded sexual language to solicit a sexual engagement as were shown using a romantic approach.

Not surprisingly, given these representations of black females' presentation of self as sexually-eager objects, the male characters in the films analyzed overwhelmingly viewed the women as almost exclusively sex partners. Fifteen of the 16 female characters were regarded by the males as sex-objects, and only one female was viewed as a friend by any of the males with whom she came in contact. Similarly, the males related to 12 of the females as predominantly sexual beings, as well as used demeaning sexual language to refer to 14 of the 16 women. Four women were also viewed as outright sluts or call-girls, with one of the latter coded as "mistress" to cover her prostitution role. Finally, only two of the four "girlfriends" were actually viewed by the males as unqualified girlfriends.

Comparison of Black and White Male Filmmakers' Depictions—1986 to 1995

Within the general pattern of similarity described above, there were fairly notable differences in how black and white male filmmakers represented black women's sexuality. A comparison indicates that black filmmakers and white filmmakers differed in their depictions of the females' non-sexual roles. Table 1 shows in column 1 that where black filmmakers represented only three different familial roles among five females (predominantly those of daughter or sister), white filmmakers depicted the women in a greater diversity of familial relationships—6 different roles among five women (including the extended familial roles of aunt, niece and cousin). Black filmmakers appeared to have valued friendship over family, depicting eight females in the role of friendships with other women. By contrast, white filmmakers depicted only one female who was a friend to another woman.

Black filmmakers gave no attention to black women's community or educational roles (Table 1, column 2), and white filmmakers referred to these in only two instances. The females' work roles, however, fared somewhat better (column 3). While none of the females' occupations in any film was in education, law, or medicine, and while both sets of filmmakers portrayed the females in "stereotypical" occupations traditionally assigned to black women in film, there were differences in the type of work assigned. In the films by black filmmakers, most of the females depicted as working (four of six) held low-paying positions requiring little education or training. These women were constructed as primarily waitresses and beauticians. By contrast, the majority of working women in the films of white filmmakers (four of five) held positions of higher status, primarily entertainers and one as businesswoman (Table 1, column 3). Nonetheless, both sets of filmmakers depicted one female each as strippers, seemingly subtle versions of the typical filmic black female "prostitute." It is worth noting that, though depiction of the diversity of work roles was fairly similar, white filmmakers depicted nearly twice as many females who had interest in their careers; black filmmakers coded only one female who had such interest.

Table 1: Nonsexual Roles of Black Females on Film, 1986–1995

1

Familial/Friendship Roles	Filmmakers	
	Black	White
Mother		3
Daughter	3	2
Sister	2	2
Aunt		2
Granddaughter	1	
Niece		1
Cousin		1
Friend	8	1

2

Community/Education Roles	Filmmakers	
	Black	White
Volunteer		1
Student		1

3

Career Roles	Filmmakers	
	Black	White
Entertainer		3
Business Woman	2	1
Waitress	2	
Beautician's Asst.	1	
Stripper	1	1

Among the several behaviors examined were black women's roles with men (Table 2, column 1), their attitudes about sex, and their sexual aggressiveness. According to the findings, it appears that black male filmmakers make these behaviors more explicit than do white filmmakers—especially behaviors of sexual aggressiveness (Table 3). The filmmakers' portrayals of the nature of the females' roles with men differed to a large extent. While the role of lover predominated among both set of filmmakers (Table 2, column 1), white filmmakers portrayed women in

Whitney Houston stars as singer and actress Rachael Marron, triumphant on stage just prior to the crowd's closing in on her, when she will be rescued by her bodyguard in Warner Bros.' *The Bodyguard* (1992).

the somewhat more committed or exclusive sociosexual relationships of mistress and wife. More than twice as many females (five of seven) were depicted by white filmmakers as having multiple roles of both positive and negative sexual behaviors with men (including roles of wife and platonic friends) as were depicted by black filmmakers. Black filmmakers depicted less than a quarter, or two of nine females, as having a similar complexity of role relationships with men. But even here, the two women's roles were given only cursory treatments. And in no instance were the women portrayed by black filmmakers as platonic friends of men.

The most notable differences found with respect to the females' roles with men were the females' depictions as equally aggressive or assertive as the males in initiating the sex act (Table 3, column 5), and in initiating sexually oriented contact—the "pick-up" (Table 3, column 2). Black filmmakers depicted the female subjects as almost always initiators of the sex act. These filmmakers portrayed seven of their nine female subjects as initiators of sexual intercourse, but white filmmakers were generally less obvious, depicting only two of seven females as initiators of the sex act. The females' sexual aggressiveness was further amplified by black filmmakers' depiction of nearly five females who were initiators of the "pick-up," versus white filmmakers' depiction of only three females as initiators. Additionally, more females (seven to one) were portrayed by black filmmakers (Table 3, column 1) as viewing the males initially as sex partners or sources of money than were shown by white filmmakers. These latter filmmakers depicted the females' view of the males they approached as potential lovers or mates (i.e., partners in longer-lasting or exclusive sexual and romantic relationships) and friends, suggestive here of interest in a more committed monogamous relationship.

Table 2: Depiction of Black Females' Sexual Relationships with Men, 1986–1995

1

	Filmmakers	
Roles	*Black*	*White*
Lover	6	4
Mistress	0	2
Wife	0	1
Fiancée	1	0
Girlfriend	2	2
Call-Girl/Slut	2	1
Flirt	1	3
Friend	0	2

2

	Filmmakers	
Nature of Interest	*Black*	*White*
Sexual	8	6
Romantic	2	1
Platonic	0	2

3

	Filmmakers	
Females with One/Many Sexual Partners	*Black*	*White*
One Partner	3	2
Many Partners	6	4

4

| Females Showing | Filmmakers | |
Anger/Hostility with Men	Black	White
Anger/Hostile	5	4
Not Angry/Hostile	3	3

5

| Females Showing Interest | Filmmakers | |
In Men As Persons	Black	White
Interest	1	2
No Interest	5	3

6

| Instances of | Filmmakers | |
Dating	Black	White
Yes	4	3
No	5	4

Table 3: Depiction of Sexual Aggressiveness in Black Females, 1986–1995

1

| Females' View of | Filmmakers | |
Male Initially	Black	White
Sex Partner Only	4	0
Money Source Only	1	1
Sex Partner & Money Source	2	0
Lover	0	3
Mate/Friend	0	1
No Interest	1	0

2

| Who Picked | Filmmakers | |
Up Whom	Black	White
Male	2	1
Female	3	2
Mutual	1	1

3		
Frequency of Sex Act	*Filmmakers*	
	Black	*White*
Occasionally	1	2
Frequent	6	4
Only Once	1	0

4		
Depiction of Sex Act	*Filmmakers*	
	Black	*White*
Explicit	6	2
Implied	2	4
None	1	0

5		
Initiator of Sex Act	*Filmmakers*	
	Black	*White*
Male	0	2
Female	5	2
Mutual	2	0

6		
Reason for Sex Act	*Filmmakers*	
	Black	*White*
Pleasure	4	3
Pleasure & Money	3	2
Love & Pleasure	1	1
Revenge	0	1

7		
Did Female Present Herself With Strong Sexual Overtones?	*Filmmakers*	
	Black	*White*
Yes	8	6
No	1	1

White filmmakers were not merely distinguished from black filmmakers in the degree of their negative portrayals of the black females as sexual aggressors. White filmmakers were more apt to depict the females in less negative terms where it concerned these females' explicit sexual engagements. Iverem's (1997) contention that film audiences are usually met with "loose sexuality" of black female subjects is meritorious to this study's findings that three times as many females in black filmmakers' films (six versus two) were explicitly depicted in the sex act as were depicted in white filmmakers' films (Table 3, column 4). Moreover, three of the six were depicted by black filmmakers as selfish and cold during the sex act (Table 4, column 5), while no female was depicted by white filmmakers with either quality during the act. Differences also emerged where the means through which the females experienced sexual pleasure were concerned (Table 4, column 6). Black filmmakers portrayed five females as finding pleasure either through lust or a combination of lust and anger. White filmmakers, on the other hand, portrayed just two females as experiencing pleasure through lust or lust and anger.

Black filmmakers were also more explicit in their treatment of the females' display of nudity (16 versus 14). And though both sets of filmmakers portrayed the females as comfortable with disrobing, the angles from which white filmmakers shot some of the females' nude bodies (Table 4, column 3) suggested that these filmmakers attempted to transmute the graphic depictions into more tasteful portrayals. This attempt did not appear to be the case with black filmmakers.

Differences between the two sets of filmmakers also emerged where sexual victimization was concerned. While black women were consistently depicted in both sets of films as willing participants in the sex act (Table 4, column 1), four women were also victims of sexual harassment and one was raped. However, the sole rape victim in a film by a black filmmaker was portrayed as treating the assault less than seriously. She neither vigorously fought back, pressed charges, sought professional help specific to the rape, nor sought help from family or friends. In fact, viewers were never shown this female character as emotionally distraught about the rape. When she did raise the issue with the lover who was her rapist, she was depicted as accepting his placing blame onto her. Similarly, of the two other women depicted by black filmmakers as victims of sexual harassment, only one responded by fighting off her attacker. The other was shown to accept the assault. By contrast, the two females portrayed by white filmmakers as victims of sexual assault were shown to fight back.

Though sexual rivalry among women was not systematically examined in either study, one item on the SBFA instrument did indicate that such rivalry was consistently, if not strongly represented in the two sets of films. As Table 4, column 8 indicates, one-quarter of the female characters demeaned other women verbally in their pursuit of sexual pleasure. It should also be noted, however, that sexual rivalry was depicted as a motive for the seduction of a male in only one instance, in a film by a white filmmaker. There were also differences in how the women presented themselves to others as comfortable with their own sexuality—that is, as women who enjoy sex and sexuality for their own sake or for their own personal gratification (Table 4, column 9). A larger percentage of the women in the films of black filmmakers (50 percent, as opposed to 20 percent in the films of white filmmakers) presented themselves as idealized sexual selves—i.e., women who take pride in their own sexual prowess, in their ability to please the male, or in their knowledge of various sexual techniques. Only one female, in a white filmmaker's film, presented herself as sexually degraded—i.e., as damaged, shamed, or humiliated by sex and her own sexuality.

Notable differences also emerged in black and white filmmakers' treatment of black females as romantic figures. In fact, sexual interest in men outweighed romantic and platonic interest (Table 2, column 2) in both sets of films (eight to two in the films of black filmmakers and six to three in those of white filmmakers). Indeed, the minimal instances of dating (Table 2, column 6) suggest a near devaluation of "romance" in favor of more sexually-oriented encounters. Iverem (1997) has decried the dearth of a "romantic sympathy or sensibilities" developed for most black women on screen. While white filmmakers depicted only one female as a romantic character, black filmmakers depicted twice as many females who were romantic subjects, seemingly more positive portrayals. But if the romantic imagery as depicted by both black and white male filmmakers is examined against their depictions of the sexual imagery, the treatment is not only equivocal, but confirms Iverem's (1997) charge that in film, black women are not depicted as "...wrestling with emotions and mating" (p. G4).

For example, though one "romantic" female was coded by black filmmakers as a "fiancée," the couple was never shown in a warm, tender exchange. The only scene in which this couple was shown together depicted the culmination of their break-up. In fact, while still engaged, this female was depicted as initiating a sexual contact with a second male. Such a visual coding harkens back to myths of black women as morally loose. It sends the wrong message that even when they are afforded opportunities for "legitimacy," they nonetheless revert to type. They are shown to be incapable of fidelity because it is so much a part of who they are. The depiction of this female as seducing a second man while committed to another promotes the view that black women lack trustworthiness.

Male viewers, especially, may leave with the false impression that black women cannot be trusted.

Table 4: Sexual Participation; Nudity; Degree and Source of Sexual Pleasure of Black Females on Film, 1986–1995

1

Willingness of Sexual Participation	Filmmakers	
	Black	*White*
Willing	8	7
Reluctant	0	0
Harassed	2	2
Raped	1	0

2

Response to Assault	Filmmakers	
	Black	*White*
Treats Lightly	1	0
Accepts	1	0
Fights Back	1	2

3

Appeared Nude	Filmmakers	
	Black	*White*
Full	1	1
Partial	4	3
Frontal	2	3
Back	3	3
Side	1	2
Breasts	5	2

4

Reasons for Nudity	Filmmakers	
	Black	*White*
Seduction	2	3
Sex	6	4

5

Sexual Response	Filmmakers	
	Black	White
Aggressive	7	2
Assertive	3	2
Passive	0	0
Selfish	3	0
Warm	3	4
Cold	3	0

6

Finds Sexual Pleasure Through	Filmmakers	
	Black	White
Love & Affection	1	2
Affection	1	1
Lust	3	1
Lust & Anger	1	1
Anger	1	

7

Gains Pleasure By	Filmmakers	
	Black	White
Overt Seduction of Males	6	4
Covert Seduction of Males	0	1

8

Verbally Degrades Women	Filmmakers	
	Black	White
Yes	2	2
No	7	5

9

Sexual Presentation of Self	Filmmakers	
	Black	White
Idealized	4	1
Comfortable	4	5
Degraded	0	1

The second female portrayed by black filmmakers as a "romantic" figure was principally depicted in graphically explicit sexual acts, where few signs of warmth or romantic love as is understood in cinematic representations of the 20th century were shown. Prevalent was the portrayal of a female who was preoccupied only with fulfilling her own sexual pleasure.

Lyn Whitfield stars as exotic and provocative dancer Josephine Baker in HBO Pictures' *The Josephine Baker Story* (1991).

Moreover, save for her sexual interest in her lover, this female was depicted as having much hostility toward men generally. What surfaced in the films of black filmmakers was an ambivalent imagery of both women as romantic characters.

White filmmakers fared only slightly better in their "romantic" portrayal of a black female, going beyond the usual depiction of black women as depraved sluts to assign this female what for many is viewed as the culturally desirable role of legitimate wife. This characterization was marred, however, by the female's heavy focus on the sexual, on the one hand, and by her sudden shift in character to a near matriarchal one, on the other hand. Prior to her marriage, she was depicted as having much interest in sexual engagement; after her marriage, her focus inexplicably shifted to obsession with motherhood, thereby avoiding romantic intimacy. Hooks (1981) contends that "the predominant image of black women is that of the sex object, prostitute, and whore, etc. The second image is that of the ... nagging maternal figure" (p. 66). By constructing this female as moving from the role of "hypersexed" to "matriarch," the film crystallizes these two stereotypes of negative extremes. And because in the marital union this female was coded as the party having the economic power as against the male, the predominant image which surfaced of this female was that of matriarch. Thus, even when the shift is away from the "sexual," black women on screen continue to be devalued as unfeminine women. There are serious gaps in these representations because neither role presents an image of a sexually-balanced black woman, and both roles are mere extremes of the other. This study's findings suggest that any attempt on the part of either set of filmmakers to portray black women as "romantic" figures; any attempt to present them as women who possess qualities of tenderness, gentleness, compassion, and emotional depth is met with serious discrepancies.

Hooks (1992), Jones (1992), and Iverem (1997) have tirelessly complained of the limited range of characterizations assigned to black women in film. Indeed, Iverem contends that over the past three decades, "...the most consistent image of black sexuality shown ... has been that of a black prostitute" (G4). Black and white male filmmakers' depictions of two females each as prostitutes differed only in the type portrayed (Table 2, column 1). Black male filmmakers depicted two females as outright sluts, while white male filmmakers masked the role by depicting one female as unqualified call-girl, with a second euphemistically coded as "mistress."

While still a prostitute role, the representation of "mistress" was seemingly a less sleazy image than was that of "slut," which presented the females as exhibiting loose, depraved sexual behaviors. Presumably, the

role of mistress was meant to soften this particular black female character's role. Still, she was nonetheless portrayed as dependent on male support and reliant on his contacts to further her acting career. Such coding supports Baker Jr.'s (1993) lament of the lack of independence in black women on screen. Nowhere was she given agency as an independent woman who made prudent decisions which would determine her own destiny. But while she was coded as incapable of "legitimately" providing for herself, she was given ample agency in the seduction of men; the metames-

Halle Berry appears as exotic dancer Cory in Geffen Films' *The Last Boy Scout* (1991). Here, Berry is seen at her strip club looking toward Jimmy Dicks (Damon Wynon), her lover and financial supporter.

sage sent was that her achievements lay primarily in matters of sexual know-how. Thus, although this female appeared less crass in her sexual construction, there was no mistaking that she was nonetheless a prostitute. Appearance aside, the recurrent pattern of negative portrayals of the black female characters as prostitutes and, by extension, as embodying culturally undesirable traits suggests that black female subjects who possess qualities of self-restraint are of no interest to filmmakers, black or white.

That the black females are devalued in these ten films is further seen in negative depictions of their nonverbal behaviors. Most of the women were depicted within the framework of unflattering stereotypes where it concerned their mode of dress, for example. Many were shown to wear tight, revealing clothing which emphasized certain body parts typically related to the "sexual." When the camera did not emphasize their buttocks or breasts, the depictions focused on the women's preoccupation with using their bodies to gain male attention. Both sets of filmmakers depicted the females as using a variety of body parts to seduce the males, including puckered lips, suggestive use of tongues, eyes, and so

Tracy Camila Johns appears as seductress Uniqua, out to win the attention and money of drug-pin Nino Brown (Wesley Snipes) in Warner Bros.'s *New Jack City* (1991).

forth (Table 5, columns 2, 3, and 4). Differences between the two sets of filmmakers emerged, however, in the tactile behaviors of the black female characters. White male filmmakers tended to depict the kissing and hugging of the males by the females as loving acts, while black male filmmakers tended to depict these same acts by the females as primarily sexual. White male filmmakers also depicted one female who nestled a male's face in her bosom, again, suggestive of a maternal figure. No female was shown to engage in this behavior by black male filmmakers, whose stress on the "sexual" further resonated in their portrayal of one female subject who caressed a male's genitals. In contrast, white male filmmakers depicted no female as engaging in this behavior.

Sheryl Lee Ralph stars as seductive Beverly Dumont, mistress to rich and jealous married boyfriend Evan Wright (Robert DeNiro), who will invest in a movie only if Beverly will get the starring role, in Tribeca Productions' *Mistress* (1991).

Table 5: Nonverbal Sexual Behavior of Black Females on Film, 1986–1995

1

Appearance	Filmmakers	
	Black	White
Attractive	4	4
Seductive	5	5
Sexy	2	4
Clean	2	0
Sleazy	1	1

2

Type Dress	Filmmakers	
	Black	White
Revealing Cleavage	8	6
Clingy Dress	7	4
Micro Mini Skirt	4	4
Tight/See-Thru Blouse	6	6
High Heels	5	6

3

Uses of the Face: Lips	Filmmakers		Eyes	Filmmakers	
	Black	White		Black	White
Licks Lips with Tongue	3	2	Winks Suggestively	3	2
Sticks Out Tongue	2	2	Eyes Male Lustfully	5	4
Coyly Bites Lower Lip	4	6	Eyes Male While Stroking		
Puckers Lip as			a Phallic Object	3	4
"Come On"	2	3	Bats Eyelids Suggestively	4	3
			Stars at Male's Genitals	5	3

4

Uses of the body	Filmmakers	
	Black	White
Calls Attention to Buttocks While Walking	4	5
Thrusts Chest forward	4	4
Reveals Legs/Thighs	6	4
Makes Graphic Pelvic Thrusts	2	3

Uses of the body	Filmmakers	
	Black	White
Swings Head/Hair Often	7	5
Dances Sensuously; Wildly; Uninhibitedly	7	5
Straddles Male's Torso/Groin	5	3
Caresses Self	5	3
Undresses Male/Self for Sex	6	3
Caresses Male's Genitals	1	0
Kisses Male Sexually	5	6
Kisses Male Lovingly	2	3
Hugs Male Sexually	4	4
Hugs Male Lovingly	1	3
Nestles Male's Face in Bosom	0	1

Differences here may be an indication of white male filmmakers' ligatures with ideas of the "mammy" image, or it may have been their tentative, albeit awkward, attempts to add dimensions of warmth and tenderness to the black female characters, attempts that were all but absent in the films of black male filmmakers. Because rarely in mainstream films are black women portrayed in their male-female relationships as caring and loving characters, depiction of the black women as warm characters is no small point. Indeed, it is precisely because of this lack that such depiction, when present, is noteworthy. Aligning qualities of warmth and tenderness to black female subjects is also noteworthy, since such portrayals illustrate that black women indeed possess feminine qualities, despite film's routine suppression of these characteristics. These differences may not seem large at first glance; yet, they could have genuine and important implications for how black women fare societally; such depictions could work to direct viewers in how to define actual black women.

But a surprising difference found in black and white male filmmakers' portrayals was the females' lack of interest in men as persons (Table 2, column 5). Brent Zook (1996) laments that "at present, not a single film in production promises to present black women sexually and in relationships, in all [their] full … human … complexities" (p. 6). White male filmmakers were less negative here, depicting more than twice as many females who had interest in men as persons as did black male filmmakers. These latter filmmakers' depictions of females who had no interest outweighed females who did, five to one, despite the uninterested women's sexual attraction towards and pursuit of the males. In fact, black male filmmakers depicted no female who pursued a platonic friendship with a male; these filmmakers portrayed eight of the nine females' interest in men as primarily a sexual one. And while only in white male filmmakers' films were two females shown to have platonic friendships with men, white male filmmakers also portrayed six of their seven female subjects' primary interest in men as also a sexual one.

Given the black female characters' indifference to men as persons, the portrayal of the females as having such intense sexual interest in men was even more striking when the number of females depicted as angry or hostile toward men was considered (Table 2, column 4). The filmmakers each portrayed more than half the females as having hostility toward the males in the films, indicating some ambivalence on the part of the filmmakers. In fact, even both sets of filmmakers' portrayal of one female each as "in love" did not add warmth or tenderness to the females' general attitude toward the males. Indeed, not one female in either set of films was shown to utter the meaningful words "I love you" to a male character. Instead, black and white male filmmakers each depicted five and four females, respectively, as using crass and degrading language to ask for sex (Table 6, column 1). Rather than seeking emotional intimacy with or being invested in the males, the black female subjects were portrayed as sexual predators, whose sole interest was with carnal pleasure.

Table 6: Verbal Sexual Behavior of Black Females on Film, 1986–1995

1		
Direct Use of	*Filmmakers*	
Sexual Language	*Black*	*White*
Crass	3	2
Degrading	2	2
Humor	1	0
Romantic	1	0
Threatens to Withhold Sex	3	1

2		
Indirect Use of	*Filmmakers*	
Sexual Language	*Black*	*White*
Sexual Jokes	6	2
Sex-Code Words	7	6
Sexual Teasing	6	3
Sexual-Innuendo	4	3
Sexual-Flattery	2	1

Table 7: Males' Attitudes Toward Black Females

1

Males Viewed Women As:	Filmmakers Black	White
Sex Object	9	6
Tease	2	3
All Women	2	3
Girl Friend	2	2
Friend	0	1
Nympho	1	0
Prostitute	2	2
(Call-Girl)	0	(2)
(Slut)	(2)	0

2

Males Related to Women As:	Filmmakers Black	White
Predominantly Sexual	8	4
Predominantly Nonsexual	1	3

3

Number of Women Males:	Filmmakers Black	White
Used Demeaning Sexual Language to Refer to	9	5
Leered at	5	5
Ogled	8	5

The findings of this first study—that black female subjects are characterized in film as symbols of sexual aggressiveness while at the same time, inimical toward and demeaning of men—lend support to Jones' (1992) polemics of the ambiguous portrayal of black women's filmic roles as "bitch" and "ho." Results of the study also appear to confirm black feminists' claims that films of the 1980s-1990s are reminiscent of those of the 1970s: hooks' (1992) contention that black women are depicted as "sexually ready" and "on the make" (pp. 66, 69) echoes Bogle's (1973/1989) past argument that the macho-goddesses in films of the 1970s were portrayed as "ready and anxious for sex as any man" (p. 251). These images, long remembrances of the old myth, "Jezebel," resonate in the ten films analyzed in this first study.

Black Females as Depicted in the Six Films in the Second Study (1997 to 2001)

As was the case in the first set of films (1986-1995) by black and white male filmmakers, the content of the six films from 1997 to 2001

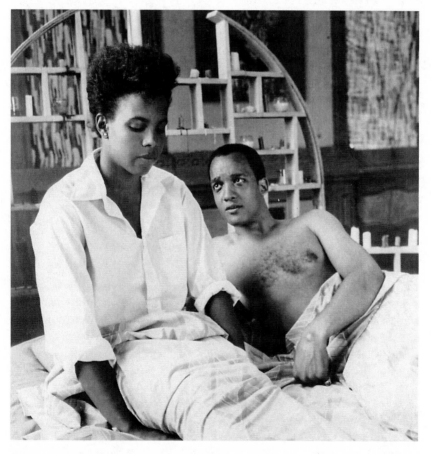

Tracy Camila Johns stars as Nola Darling, a woman sexually involved with three very different men. Here, she and Jamie (Redmund Hicks), who wants her to give up the other two lovers, discuss her disinterest in a monogamous relationship, in *She's Gotta Have it*, Island Pictures (1986).

was analyzed for their depictions of the sexuality of their major black female characters—six (6) in the films of black male filmmakers and three (3) in those of their white male counterparts. Again, although it is not noteworthy that the black female characters were found to be "sexual," what is remarkable is the degree to which the women were portrayed as almost exclusively sexual.

Results of the study again support criticisms of popular films' representation of black female sexuality. Unlike in the earlier study where the black female characters were often identified as having diverse familial roles, this present study identified just four characters who occupied two role relationships only—those of daughter and mother. None of these familial roles was given serious attention, however. The females' career roles, on the other hand, fared far better. Five of the nine black females held professional roles, with only one of the nine portrayed as a stripper, and four females were also coded as having interest in their careers. Career interest notwithstanding, however, the black female characters' interest in men was portrayed as at least equal with that in their professions. Their interest in men, moreover, was depicted as quite strongly sexual: only four of the nine female subjects showed any interest in men as persons, and only one had a platonic friendship with a male in addition to her implied sexual interest. Moreover, just four females showed any romantic interest in the men, underscored by the fact that less than half of the nine females was shown on a formal date. For the most part, the women were portrayed in the sexually-motivated roles of short-term lover or girlfriend, with three females characterized as sluts or call-girls and one as lesbian.

Hooks' (1992) complaint that black women are typically represented as "sexual outside the context of marriage," and are "sexually ready," is again confirmed by this present study's finding that three times as many females were depicted as having multiple sex partners as were portrayed as having one partner only, and six were depicted as having sex "frequently," as opposed to "occasionally" during the course of the films. Depictions of the female characters' sexual attitudes also support Jones' (1993) contention that black women are depicted as "initiating sexual encounters." The females not merely outnumbered the males as initiators of sexual "pick-ups," but they also initiated sexual intercourse more frequently than did the males. Seven of the nine females presented themselves throughout the films with strong sexual overtones, and six were represented as either aggressive or assertive during sex. A large proportion of the females (seven of nine) also took pleasure in overtly seducing men. Yet, while seven of the nine were portrayed as having strong sexual interest in the males, with the same number having multiple sex partners, more than half of the females (five of nine) simultaneously displayed anger or hostility toward males.

Indeed, in their initial contact with the men, five of the nine females viewed the males only as potential sex partners or sources of money, and just one female viewed a male as a potential friend of sorts. Such ambiguous depictions once more confirm Jones' (1992) observation of the narrowness of black women's filmic characterization, what she terms is black women's simultaneous representation both as "bitch" and "ho."

Both the nonverbal and verbal behavior of the black female characters in the films analyzed indicates the sexual "readiness" and aggressiveness that hooks (1992) and Painter (1992) complain of. Not only did the majority of the females wear tight, revealing clothing, including clingy dresses and sexy high heels, but they also used, as a "come-on," a variety of body language, including uses of the eyes and body to seduce the men: four of the nine women stared intently at the males with lust and the same number swayed their hips and called attention to their buttocks when they walked, while three leaned forward with their chests protruded. And while five kissed the males in a sexual manner, only three kissed the males lovingly. Similarly, most of the women (six of nine) hugged the men in a sexual way, while only three hugged the men lovingly.

Painter's (1992) contention that black women are routinely shown in film as "...unclothed, in bed, and in the midst of coitus" (p. 210) is again supported by depictions of the black females' display of their nude or partially naked bodies both in and out of bed. Five female subjects were nude exclusively for sex; five were nude to seduce men; and four were explicitly depicted during the sex act. Moreover, Guerrero's (1993) complaint that black women are represented in film in the "most distorted and perverse terms and images" (p. 238) is confirmed by this study's findings that more than three times as many women were depicted as using crass and degraded sexual language to solicit a sexual engagement as were shown using a romantic approach.

Given the black females' presentation of self as sexually-eager objects, it is not surprising that the male characters in the films analyzed overwhelmingly viewed the women as almost exclusive sex-partners. Seven of the nine females were regarded by the males as sex-objects, and only one was viewed as a friend by any of the males with whom she came in contact. Regrettably, because of interest in her career, one female was regarded by the males as a lesbian, and the males expressed great fun over this speculation. The males related to six of the nine females as predominantly sexual beings, and used demeaning sexual language to refer to seven of the nine women. In fact, when taken together, the males tended to use degraded sexual language to refer to women generally. Three women were viewed by the males as outright sluts or call-girls. Finally, only one of the three "girlfriends" was actually regarded by a male as an unqualified girlfriend, while two males struggled with the idea of having to remain monogamous with their alleged girlfriends.

Comparison of Black and White Male Filmmakers' Depictions—1997-2001.

A comparison of the depictions of both sets of filmmakers indicates that while they portrayed black female sexuality similarly, they also differed in their depictions of the female subjects' representations. But unlike in the earlier study, differences emerged in the reverse between them in a number of cases. Regarding the women's non-sexual roles, Table 8, column 1 shows that where white filmmakers represented only one familial role (that of mother), black filmmakers depicted three women each as having familial (daughters) and friendship roles. As in the earlier study, however, these latter filmmakers appear to have valued friendships with other women over familial relationships. By contrast, their white counterparts depicted no female who was a friend to another woman. White filmmakers also gave no attention to black women's community or educational roles (Table 8, column 2), and black filmmakers referred to educational roles in only two instances. Representation of the females' career roles differed in the reverse, however, between the two sets of filmmakers in this present study (Table 8, column 3). In the films of white filmmakers, all three females held low-paying positions, requiring little education. They were constructed as primarily waitresses and criminals. By contrast, the majority of the women in the films of black filmmakers (five of six) held positions of higher social status, primarily professionals. Nonetheless, black filmmakers also depicted one female as a stripper, a subtle version of the typical filmic black female "prostitute." Though never shown as engaged in studying of any kind, she was, however, also depicted as a student. It should also be noted that while white filmmakers portrayed no female as having strong interest in her work, black filmmakers depicted four females who had such interest, a clear improvement over findings from the first study. Even so, it is noteworthy to comment here on the view of the males toward one female regarding interest in her career. Most of the males in *The Best Man* found it

Table 8: Nonsexual Roles of Black Females on Film, 1997–2001

1

Familial/Friendship Roles	Filmmakers Black	White
Mother		1
Daughter	3	
Friend	3	

2

Community/Education Roles	Filmmakers Black	White
Volunteer		
Student	2	

3

Career Roles	Filmmakers Black	White
TV Producer	1	
Photographer	1	
Caterer	1	
Publishing Asst.	1	
Actress	1	
Stripper	1	
Waitress		1
Criminal		1
Flight Attendant/Criminal		1

unnatural that the female was career-focused. They speculated that she must be a lesbian, since she was unattached, yet so driven. A sole male pointed out to his pals that they were being hypocritical because on the one hand, they accuse women of being gold-diggers; yet, when they meet a woman who is self-sufficient on the other hand, they then deride her efforts. The point was settled with one of the males admitting that he was indeed chauvinistic.

Table 9, column 1 examined the black females' roles with men, but again, differences emerged in the reverse between the two sets of filmmakers in this present study. According to the findings, while the role of lover predominated among both sets of filmmakers, black filmmakers portrayed the women in the more committed or exclusive sociosexual relationships

Monica Calhoun stars as frustrated and hurt Mia whose fiancé, pro-football player Lance Sullivan (Morris Chestnut), has cheated on her one too many times. To get back at him, she here initiates the seduction of his best friend, Harper (Taye Diggs), in Universal Studios' *The Best Man* (1999).

of fiancée, girlfriend, and wife. In fact, twice as many females (4 of 6) were depicted by black filmmakers as having multiple roles of both positive and negative sexual behaviors with men (including roles of wife and girlfriend) as were depicted by white filmmakers. These latter filmmakers coded just two of three females as having a similar complexity of role relationships with men. Yet, in no instance were the women portrayed by black filmmakers as exclusively platonic friends with men, unlike in the case of white filmmakers who coded one female as occupying such a role.

Table 9: Depiction of Black Females' Sexual Relationships with Men

1

| | Filmmakers | |
Roles	Black	White
Lover	4	3
Mistress	0	1
Wife	1	0
Ex-Wife	0	2
Fiancée	2	0
Girlfriend	2	1
Call-Girl/Slut	1	2
Flirt	2	2
Date	1	0
Friend	0	1

2

| Nature of | Filmmakers | |
Interest	Black	White
Sexual	4	3
Romantic	3	1
Platonic	0	1

3

| Females with One/Many | Filmmakers | |
Sexual Partners	Black	White
One Partner	1	1
Many Partners	5	2

4

Females Showing Anger/Hostility with Men	Filmmakers Black	White
Angry/Hostile	3	2
Not Angry/Hostile	2	0
Can't Determine	1	1

5

Females Showing Interest In Men as Persons	Filmmakers Black	White
Interest	3	1
No Interest	3	2

6

Instances of Dating	Filmmakers Black	White
Yes	4	0
No	2	3

The most notable differences which emerged with respect to the females' roles with men were the females' depictions as equally aggressive or assertive as the males in initiating the sex act (Table 10, column 5) and in initiating sexually-oriented contact—the "pick-up" (Table 10, column 2). As was the case in the earlier study, black filmmakers again depicted the females as almost always initiators of the sex act. Whether or not the "act" came to fruition, five of the six females were portrayed by black filmmakers as initiators of sexual intercourse; their white counterparts also depicted all three females as initiators in this regard. The female subjects' sexual aggressiveness was further accentuated by both sets of filmmakers' depiction of three females each who were initiators of the "pick-up." White filmmakers, however, were generally less obvious in depictions of the females' view of the males initially (Table 10, column 1). Where black filmmakers portrayed the females as viewing the males initially as sex partners or as sources of money, white filmmakers tended to depict the females' view of the males they approached as neutral or as friend.

Nia Long stars as Jordan, who desires to finish what was started between her and Harper (Taye Diggs). Here, she prepares the scene for the seduction of Harper in Universal's *The Best Man* (1999).

Table 10: Depiction of Sexual Aggressiveness in Black Females, 1997–2001

1

Females' View of Males Initially	Filmmakers Black	White
Sex Partner Only	2	0
Money Source Only	1	0
Sex Partner & Money Source	1	0
Lover	1	0
Co-Conspirator & Sex Partner	0	1
Mate	0	0
Friend	0	1
Can't Determine	1	1

2

Who Picked Up Whom	Filmmakers Black	White
Male	3	
Female	3	2
Mutual	0	1

3

Frequency of Sex Act	Filmmakers Black	White
Occasionally	1	0
Frequent	3	3
Once Only	1	0
Can't Determine	1	0

4

Depiction of Sex Act	Filmmakers Black	White
Explicit	3	1
Implied	1	2
None	2	0

5

Initiator of Sex Act	Filmmakers	
	Black	White
Male	0	0
Female	4	3
Mutual	1	0
Can't Determine	1	0

6

Reason for Sex Act	Filmmakers	
	Black	White
Pleasure	2	1
Pleasure & Money	2	0
Affection	0	1
Love & Pleasure	1	0
Revenge	1	0
Coercion	0	1

7

Did Female Present Herself With Strong Sexual Overtones?	Filmmakers	
	Black	White
Yes	4	3
No	2	0

Regarding the females' explicit sexual engagements, white filmmakers were also more likely to depict the females in less negative terms than were black filmmakers. Here, loose sexuality of the black females was amplified by the fact that three times as many females (3 vs. 1) were explicitly depicted in the sex act by black filmmakers as were depicted in white filmmakers' films (Table 10, column 4). Moreover, two of the three females in black filmmakers works were depicted as selfish and cold during their sexual engagements (Table 11, column 5), whereas only one female was depicted by white filmmakers as possessing these qualities. Differences also surfaced with respect to the means through which the females experienced sexual pleasure (Table 11, column 6). Black filmmakers depicted three females as finding pleasure either through lust, lust and anger, or a combination of lust and violence. White filmmakers, on the other hand, portrayed just one female who experienced pleasure through lust. However, these latter filmmakers also portrayed one female who experienced pleasure through greed which was not the case with black filmmakers. Black filmmakers were also more explicit in their treatment of the females' display of nudity—six versus two respectively (Table 4, column 3). And though both sets of filmmakers portrayed the females as comfortable with disrobing, black filmmakers depicted nine different instances of various stages of undress, while white filmmakers depicted only six such instances. Black filmmakers depicted four females as nude for the purpose of having sex and three of the four were also nude for the purpose of seducing the males they encountered. Similarly, white filmmakers depicted two females as nude for seducing males and one of the two was nude for having sex.

Table 11: Sexual Participation; Nudity; Degree and Source of Sexual Pleasure of black Females on Film, 1997–2001

1

Willingness of Sexual Participation	Filmmakers	
	Black	White
Willing	5	3
Reluctant	0	0
Harassed	0	0
Raped	0	0
Can't Determine	1	0

2

Response to Assault	Filmmakers	
	Black	White
Treats Lightly	0	0
Accepts	0	0
Fights Back	0	0

3

Appeared Nude	Filmmakers	
	Black	White
Full	0	1
Partial	4	0
Frontal	1	2

Appeared Nude	*Filmmakers*	
	Black	*White*
Back	0	1
Side	1	0
Bare Breasts	3	2
Does Not Apply	0	1

4

Reasons for Nudity	*Filmmakers*	
	Black	*White*
Seduction	3	2
Sex	4	1
Bath	0	1
Does Not Apply	1	0

5

Sexual Response	*Filmmakers*	
	Black	*White*
Aggressive	2	2
Assertive	1	1
Passive	0	0
Passion	1	1
Selfish	1	1
Warm	2	0
Cold	2	1
Can't Determine	2	1

6

Finds Sexual Pleasure Through	*Filmmakers*	
	Black	*White*
Love & Affection	1	0
Affection	0	1
Lust	1	1
Lust & Anger	1	0
Anger & Violence	1	0
Greed	0	1
Can't Determine	2	0

7

Gains	Filmmakers	
Pleasure By	Black	White
Overt Seduction of Males	4	3
Covert Seduction of Males	0	0
Can't Determine	2	0

8

Verbally	Filmmakers	
Degrades Women	Black	White
Yes	1	0
No	5	3

9

Sexual	Filmmakers	
Presentation of Self	Black	White
Idealized	2	0
Comfortable	3	3
Degraded	0	0
Repressed	1	0

Thankfully, neither set of filmmakers depicted the women as sexually victimized as in the earlier study—1986–1995. However, as with the case in that study, one item on the SBFA instrument in this present study did indicate that sexual rivalry among women was represented. As Table 11, column 8 indicates, sexual rivalry is shown as a motive for the seduction of a male in one instance, in a film by a black filmmaker. Differences also emerged in how the female subjects presented themselves to others as comfortable with their own sexuality—that is, as women who enjoy sex and sexuality for their own sake or for their own personal gratification (Table 11, column 9). A large percentage of the females in the films of black filmmakers (90 percent) presented themselves as comfortable, or as idealized sexual selves—i.e., women who take pride in their own sexual prowess, in their ability to please males, or in their knowledge of various sexual techniques. Only one female in a black filmmaker's work presented herself as a repressed dominatrix—as willing yet uncomfortable with her own violent display of sexuality.

Similarities emerged in black and white filmmakers' treatment of the black female subjects as "romantic" figures. In fact, sexual interest in men outweighed romantic and platonic interest (Table 9, column 2) in both sets of films (four to three in black filmmakers' works and three to two in those of white filmmakers). However, in this study, black filmmakers fared far better in representing the women on formal dates than did white filmmakers (Table 9, column 6), who depicted no woman on a date. Still, when compared with the women's sexual engagements, the overall minimal instances of dating also suggest a downplaying of "romance" in favor of more sexually-oriented encounters (four women were shown on a formal date versus five who were not). Iverem's (1997) complaint of the dearth of "romantic ... sensibilities" developed for most black women on screen resonates with the treatment of only four of nine black females who were depicted as unqualified romantic characters (Table 9, column 2). Indeed, when examined against their coding as highly sexually-charged women, their romantic treatment as depicted, especially in the films of black filmmakers, is more than ambiguous.

Though three black females were coded by black filmmakers (versus one by a white filmmaker) as romantic characters, much ambivalence was displayed by two males toward the objects of their interest. In each case, both men openly expressed disinterest and disdain in being expected to adhere to the dictates of marriage—i.e., having to sleep with one woman only. Each man was shown to view women generally as primarily sex-objects, and each indicated to his respective "girlfriend" his deep reluctance regarding involvement in a monogamous relationship. In fact, one of the men accepted calls from other women late into the night and into the early mornings, even while his "girlfriend" was present and sharing his bed. And as if to underscore his disrespect for his girlfriend, this male expressed utter disgust when she attempted to address the issue with him, leading to their second break-up which lasted a year. In the second case, the male was depicted as shamed by having to confess to his "girlfriend" his earlier infidelity with his best friend's fiancée, resulting in the best friend calling off his wedding, scheduled for that very morning. Having begged the "girlfriend" to help him correct the problem, her loyal response apparently won him over; afterward, he was shown making a grand stand as he asked her, on bended knees and in public, to marry him. It should also be noted that both men were shown to use strong demeaning sexual language to refer to women generally. Much like in the madonna-whore model, these men apparently reserve respect for their individual mates; other women, on the other hand, are still viewed as depraved sex-objects.

Considering the males' overall negative attitude toward the females, it is illuminating to note that one black male filmmaker in *Loving Jezebel* did humanize the black male protagonist, who was shown to genuinely regard the black female as his unqualified girlfriend. She, however, was depicted as exploiting the male for room, board, and sex. Save for her exploitive interest in this male, she was depicted as having much hostility toward men, along with simultaneous preoccupation with fulfilling her own sexual pleasure. Her portrayal was that of a cold insensitive woman whose repressed sexuality emerged as violent and domineering.

Black and white filmmakers depicted one and two females respectively as sluts, but each differed in the type portrayed (Table 9, column 1). The one female depicted by a black filmmaker as a "slut" was also shown to be a student. But as in the earlier study, white filmmakers again masked one of the "slut" roles by depicting the female as a kind of "call-girl" or criminal. In fact, white filmmakers depicted two of their three black female characters as not only sexual beings, but as engaged in criminal activity. These two representations are illustrative of the traditional roles mainstream filmmakers typically assign to black women. It should be noted, however, that depictions of criminality were absent in black filmmakers' works.

Pam Grier stars as Jackie Brown in Miramax's *Jackie Brown* (1997). Here, Jackie confronts Ordel (Samuel L. Jackson) about being set-up and subsequently arrested while trafficking his drug money into the country.

In both set of films, the black females' nonverbal behaviors worked to underscore their sexual interest in men. Most were shown to wear tight, revealing clothing which emphasized certain body parts related to the sexual (Table 12, column 2). Depictions focused on the women's use of the eyes, lips, and body to seduce the males (Table 12, columns 3 and 4). But unlike in the earlier study where white filmmakers tended to depict the women as engaged in loving acts of hugging and kissing, depictions in this present study between the two sets of filmmakers were almost equal. Here, black filmmakers depicted two women who hugged and kissed the men in loving ways versus four who hugged the men in a sexual manner, while two of these four also kissed the men sexually.

White filmmakers also coded two women who kissed the men in a loving manner and one of these two hugged the men in a similar fashion. Two, however, hugged the males in a sexual way and an additional female also kissed the male in sexually-oriented ways. It is worth noting that only in black filmmakers' films did a female straddle a male's torso or groin area, unzip a male's pants for sex, or make pelvic thrusts. Similarly, only in white filmmakers' works did two females bare their breasts to seduce the males.

Table 12: Nonverbal Sexual Behavior of Black Females on Film, 1997–2001

1

Appearance	Filmmakers	
	Black	White
Attractive	4	1
Seductive	1	1
Sexy	3	3
Sleazy	1	0

2

Type of Dress	Filmmakers	
	Black	White
Revealing Cleavage	3	3
Clingy Dress	4	2
Mini Skirt	1	2
Tight Blouse	4	2
Bare Shoulders	3	0
High Heels	2	2

3

Uses of the Face: Lips	Filmmakers Black	White	Eyes	Filmmakers Black	White
Bits Lower Lip Coyly	1	1	Eyes Male Lustfully	1	1
Puckers Lip as "Come On"	0	2	Looks Male Up and Down While Stroking a Phallic Object	1	0
Chews Gum Seductively	0	1			
Smokes Cigarettes Seductively	0	1	Stars Intently at Male with Sexual Interest	2	2
			Sustains Eye Contact with "Knowing" Look	4	1
			Smiles Suggestively	1	1
			Stares at Male's Genital Area	1	1
			Stares at Male with Helpless Expression	1	1

4

Uses of the Body	Filmmakers Black	White
Dances Sensuously or Wildly	3	0
Swing Hips When She Walks	2	2
Leans Forward with Protruding Chest	2	1
Sucks Her Finger	1	0
Sucks His Finger	1	0
Calls Attention to Buttocks When She Walks or Dances	2	2
Raises Skirt to Reveal Legs	1	1
Makes Pelvic Thrusts	1	0
Raises Shoulders Coquettishly	1	0
Fondles Male's Face/Lips/Thighs/Torso	3	3
Fingers Hair While Talking	1	1
Hugs Male Sexually	4	2
Hugs Male Lovingly	2	1
Kisses Male Sexually	2	3
Kisses Male Lovingly	2	2
Caresses Self (Arms, Breasts, Lip, etc.)	2	1
Sits on Male's Lap in Sexual Manner	2	0
Brushes Up Against Male Suggestively	2	0
Pulls Male to Her for Sex	2	2
Snuggles Up to Male	1	2
Straddles Male's Torso/Groin	1	0
Undresses Male for Sex	1	0
Undresses Self for Sex	1	1

Uses of the Body	Filmmakers	
	Black	White
Unzips Male's Pants	1	0
Bares Breasts	0	2
Cocks Head to One Side While Rocking Body in Suggestive Manner	0	2

As with the first study, the females in this study were also portrayed as characters who lacked interest in men as persons (Table 9, column 5). Here, again, differences emerged in the reverse between the filmmakers. Black filmmakers depicted three times as many women who had interest in men as persons as did white filmmakers, who coded only one female as having such interest. These latter filmmakers' coding of females who had no interest outweighed females who did two to one, despite the uninterested woman's sexual pursuit of the male. And while only in a white filmmaker's work was one female depicted as having a platonic friendship with a male, white filmmakers also depicted two of their three female characters as hostile or angry with men (Table 9, column 4). In fact, the filmmakers each portrayed at least half the females as having hostility toward men generally, even as they also actively sought out sexual encounters with the men. Indeed, black and white filmmakers depicted five and two females, respectively, as using crass and degrading language to solicit a sexual engagement (Table 13, column 1).

Table 13: Verbal Sexual Behavior of Black Females on Film, 1997–2001

Direct Use of Sexual Language	Filmmakers	
	Black	White
Crass	3	1
Degrading	2	1
Romantic	1	1
Humor	0	1
Threatens to Withhold Sex	1	0

2

Indirect Use of Sexual Language	Filmmakers	
	Black	White
Sexual Jokes	1	0
Sex-Code Words	2	1
Sexual Teasing	1	0
Sexual Innuendo	1	2
Sexual Flattery	0	0

Table 14: Male's Attitudes Toward Black Females on Film, 1997–2001

1

Males Viewed Women As:	Filmmakers	
	Black	White
Sex Object	5	2
Tease	0	1
All Women	1	0
Girl Friend	2	1
Friend	0	1
Prostitute		
(Call-Girl)	0	1
(Slut)	1	1
Kook/Crazy	1	0
Lover	1	0
Lesbian	1	0

2

Males Related to Women as:	Filmmakers	
	Black	White
Predominately Sexual	4	2
Predominately Nonsexual	2	1

3

Number of Women Males:	Filmmakers	
	Black	White
Used Demeaning Sexual Language to Refer to	5	2
Leered at	2	2
Ogled	3	0

Portrayals of the women in both studies were found to be sexual, vindicating black feminist writers who have long complained of the all-too-familiar requisite black Jezebel. Moreover, in both studies, black male filmmakers emerged as at least equal with, if not more negative than, their white counterparts. Considering black filmmakers' negative role constructions of black women in the films of both time periods (1986-1995 and 1997-2000), Leab's (1975) argument that films of the 1970s did not accurately reflect black visions of the world because black directors had little control of the images seems to have little merit. Black filmmakers now have some artistic control of the content of their films, as in the case of Spike Lee and John Singleton, for example. Yet, the negative sexual themes and images persist. Wallace (1996) has commented that "...the notion of blacks making their 'own' films presupposes the existence of a monolithic community, unified enough to possess a common ideology, ... sufficient to override ... class, gender, [and] sexuality..." (p. 10). Perhaps racial affiliation is not as powerful a factor in influencing individual belief as was previously thought afterall. Given black male filmmakers' sexual construction of the women of their group as sexual initiators; as sexually explicit; and as ambiguous romantic characters, such would not appear to be the case. The portrayal and, therefore, perception of black womanhood has not, in fact, changed with the race of the filmmaker.

While the treatment of black female sexuality in the films of both black and white male filmmakers was consistent in their negative depictions, overall, white male filmmakers were somewhat less negative in their portrayals than were black male filmmakers. In fact, white male filmmakers have traditionally produced their share of scurrilous images of black female sexuality; but in terms of sheer dreadfulness, black male filmmakers have heightened the sexual exploitation of black female subjects, to the distress of many. Moreover, in addition to depicting debased images of black female sexuality, black male filmmakers also portrayed the males as exhibiting deep disrespect for black women, evident in the men's demeaning attitude and the language used to characterize the women. Therefore, so far as filmic representation of black female sexuality is concerned, if black female subjects must be represented in film, it appears that it is probably less insulting for black female characters to be represented by white male filmmakers than it is to be represented by black male filmmakers. Certainly it is less painful, for to have one's moral character assassinated by members of one's own group is nothing short of a slap in the face. In the next chapter, I will provide a discussion for the incongruity of the images in black male filmmakers' depiction of the black women's non-sexual roles. I will also speculate about how media images can adversely impact the self-image of young black girls. Finally, I will examine three issues regarding depictions of black female sexuality as articulated by the two sets of filmmakers: Why the difference in portrayals of black female sexuality between black and white male filmmakers? Why the stress on black female sexuality? and Why is the deviation in images made more sexually explicit by black male filmmakers?

6

Implications of the Incongruity in Black Filmmakers' Depictions of the Black Female's Nonsexual Roles

It has been said that images are often more important than reality in shaping perceptions. One way of determining what has imagistic relevance is to observe what is suppressed versus what is highlighted. A major finding in both studies was that black male filmmakers depicted the black female characters' roles with friends as predominating. In fact, black male filmmakers portrayed the women as valuing their relationships with friends over their familial relationships. This point is evidenced by the time spent and quality of interactions shared with friends versus that with family. In the second study, for example, only one woman coded as having familial relations was shown interacting with her father. And even here, viewers were left to deduce that the male accompanying her down the aisle was the father. Considering that this was a wedding, one would expect to see images of the bride-to-be interacting with her mother, whose absence was not explained by a death. Where was the mother? Why, for example, was

Jordan, a friend of the bride's, given the responsibility of assuming the role of "mother" by taking care of last minute wedding snafus?

Though research shows that within the black community, extended family systems, including "fictive" kinship, have been cultural mainstays in the lives of most black Americans (Feagin, 1968; Gutman, 1976; Dilworth-Anderson, 1992; Staples & Johnson, 1993; Cherlin, 1996), these familial systems have generally been denigrated by the dominant culture. That culture has tended to view extended family systems within the black community as "pathological" (Herrnstein, 1994; Moynihan, 1965). Moynihan's characterization of the black family, for instance, has come to define black cultural life for the populace (St. Jean & Feagin, 1998), even as "extended family" systems and "fictive" kinship continue to serve as a core network of support within that culture. McAdoo (1993) defines "extended family" as one where not all members live in the same household, but "nonnuclear family members are in close interaction with one another, exchange goods and services and keep in close or periodic contact with one another" (p. 10).

Despite this reality, critics of the black family continue to perceive the structure of black family life as inconsistent with the dominant culture's definition of an intact familial structure (Herrnstein, 1994). Moynihan's (1965) view of black female-headed households as the primary cause of family disruption within the black community has been particularly troubling; for it dismisses the possibility that other structural inequities might be prime determinants. Given such cultural (mis)perception of black family life, therefore, black male filmmakers might have incorporated familial exchanges among the female characters. Failing that, they might have made clear in their filmic narratives the point that friendship within black communities is often viewed as "fictive" kinship. Had this point been sensitively attended to, the black female characters in the black filmmakers' works analyzed might have fared somewhat better as women who value family life. This point is especially important given that the black male filmmakers are products of the black community and so are cognizant of the various family systems within that culture. Presumably, they are aware of the negative views held by whites regarding black women and their "pathological" family structures. If these filmmakers are unaware of this ideology, and I cannot imagine why they would be, they needed to have made it their business to learn about such cultural stereotyping in the research stage of their filming. This lapse seems to me more than perplexing.

Having close friendships is not undesirable; what is problematic is the emphasis placed on closeness with friends to the exclusion of that placed on "family." When this occurs, an imbalance is introduced that has the potential to convey the wrong message. Such public airing of the women as having little interest in family life sends an erroneous message that beliefs held about black women have merit. The images feed into popular myths that black women lack family values, which is merely a slippery slope to arriving at faulty explanations for the social phenomena that beset many poor black women's lives: single status and out-of-wedlock births.

Compounding the problem further was that in the earlier study (1986–1995), black male filmmakers portrayed black women as having little interest in their work. Six of the nine women in black filmmakers' films were depicted as working, but of these, only two held positions that require any training. The remaining four (all of whom were poor, and none of whom valued their work) included two waitresses, one beautician's helper, and a stripper. But again, these depictions feed into the faulty cultural belief that black women, coming as they do from a subculture of laziness and welfare dependence (Collins, 1990; St. Jean & Feagin, 1998), need to adopt a stronger work ethic in order to lead more successful lives. The depictions also have the potential to solidify belief that black women's depressed social and economic position is founded in their own individual failures, rather than in structural and socio-economic inequities (Manatu et al., in press). The reverse side of this argument is that culturally speaking, more black women are college educated when compared to black men (St. Jean & Feagin, 1998). Yet, given the kinds of work the black male filmmakers depicted the black female characters as engaged in, the impression left with viewers is that strippers, entertainers, and waitresses are still the main province of black women generally.

In the later study (1997–2000), black filmmakers greatly ameliorated the kind of work black females were engaged in, as well as heightened the women's interest in their professions. And indeed this is an improvement. Yet, there is an unsettling trend which accompanies this change. In spite of their supposed entry into mainstream professions and mainstream living, black male filmmakers still depict black female subjects as frequently exhibiting vituperative and crass verbiage. It is not enough to improve their professional status; black women's personal conduct must also reflect a strong sense of propriety both inside and outside their workplace. Degrading language of the type and frequency displayed by many of the women in black filmmakers' works sends the wrong message: the implication is that even when they become educated and professionals, black women merely mimic appropriate comportment, but eventually revert to debased type because that is who they essentially are. More effort, therefore, must be made to correct this imaging because it perpetuates false perceptions of all women of the group.

On another note, the earlier study (1986–1995) revealed that black filmmakers gave no attention to community or educational roles, even though the women were shown to be underskilled (in 4 cases) or unemployed (in 3 cases). It can legitimately be said that within most black families, education is highly valued (St. Jean & Feagin, 1998). Education, in fact, is viewed as a vehicle toward achievement and success, and therefore is stressed by most poor black families. That not one black female character was shown to be pursuing an education; that not one family member was depicted as urging on any of the women to pursue an education; that not one black female was depicted as even interested in an education is inexplicable. One wonders what these earlier black male filmmakers were thinking! How can they reconcile such images with the values with which they were raised? Did they, in fact, think at all, or were they driven by greed? Depictions of the women's interest as primarily centered in sexual pleasure prompts this question, for as is commonly known, sex sells! This point, in fact, is troubling to many in the black community who are concerned about how the general media images projected might impact black children's perceptions of themselves (hooks, 1981; Cosby, 1994; St. Jean & Feagin, 1998). And despite that the later study (1997–2000) showed improvement in black women's educational and professional interests (2 females were depicted by black filmmakers as students), depictions of debased personal conduct still persists. What messages are young black viewers to take away from the various negative media images assigned to black women?

Cosby (1994) asserts that, generally, negative images of blacks have adverse effect on the self-esteem of young black viewers who are more likely to accept the validity of the images they view. In the case of young black girls, one need consider how images of black women as simultaneously displaying professional, yet, inappropriate personal conduct can impact the sense of self for these girls. This point is of extreme importance, especially when considered alongside balanced images symbolic of other women. The juxtaposing of certain seemingly innocuous media images against unseemly images of black women may serve to confuse and, thus, lower young black females' self-esteem. Take the case of fairy-tales, for example, a favorite among American girls—tales which espouse, among other attributes, feminine virtue (Ivy & Backlund, 2000; Downey, 1996; Lieberman, 1986; Rowe, 1986), one of the many attributes that black girls are believed not to possess. Constant exposure to images of *Cinderella*, *Sleeping Beauty*, and other such American female icons can produce problems for these girls because the ubiquitous fairy-tale genre "ha[s] been made the repositories of the dreams, hopes, and fantasies of generations of girls" (Lieberan, 1986, p. 187).

In U.S. culture, for example, images of Cinderella have been magnified into a cultural mainstay, where most all girls are psychologically socialized to want to be Cinderella, complete with the handsome prince, the romance, and wedding (Lieberman, 1986; Rowe, 1986). Ivy and Backlund (2000) argue that the romantic themes girls first learned from fairytales as children have likely become a "standard" for how women think relationships should be (p. 440). If this is not the case, the authors wonder, why did "so many people worldwide tune in to [watch] the marriage ceremony of Prince Charles and Lady Diana?" (pp. 439–440). And indeed, that Charles and Diana's fairy-tale wedding enjoyed a worldwide audience strongly suggests that women especially "internalize romantic patterns from ancient tales" (Rowe, 1986, p. 222). Mass internalization further suggests that black girls likewise internalize such cultural scripts, for black girls do not live in a vacuum. But whether the tale is disseminated through print or through film, a disconnect surfaces for many, if not most, black girls: the classic heroine bears little resemblance to black girls generally. Rowe and Lieberman note that beauty is presented as a necessary attribute in order to be worthy of romantic love; yet, the authors fail to make the obvious distinction: that the requisite beauty is centered in the white beauty ideal. Perhaps to help redress this contradiction, singer and actress Whitney Houston produced a black version of *Cinderella* which aired on television in the late 1990s. There was no mistaking that the actress who represented Cinderella was black; she looked much like the average black girl. Response from white viewers suggests that many rejected this new imaging, since the black Cinderella did not resonate with their cultural vision of what the heroine should look like. For these naysayers, Cinderella could only be blonde and blue-eyed—this despite the fact that Cinderella, whose presence is ubiquitous as a cultural icon, is also a major cultural role model for many young girls, including young black girls. One wonders how these detractors expect black girls to respond to an ever-present white role model. That white viewers were outraged by the one-time on-screen presence of a black Cinderella begs the question: have they ever thought black girls might also be outraged and confused by the constant bombardment of images of a white icon presented as the image for which to strive to become?

It is safe to assume that the new film version of *Cinderella* failed to leave an indelible, positive imprint on most of white America. What of young black girls, however? Studies might be undertaken to discover how the black Cinderella was received by these young girls. Did they celebrate such a viewing, or did they, too, reject it? It would be instructive to learn what, if any, positive effect the film generated in young black girls.

Because on the cultural level, no positive filmic images of a "feminine" black female character have yet been projected to rival images of *Cinderella*, the white beauty symbol continues to permeate the psyche of young black girls all across this country. When the realization sets in that they look nothing like the cinematic role model; that behaviors consistent with those of Cinderella are not expected of them (especially when viewed against routine media images of black females as boisterous and debased); nor might a slice of the rewards granted to Cinderella be granted to them, what is the cost to young black girls' psyche? Like Pecola in Morrison's *The Bluest Eye* (1993) who desired blue eyes, since as created by the media, that is what symbolizes feminine beauty, might not young black girls also become confused? The point to remember is that Pecola rejects herself and thereafter develops psychological problems. How many Pecolas might there be among us? Where are their black heroines? Despite that film in particular has not provided young black girls with an iconic black heroine, society expects black girls to be accepting of this similar but unequal female socialization. One must concur with Cripps' (1977) argument that "it [U.S. society] encourage[s] cultural assimilation while denying social integration" (p. 313). And how ironic! For if such a practice poses dilemmas for adult black females, how are young black girls to cope?

It was Du Bois (1961) who coined the phrase "double consciousness" to explain the schizophrenic existence blacks generally must endure in U.S. culture. Must our children also suffer such undue psychological trauma? Given the continued devaluation of black womanhood in U.S. culture, are there not more than enough social indignities these girls will have to abide in their adult lives? Socializing young black girls to respond to an unattainable symbol not of their own likeness while offering up that symbol as the model for which to aspire seems to me more than cruel and unusual punishment. Because all media have the potential to influence behavior (Berne, 1961/1974; Erikson, 1963; Bandura, 1977, 1986), and because most young children tend to be accepting of what they see (Bandura, 1986; Villani, 2001), it is especially urgent that filmmakers provide young black children, but especially black girls, with images of hope rather than hopelessness.

Yet another potential negative impact of film's imaging on young black girls concerns how they may respond to images of sexuality. Indeed, a major concern for many black parents is the negative lessons young black teenage girls may be learning about black female sexuality. St. Jean & Feagin (1998) suggest that the negative imagery as portrayed by black actresses "can become role models for black children who have few hero[ine]s..." (p. 114). Young black girls who lack a strong father figure as model, or those who, because of economic constraints, lack consistent parental supervision (Astone & McLanahan, 1991) may be especially susceptible to such negative sexual imaging as those offered in films. For these girls especially, negative attitudes associated with hypersexuality may replace positive attitudes associated with education, for example. Wilson & Russell (1997) note that negative attitudes toward the value of education contribute to high dropout and suspension rates among many black female students overall (p. 61). Perhaps for many of these girls, the search for male-female relationships through the ethos of hypersexuality may have come to be viewed as more achievable than the search for education. Certainly, popularity of the sexual imagery in the media is presented as the province of black women. It is possible that many young girls buy into such beliefs, learning to over-emphasize sexual behaviors. In fact, Cosby (1994) suggests that such negative images may not encourage young black girls to envision themselves as achievement-oriented adults. This is why it is so urgent that filmmakers, but especially black filmmakers, begin to offer positive images of black female subjects. The social ramifications for the choices young black girls may make based on dysfunctional role-modeling are much too ominous. St. Jean & Feagin (1998) contend that images of black women as prostitutes and as hypersexed can be dangerous for present and future generations who might come to perceive the sexual imagery as typifying black women, generally. Indeed, because young black girls are a major audience for film, the ways in which their sexuality is portrayed may come to condition their own attributes and behaviors.

What a shame it would be if, after finally achieving control of their filmic images, black male filmmakers' disparaging stereotypes of black women were to come to permanently define black women as hypersexed and lacking in comportment! How ironic it would be if the message young black girls were to learn from such imaging is a resulting valuation of hypersexuality as opposed to education! And how tragic it would be if the message young black boys glean from the images is the continued devaluation of black girls! For it has been suggested that the denigrating language used by many black males to refer to black women, generally, may be a consequence of images found in the general media fare (Jones, 1992; Williams, 1992).

Why the Difference in Overt Sexuality Between Black and White Male Filmmakers?

Given that white male filmmakers were revealed to be somewhat less negative in their portrayals of black female sexuality than were black male filmmakers, the question is, what accounts for the difference? One answer might lie in the greater sensitivity of white filmmakers to political correctness. Much public debate continues to center around derogatory remarks made about, or inflammatory symbols used as weapons against, members belonging to under-represented groups. In a number of cases, punitive measures of various kinds have been taken against perceived offenders. Considering this racial-political climate, white filmmakers might be engaging in self-monitoring behaviors, taking care not to offend, by avoiding going too far in their negative portrayals of black female sexuality. I previously shared with you that, in my search for films for this study, I had difficulty finding works by white male filmmakers featuring black women as central characters. While they are conditioned to "see" black women in sexual terms, the dearth of roles may be explained by the racio-political climate which may restrict white male filmmakers from producing more films containing negative images of black female subjects. The rationale may be that, absent the sexual, producing images of black women is hardly cost-effective; thus, there are far fewer films with black women in central roles. On the other hand, their depiction of less inflammatory images could also be founded in the notion that one is at times apt to be more kind to members of other groups than one tends to be toward members of one's own group. The sentiment here being that only members of a given group are allowed to make fun of members of that particular group.

One might ask, why then, if white male filmmakers can present members of their group in lurid terms, should black male filmmakers not have the same inherent right? The obvious answer is that if all things and people were equal, they should. But as a marginalized group, blacks simply do not have that luxury—at least, not presently! The potential to define members of a group based on the beliefs which fostered such stereotypes in the first place is far too tempting. If black male filmmakers are allowed a broad canvas upon which to paint negative images of black female sexuality, culturally, perceptual distortions of and negative attitudes toward black women cannot then be obviated. Arguably, restrictions of this kind limit black male filmmakers' "creativity," and on this point I empathize. Alas, this, unfortunately, is one burden all marginalized groups must bear. For until their group assimilates into the mainstream proper, it does that group little good to reinforce already deep-seated prejudices.

Group-bashing aside, the question remains: Why did black male filmmakers construct black women in such graphically-debased terms? From the point of view of these filmmakers, a number of social factors could have been operating. First, it is quite possible that they are more negative in their portrayals of black female sexuality because their worth as "equals" is attached to their perceived competence. Thus, for example, if black men are to be perceived as good at what they produce, these men will have to outperform their white counterparts in any given job situation (Cose, 1993). The logic would read something like the following: since constructing images of black female sexuality is the norm, to be perceived as competent, black filmmakers will need to be more extreme in their sexual exploitation than their white counterparts. Hence, their images of black female sexuality would become more exaggerated.

But beyond that, film's formulaic structure must be considered. Hollywood operates from a cookie-cutter formula, staying close to that which has worked in the past (Jowett & Linton, 1980). Granted, black male filmmakers could have embarked on a narrative of resistance, thereby challenging the cultural belief (we will return to this point shortly). But filmmakers, black or white, are in the business to make a profit. If in the process, the formula happens to raise the public's consciousness, this may be a plus; but the primary aim is to make money and lots of it. Rhines (1996) contends that "the main goal of any feature filmmaker, regardless of race or gender, is making money" (p. 6). But a major problem for most black filmmakers is acquiring funding for their ventures. If their works are to be showcased, they must often conform to the agenda of studio executives. However, what executives want to see versus what black filmmakers may want to create about black women often can become conflictive. While racial ideology is a driving factor undergirding the conflict, at bottom also is the question of distribution. Apart from financial concerns, black filmmakers have difficulty getting their products distributed on both the domestic and international scene. Rhines (1996) argues that:

> Distribution is the greatest obstacle to broad-based success for African-American feature filmmakers.... From the early twentieth century until the present, the lack of enthusiasm that distribution companies, the overwhelming majority of which are controlled by whites, have shown for handling films controlled by Blacks has meant a paucity of Black entrepreneurial ... success in the Hollywood film industry (p. 13).

Domestically, if a film by blacks is not expected to make a profit, distributors are unlikely to finance its promotion or advertising. Successful black films in Hollywood generally mean denigrating images of sexuality or social deviance. Where international distribution is concerned, the picture is even more grim for black filmmakers. While blockbuster films containing images of black women, such as *The Bodyguard,* are distributed overseas, most generally are not. *Eve's Bayou*, for example, a recent film produced by black women, contains positive images of black women, but such films rarely move to the international scene. One view is that because such films are viewed as "black culture" based, it is believed they have no audience (Rhines, 1996, p. 172). Yet, because his works are perceived as having an artistic element, much of Spike Lee's films, with their lurid images of black female sexuality, get international exposure. And it is precisely because many of Lee's films contain denigrating images of black women that their exportation problematizes the situation. Like American viewers, overseas audiences, too, are provided few images of counterexamples with which to balance their impression of black womanhood.

Still, despite the many challenges faced by black filmmakers generally, a few black male filmmakers have, since the early 1990s, attained some financial muscle whereby the negative images could begin to be altered. This point is perhaps best illustrated in the case of Spike Lee. Lee has by now made not only a reputable name for himself in the business; he should have garnered enough economic clout whether through his own resources or through connections made with others in the business, such that he can challenge, without serious fear of economic reprisals, traditional filmic images of black female sexuality. To date, however, none of his works can truly be said to have altered the negative image of black women in film.

Given that the "bottom line" is a large factor in the production of films, and given still that studio executives have a definite vision of those images they want to see of black women, it may be that some black filmmakers compromise their vision and talents by using black women's "reputed" sexual promiscuity as a convenient way to bolster their careers. Financial exigency, therefore, may act as a major factor in motivating some, for black male filmmakers are no different from their white male counterparts where it concerns profits.

Yet another possible reason for black male filmmakers' negative portrayals of black female sexuality may lie in black men's frustration regarding their social status. Attaining social acceptance has not come easily for black males in U.S. culture. Even on the strength of their educational and socio-economic achievements, black men as a group have, traditionally, been denied respectability as "men" (St. Jean & Feagin, 1998; Manatu et al., in press). Failing that effort, perhaps some black male filmmakers view status through sexual domination as one way in which to attain some measure of pretended social worth. Constructing black women as aggressively sexual, thus, may be perceived as one such avenue.

Then too, it may be that learned gender behavior is stronger than group loyalty, for black male filmmakers, like their white counterparts, are still men. Depiction of the black female characters as sexually eager for men could be a function of the male filmmakers' projecting onto black women the filmmakers' own hidden sexual desires (Haste, 1993; Mulvey, 1989). Or it could be that because film tends to reflect cultural practices generally, women who represent sexual "other" are viewed as sex objects. By contrast, men are perceived as "subjects," who, according to Mulvey (1989), control the "look" of the object, woman. Such conception has been particularly useful in the representation of the black female body, which hooks (1992) and others argue has come to occupy the space of "dualized other." Black filmmakers, perhaps more than white, may have come to view black women as even more a sexual "other" in attempts to distance themselves away from their own label of sexual "brutes" (Bogle, 1989). Diverting attention away from themselves feeds into cultural belief that women are the ones who lead men astray (Haste, 1993, p. 173). If, in fact, black male filmmakers' intent was to place responsibility for their own sexual reputation onto black women, black filmmakers' maleness may have been successful in undermining positive representations of black female sexuality in their works.

Still, considering that black men share a history of racial and sexual oppression with black women, the question should be asked, why is the deviation made more sexually explicit in black male filmmakers' films? Both belong to the same group. Why, then, are they not more "protective" of black women's reputation? These questions, in fact, raise yet another question: Just why the stress on black female sexuality in the first place? Research suggests a possible motive. A number of writers have commented on a rift between black men and women (Blakey, 1974; Wallace, 1979; hooks, 1981). Blakey (1974), for example, suggests that black men might feel they must demean black women in order to repudiate the myth of the "'castrating' black matriarch" (p. 19). Unable to secure and keep jobs, black men resent black women who assume the role of "provider." Continued economic marginality and chronic joblessness among black men (Cherlin, 1992, 1996; Wilson, 1996) suggest that black male resentment may be a likely explanation.

"Castrating" matriarch aside, black male filmmakers' negative portrayals of black women might also be a signal of self-hatred turned outward (Poussaint, 1983). Because black men have been told through daily social practices they have little worth (Ellison, 1952/1989; Wallace, 1979; McCall, 1994), the metamessages may have signalled a sense of inferiority which can become part of the sense of self (Freire, 1970; Blauner,

1972; Yamato, 1998). Combine this with the suggestion of a number of scholars that generally, a man's sense of his masculine identity is determined to a large degree by the kind of woman he chooses (Lerner, 1989; Keen, 1991; Wade, 1996). Following this suggestion and given black women's social status in film and in the culture, a black man's sense of himself may not be felt as improved by choosing that which is deemed culturally undesirable—a black woman, particularly a dark-skinned black woman. He may feel that if he were to choose such a woman, each time he looked at her, he might be reminded of who he is not. She would be his reminder that he, too, is regarded as unworthy. He may conclude that such a reminder hardly bolsters his sense of self! He, therefore, may do all he can to divorce himself from such a reminder; hence, the attraction toward lighter-skinned, if not white, women.

Wallace (1979) suggests that film has made the information that black women are culturally undesirable "very available" to black men (p. 158), which has had a negative impact on black males' vision of black women culturally. Hooks (1981) echoes a similar sentiment. She contends that media "emphasize [black women's] undesirability ... as friends or ... marriage partners ... [which] promotes divisiveness between black men and women...." (p. 67). Cleaver (1968) long ago provided us with an example of the dualism in attitude toward white and black women held by black men generally:

> I love white women and hate black women.... There's a softness about a white woman, something delicate and soft inside her. But a nigger bitch seems to be full of steel, granite-hard and resisting, not soft and submissive like a white woman.... The white woman is more than a woman.... She's like a goddess, a symbol... [p. 148].

The roots of black men's dismissive attitudes toward black versus white women may reach back even further than films. Cleaver also remarked that "every time I embrace a black woman, I'm embracing slavery, and when I put my arms around a white woman, well, I'm hugging freedom..." (p. 149). Such contradistinction has its roots in slavery, where, according to Simson (1983), black women were perceived as "objects for sexual gratification," whereas sexual "purity was considered the noblest 'virtue'" for white women (pp. 230–231).

Modern filmic construction of black female sexuality owes not a little to the long history of black women's marginalization in U.S. culture. It is likely that adaptation to their environment lies at the root of black men's dismissive attitude toward black women. Perhaps these men's early cultural training under slavery adventitiously occasioned a modification of their behaviors toward black women which suited their cultural environment. Such early cultural training likely conditioned black men to hold negative attitudes toward these women, learning to see black women as "sexual gratifiers," but not valued members of the "feminine" prototype. Given that these attitudes now routinely appear in the films of black males, it might help explain why black male filmmakers depicted black women not only as more "sexually aggressive," but also as simultaneously more angry and hostile toward men (5 of 8 women coded on this item in the earlier study; 3 of 6 in the later study). Lorde (1984), in fact, provides a compelling argument for this latter ambiguity on the part of black male filmmakers. She argues that though black men and women share racist oppression in U.S. culture, "…sexual hostility against black women is [still] … implemented within … black communities…." She adds:

> the … history of shared battle ha[s] made … Black women, particularly vulnerable to the false accusation that anti-sexist is anti–Black. Meanwhile, womanhating as a recourse of the powerless is sapping strength from Black … [women's] very lives [pp. 119–120].

I am almost inclined to agree with Lorde's miscegenation argument; however, I am also moved to consider the particular situation of the black male essence as played out both culturally and in the media generally. Deconstructing racial male-gender oppression is a complicated business, made more so when issues of the role black males have been allowed to play (or more precisely, the role they have been excluded from occupying) are factored into their cultural experience. On the other hand, when I consider the condition of actual black women in U.S. culture, I cannot resist temporarily entertaining Lorde's argument. I waver between the two dialectics because there is a repeat in my head which argues that there must be some way of resolving the animus which appears to have fractured loving and sustained relations between black men and women. Still, wavering has not blinded me to the impact of persistent negative images on actual black women in U.S. society. Too many are the black women on whose psyche the negative images wreak havoc (hooks, 1981; Lorde, 1984; St. Jean & Feagin, 1998)! One wonders, for example, if the routine and lewd proposals made by both black and white males that a great many black women must endure (while on their way to school, work, church, supermarket, theatre, interviews, etc.) are not indeed related to their cultural and on-screen construction as "hypersexed." Publicly, most black women shoulder the burden with a smile, finding whatever resources they can to avoid becoming bitter. But in appearing unshaken by the daily social assaults, an ironic twist surfaces: many nonminorities reduce black women's response to mean they are especially strong women, a further indication to them of black women's nonfeminine gender status. Indeed, nonminorities often comment admiringly on black women's "strength," oblivious to the emotional toll visited upon black women's interior lives from the multiple stresses brought about by simply living in a hostile social environment. So taken-for-granted is belief in the stalwartness of black womanhood that one can almost hear black women crying out: "We're disintegrating from the weight of utter strength!"

But whether belief in black women's lack of femininity resides in brute strength or in their alleged hypersexuality, the belief is based on pure myth. Myths, especially those depicted on screen, are deleterious to black women's psyche because such narratives continue to be popular with audiences. The myth's popularity, in fact, has been addressed by other writers: hooks (1981) as seen previously offers a political explanation, suggesting that the primary reason for popularity of the images is that they work to preserve patriarchal rule. Jones (1992) advances a different perspective. She contends that the sexual images are "functional" because they assign an accusatory space of blame to black women. Support for Jones' claim can even be found in the historical view of black women as accomplices in white men's sexual exploitation of them, even when the women were raped (Lerner, 1972; Simson, 1983). Lerner (1972) argues that despite that such exploitation was institutionalized by egregious oppressive practices; despite that the myth of black women as sluts was reinforced by such practices—different legal sanction against rape and other sex crimes committed against black and white women, for example—devaluation of black women as lacking in "virtue" became an accepted public belief. The public, in fact, viewed black women as deserving of "none of the consideration and respect granted white women" (Lerner, 1972, p. 163).

The accusatory attitude remains popular today, and it remains so because the verisimilitude inherent in filmic narratives resonates within popular memory, carrying forward the myth. This is why, even given their improving cultural status, black women's social positioning still proves difficult to compete with generational beliefs of the "oversexed" black female myth. Literary and popular cultural folklore of the past amplified by their cinematic equivalent outweigh acceptance of any new definitions of black women's social status. And it is because social time works more slowly than generational time that black women's emerging social status needs more time in which to permeate the collective unconscious. When viewers are fed with a steady diet of images of the oversexed black woman, the images merely help reinforce popular memory, essentially retarding advances in "social time."

That there has been a long tradition in U.S. culture of holding mass media culpable for various social problems (notably, media violence as the cause of violence in children; explicit sexual imageries as promoting teen pregnancies; and so forth) does not necessarily absolve film of complicity in the reinforcement process. While there remains ambiguity in the various conclusions drawn regarding film's impact on public attitude, what seems more than probable is that there is some relationship between what people watch and their attitudes toward the thing or persons viewed (White, 1983; Bobo, 1995; Robinson, 2001). A recent study helps illustrate this relationship. Though it is concerned with violent images and viewer response to such images in the mass media, a brief look at this study is useful to our discussion here.

The National Television Violence Study (1997) analyzed thousands of hours of television viewing by children. Included in the analysis were movies, dramas, and sit-coms. Researchers concluded that repeated reception of both context and style of presentation was such that learning aggressive attitude and behaviors was likely. Desensitization of feeling was also determined to be a likely result. A more recent study provides even more compelling evidence for belief in a relationship between reception and attitude. The *American Medical Association* (Robinson, 2001) studied a group of 3rd graders to determine what happens when children watch less television. The researchers determined that less television viewing significantly reduces aggressive attitudes in children; as a result, they are far less likely to behave violently. If indeed there is a relationship between images viewed and attitude toward what is viewed (and there is every reason to think there is), filmmakers have a social responsibility to become more sensitive about the images they present. Even if film's impact on viewer perception is only a minor one, repeated exposure to visual images of whatever kind clearly has some effect. It is reasonable to assume that the routine filmic portrayal of black women as morally bankrupt will have some effect, if only mass desensitization of feeling toward black women's oppressed social status.

Arguments that film has no effect on viewer perception of reality become weakened when viewed against the evidence. The shift of cultural myths to film clearly illustrates that the two effectively coalesce, despite that film's role in advancing female dualism is indirect and circuitous. The average viewer cannot be expected to determine that the medium borrows from the culture, myths about black women and then mirrors back to the culture that culture's own beliefs through magnification of its vivid images. Nor should such a viewer be expected to "see" that film's reflection invisibly, but effectively, reinforces the stereotype of black women's unworthiness. Yet it is this process which helps determine that black women will be perceived and treated as nonfeminine women. In effect, the process turns in on itself, attenuating efforts to easily identify where it begins and ends. That many black male filmmakers now project onto black women the very denigrating images mainstream filmmakers traditionally have is especially offensive and damaging to black female viewers.

The commercial success of black male filmmakers' works makes clear the point that their images resonate within popular memory. Their images provide cultural members with a potent framework within which to base members' continued denigration of black womanhood. Such images do not merely confirm perceptual distortions; the images are viewed as having merit because they emanate from males of that very group. Paradoxically, black male filmmakers also give themselves that very same framework on which to base their own dismissiveness of black womanhood, and how tragic! For up through the 1970s, both black women and men were routinely assaulted by offensive images in films produced by white males. Today, exploitation of black female sexuality by black males through the embellishment of offensive graphic images similarly assaults black women's aesthetic sensibilities, doing great injury to their social selves.

What many black male filmmakers might want to keep in mind is that while culture may be just as important a factor in shaping individual beliefs as is one's racial heritage, the entire group is undermined when they perpetuate negative images of members of their own group. Admittedly, cultural socialization helps drive individual beliefs (Bem, 1993), which certainly appears to be the case where it concerns the filmic experiences of most Americans. Tudor (1974) argues that:

> culture consists of people's beliefs, their ideas, their values, their very conceptions of reality.... It is created by men, and it helps them define what is meaningful in their world.... Movies are part of this process. They are cultural objects, purveyors of cultural fare [pp. 135–137].

As cultural objects designed to represent the "world-out-there" (Boyum, 1985), film has become a major way through which America looks at itself. Indeed, film is one of the major cultural lenses which informs blacks about how they are perceived culturally (St. Jean & Feagin, 1998). From the perspective of blacks, persistent representation of negative "other" serves as one indication that they continue to be demonized in the mythos of U.S. culture. This is not to suggest that continued marginalization in jobs, housing, and the like is not still the experience of most blacks (St. Jean & Feagin, 1998; Cherlin, 1996; Jaynes & Williams, 1989); it is rather that this larger-than-life visual medium helps magnify for blacks the inequities they experience in relation to the dominant group. On one level, film serves to publicly validate for blacks their perception of their social marginalization, even while many minimize or altogether deny that such is the case.

Cripps (1977) argues that how blacks have been situated in relation to the dominant culture's representations is at best "ambivalent." Ambivalence can be seen in the way blacks are simultaneously presented on screen as similar, yet different. In the film, *Zebrahead*, for example, the black protagonist is presented as the average American high school girl whose familial environment is a relatively healthy one. On the face of it, she is similar to the "girl next door." But she differs in the way she is coded as sexually available, sexually insatiable, and sexually uninhibited, which casts doubt on her authenticity as similar—as "pure" as that "girl next door." Her similarity, in fact, dissolves into sexual difference, so that the sameness is not at all similar. Ambivalence in this and other such films serves to perpetuate the "otherness" of black womanhood.

Such oppositional coding is apparently lost on most black male filmmakers, despite the fact that film is a mass cultural socializer which has social significance in the lives of viewers (Jowett & Linton, 1980; Stacey, 1994). One supposes these filmmakers would be more cognizant of this phenomenon. Though film is not in and of itself problematic, the uses to which filmmakers put that instrument become the point of contention. Considering the struggle it took to gain control of black images, to give up control of those images now is, in effect, symbolic suicide. Black male filmmakers might at least ask themselves, to what end have they used this instrument? Have they used film as a vehicle to reinforce cultural myths about members of their own group, or as an instrument of contestation of cultural (mis)perceptions? These are important questions because their status as men generally gives black male filmmakers an advantage over black women with respect to the power to effect change in representations of black female sexuality.

While on the aggregate, black males are also victims of racial discrimination, and even considering the obstacles they face in the film industry, their gender status has granted, to a handful, access to participation in the mainstream film industry. Such access has not generally been made readily available to black women because of the latter's gender status (Rhines, 1996). The number of films produced by black male filmmakers since the early 1990s juxtaposed with films produced by black women attests to this fact (Welbon, 1992). Welbon observes that

N'Bushe Wright stars as seductive Nikki Patterson, black girlfriend of Zack (Michael Rapaport), her Jewish boyfriend. Both characters face racial opposition to their relationship in Cinemax's *Zebrahead* **(1991).**

"of the 450 feature [films] released in 1991 by the studios and major independent companies, 12 were directed by black men and none by black women" (pp. 18–22). As of March 1995, "only about one-tenth of the fifty or so [films] released with African-American directors ha[s] been directed by women" (Rhines, 1996, p. 88). In the case of the independent studios, only a mere handful of films by black women have enjoyed mainstream distribution, most notably, *Daughters of the Dust (1992)*. In part, this is because of the alleged "soft" subject matter and slant of black women's narratives. Rhines (1996) cites Janet Grillo, vice-president of *New Line Cinema*, as claiming that where it concerns films by black female directors, "It can't just be a human story about a bunch of gals, you know. It must have a concept, a gimmick, a hook" (p. 92).

It is perplexing that films by and about black women cannot have a human storyline considering that a majority of films by and about white women manage to have as their focus a human storyline. What accounts for the difference in perspective where it concerns black and white women? Why can't black women be presented in human terms? Could it be that as St. Jean & Feagin (1998) suggest, media serve to "effectively maintain [the] cultural denigration of black women...." (p. 93)? Grillo's remarks harken back to the concept of "otherness," illustrating once again that cultural myths and film coalesce to form a particular attitude regarding black women. And given the preponderance of lurid roles assigned black female characters, it becomes apparent that the "hook" Grillo speaks of must be the "sexual."

Grillo's attitudes are precisely why, having gained participation in the mainstream, black male filmmakers might remember that the fight for control of cinematic images of blacks was not to become part of an oppressive cultural machinery; that long-hard battle was fought so as to render black filmmakers transforming agents of change. The question, therefore, the challenge for black male filmmakers is, what do they intend to do with images of black women in their next generation of films? Hollywood shows no interest in altering the negative image of black women; not even the major independent studios appear interested in reinscribing the images! Rhines (1996) notes that although there are plenty of black female filmmakers in the business, acquiring funding for their works has been particularly challenging. He indicates that this is in part because the film industry is still a male-oriented business. So despite that black female filmmakers envision transformation in images of black women on screen, their inability to raise the capital required to make feature films remains a major obstacle. Alteration of black women's on-screen images, thus, becomes a far-off dream. If not black male filmmakers, pray tell, who?

Angry Aggressive Sexual Black Women

With the noticeable rise of black male filmmakers in the cinematic mainstream since the mid–1980s, watchful and critical eyes have been trained on that medium. In particular, because whatever information viewers receive about black female sexuality is generally derived primarily through the film medium, that medium has become a site of contestation for many. While television also constructs negative images of black female sexuality, television is limited in what it can explicitly air on screen. Such is not the case with the film medium. Even with its rating system, vivid, explicit, and unsavory images still manage to make their way on screen, pushing as it were the "sexual envelope," while offending black female viewers in the process. Because of this, images black male filmmakers depict of black female sexuality are often attacked as mere imitations of those of their white male counterparts. Significantly, images of both sets of filmmakers become a primary barometer by which black female viewers measure how they are perceived in the culture at large (St. Jean & Feagin, 1998). Both studies, therefore, were designed to discover whether, as important voices in the cinematic mainstream, the emergence of black male filmmakers has altered the image of black female sexuality. To that end, it was important to determine which set of male filmmakers, black or white, conveys what sort of information to audiences about black women and their sexuality.

Results of both studies reveal black filmmakers to be not merely negative in their depictions of black female sexuality, but more negative than their white male counterparts. Yet the expectation of black female viewers was not to have their images transmuted from "mammy" to "oversexed black jezebels." However, cinematic images by black male filmmakers have extended, not displaced, the status quo. They have, in fact, added a new layer to the already lurid black female imagery: the angry oversexed black woman. Such ambiguous portrayal of black female sexuality has established a second-tier negative cultural icon of black womanhood—the "angry, aggressively-oversexed black woman," used as filmic metaphor to signify black womanhood. This new icon is actually the merging of the old Sapphire symbol with the oversexed Jezebel symbol—the blending of two old familiar images to create the new. As portrayed in film, this "new" imaging is habitually and blatantly exploited; in television offerings, by contrast, the process involved in promoting the new imagery is craftily erected, where humor is often times employed to obfuscate the construction. And so it must be; otherwise, direct devaluation of black women might prove too much even for mainstream America were the process to be fully exposed during prime time. In its pretense to project a homogenized America, such overt airing would not be a welcome one on TV. The illusion of an homogeneous culture must be maintained.

But this new offering by most black male filmmakers amounts to their having found yet another means through which to render black women signifiers rather than subjects. They have provided yet another excuse to exclude black female subjects from participating in the verisimilitude inherent in serious, dramatic roles. This new trend since the mid–1980s continues to permeate the films of black male filmmakers; yet, few seem concerned that such a metaphor can damage black women's psyche, or that of the entire group. Certainly, the foregone analysis of the social impact of the images suggests that stereotypes about black women as oversexed are potentially damaging to the lived cultural experiences of these women. As well, we have seen how the images also work to exclude black actresses from representing serious characters in dramatic roles. Still, the negative sexual image is given vivid public airing.

Yet, it is interesting to note that one of the more recent films, *The Best Man* (1999), produced by the "godfather" of the new black commercial film culture, Spike Lee, and written and directed by Lee's cousin, is said to represent blacks in what Parker (1999) suggests is a multifaceted portrayal. The film attempts to debunk old stereotypes about black men by portraying images of these men as professionals. Notes reviewer Parker (1999):

> This smart debut ... centers around a group of old friends [young black professionals] who unite in New York for a wedding.... Although the film is produced by Spike Lee, don't expect racial politics.... In a world of popular Hollywood cinema, black characters rarely seem to be more than cardboard cutouts: the requisite hoodlum, ghetto goddess or chief security. Not so in *The Best Man* [pp. 46, 54].

Parker suggests that though "godfather" Lee is reputable for reducing blacks to stereotypes, he somehow manages to veer away from such representations in this film, especially as they relate to black males. While I appreciate Parker's observation, I want to again suggest that if the on-screen behaviors are presented as stereotypical, merely improving the career status of blacks does not go far enough in improving perceptual awareness of them. Having said this, I applaud newcomer Lee for uplifting the professional status of the majority of characters in his film, black women's negative sexual depictions notwithstanding.

One wonders what accounts for the positive shift in representation of the characters' professional roles. Could it be that because Spike Lee himself only produced, but did not write or direct the film, images of blackness were depicted more sensitively? Or is a more positive view that he is slowly maturing into a more socially responsible filmmaker? If so, might this film signal a more positive direction in depictions of black females in the next generation of films by this "godfather" of the new black film culture? It must be remembered that Spike Lee first set the tone for the proliferation of films featuring negative images of black female sexuality, which was adopted by other black male filmmakers starting in the early 1990s.

Might other black male filmmakers also improve upon what is arguably an ambivalent representation of black female subjects in *The Best Man*? With one clear exception—two, if we are sympathetic to another of the black female's plight—*The Best Man* depicted most of the black females as sexual predators, albeit educated ones. Although actress Marlene Warfield (2002) is more hopeful about images of blacks in the present film culture, she also notes that what blacks "need [now] is a good script." And indeed, a more favorable shift in depictions of black female sexuality in the future works of black male filmmakers is sorely needed. Yet, such a positive reinscription of images of black female subjects has not thus far become the norm. And so this chapter ends near where it began: at the nexus of lurid visual on-screen images of black female sexuality and false age-old cultural myths and beliefs, where a narrative of contestation is all but absent from the works of black male filmmakers. Still, we dare not give up hope! Perhaps there is still time in which to have a substantive transformation of black women's imagistic portrayals.

7

Conclusion

American popular film has been roundly criticized in recent years for its stereotypical and negative characterization of black American women in general, and of their sexuality in particular. The emergence of black male filmmakers in the media mainstream has only served as further fuel in the heated debate regarding these women's portrayals. As recently as the 1960s, media representations not reflective of black cultural life sparked critical debate among black scholars. In 1967, Harold Cruse called for segregation in black cultural products as a response to criticisms about the negative portrayals of blacks in film. Twenty years later, the mood shifted when, in a counter-response to Cruse's call, Tate (1986) asserted that blacks need not abandon European influences to advance black identity. What blacks needed to do, Tate insisted, was to incorporate European filmic strategies into black versions of historical narratives. Tate then pointed to the film *She's Gotta Have It* as the example of the new black film aesthetics.

Presumably, this new aesthetic would be the answer to the negative portrayals of blacks in film. Yet, neither perspective held. For given the many criticisms that have centered around *She's Gotta Have It* for its negative depictions of black female sexuality, and given the findings of this study, not only does Tate's new aesthetic contain serious flaws, but Cruse's segregation theory assumes differences between black and white filmmakers not supported by the evidence. The findings of this study strongly indicate that both black and white male filmmakers routinely construct negative sexual imagery of black women, with only relative differences in the degree of negativity.

Based on results of both studies, findings suggest that, given the new shift in depictions of black women in films from "mammies" of the pre-1970s to "oversexed bitches" of the mid-1980s and beyond, there is an urgent need for modification of the sexual imagery of black women by filmmakers, black and white. On closer inspection, the shift, in fact, is no shift at all. Both images are negative ones, differing only in degree of negativity, much the way black and white male filmmakers differ in their degree of negativity.

Popularity of the films in these studies also suggests that there is an equal need for understanding by viewers of film's dynamics. If audiences fail to bring proportionality to their consumption of media images or fail to define for themselves a moral compass in that consumption, it leaves them vulnerable to an immoral dualized world evoked by a sensational industry. Viewers need to realize that film not only entertains, but it also transmits metamessages about how people should live, what they should value, and who they should value. Accordingly, female viewers, especially, need to become critical consumers of negative filmic images of women generally. As a communications professor, I am constantly amazed at the level of acceptance of negative filmic images of women among many of my female students, some of whom seem undisturbed by the images. Yet, I have also witnessed, after much thinking and talking, changes—sometimes small, sometimes profound—in students' perception of the images. It is because of this and many more such occurrences in my other walks of life that I urge those who understand the various levels on which filmic influence operates to help their sisters, daughters, aunts, mothers, cousins, and friends understand the consequences for all women when just one woman's debasement on screen becomes an acceptable norm.

One of the ways women, black and white, can help to effect change in representations of women's on-screen imaging is to become towering voices by boycotting those films that contain degrading images of the objectification of women. Before such mobilization can take place, however, women all across this country must begin an open dialogue among themselves regarding this issue. Each subgroup of women must become courageous visionaries in their willingness to provide the other with a fair hearing.

Certainly, various disparate women's groups have long argued for change in media depictions of "women" generally (Brownmiller, 1975; hooks, 1981, 1992; Modleski, 1991; Haskell, 1995). What has not occurred is a coming together of all women in a united effort for change in the encoding of women as subjects and not mere objects. Arguably, unity among black and white women has been an uphill battle; yet, it is this possibility which holds the most promise for positive depictions of women, or else we risk continued misrepresentation of all women. If we are ever to experience change in on-screen representations of women, black and white women must begin to empathize with each others' filmic subordination. Both must begin to see that in different ways and with different consequences, each has suffered opposite, but oppressive positions in film as well as in the culture.

White women must begin to "hear" black women's just complaint concerning the latter's oppressive place in almost all social institutions in U.S. society, including the film institution; black women also must begin to view much of white women's social experiences in society (particularly poor white women) as also a subordinate one. The degree of marginalization between the two groups must come to be seen as less important to the larger issue of women's subordination than which group has suffered more. This latter point, while important, has for too long prevented both groups from uniting in efforts to effect change in women's cinematic imaging. Not until these marginalized voices begin to join in the national debate about women's negative media representations can the potential space for substantive change be realized.

Such effort is only half the battle, however; the discussion must be extended such that men are also brought into the conversation. An enormous burden to be sure; alas, it is up to women to initiate this discussion. The onus falls onto women because women, not men, are the objects of the negative imaging. Men must be engaged in conversations about the potential harm of such imaging, menfolk from fathers, to husbands, to sons, but especially sons. How young men are taught to perceive women ultimately has enormous effect on how future generations of men will come to view and treat women. Throughout this book, we have discussed how repetition of negative cultural perceptions of women, black and white, perpetuates in one way or another, negative imaging of women in film, which likely leads to acceptance of such imaging. It is crucial, therefore, that young men become part of the discussion regarding women's imaging on screen. It is equally important that young girls also be included in the conversation. In an earlier discussion of media effect on young black girls' self-image, I noted that one of the concerns within the black community is the distorted messages film transmits to young black girls about sexual appropriateness. Filmic images that transmit messages of hypersexuality among black women may work to adversely influence young black women who lack positive role models. Because of the potential for such distorted modeling, altering the negative images becomes of paramount importance.

A second motivation for modifying the negative images of black female sexuality is the changing face of America. It is still not clear whether the U.S. will become a multicultural society or remain a multiracial culture. However, having entered the 21st century, American society finds itself confronted, more and more, with a pluralistic present. The races, hence, are going to be forced to find workable solutions toward harmonious living. As the complexion and composition of U.S. culture continue to change, how diverse groups are represented in the next generation of films is an issue that must be rigorously attended to.

Black audiences are a large ticket draw. Bobo (1992) asserts that in 1988, blacks spent $1.1 billion on films, which translated into approximately one-fourth of $4.5 billion spent nationally that year. Considering their 12 percent of the population, that figure is an impressive one. Blacks are drawn to film in a compelling way because, as has been suggested, blacks receive much of their "cultural sustenance" from films (Parks, 1995). Perhaps, too, because blacks come from a tradition of oral culture (Bobo, 1992; Hall, 1992) where storytelling functions as an inherent part of that community, narratives are highly valued (Young & Young, 1993). But as the tastes of this audience change in response to negative images of themselves, as was the case with Blaxploitation movies of the 1970s (Leab, 1975), black audiences will not accept for long these negative filmic images. If the 1970s are any indication, it may only be a matter of time before black audiences begin to reject and demand filmic representations that are reflective of their cultural status. And, indeed, the process has already begun.

The NAACP has publicly put filmmakers and other media markets on notice, with some success. Generally, the major television networks have responded to some degree to the call for changes in portrayals of blacks overall. Although debate continues regarding the degree of change that has taken place in television (Farley, 1993; Randolph, 1994; Inniss & Feagin, 1995; Braxton, 1997), it is generally agreed that the film industry has been slower in responding to the charges (Rhines, 1996; Welbon, 1992). But within the parameters of this research project, the evidence suggests that the industry might want to take notice. This research study has implications, not just for academicians as it concerns curricula and pedagogy; the project also has implications for studio executives and filmmakers, most of whom rely on market research analysis as guides for production of their output.

Given the desires of black female viewers who, as cultural consumers, want transformation in their imaging, profit will likely emerge as an issue. Filmmakers are in the business to make money and blacks generally contribute handsomely to film's market share (Bobo, 1992; Rhines, 1996). Rhines (1996) estimates that blacks comprise one-third of the total paying audience for films (p. 7). At 6 percent of the total population, even if only half that number of black women frequent filmic offerings, that translates into a hefty share of viewers who want improvement in their imaging. Results of both studies make clear the point that these women's cinematic representation is far from positive. If profit is of interest to filmmakers, they might want to seriously consider black female viewers' displeasure. Interestingly enough, though a few of the studios recognize that the black middle class want to see images of themselves on screen, the studios appear to misunderstand the desires of black female viewers generally. Rhines (1996), for example, observes that one of the reason *She's Gotta Have It* was released in the Lincoln Center neighborhood in New York City was because studio executives did not want to "ghettoize" the film's release. He suggests that had the film been released in Harlem, it would never have seen the success it enjoyed.

Of course, the majority of the audiences for the film were white viewers, a point which may say more about what white audiences want to see regarding images of black women and what they are comfortable with than what black audiences want to view of themselves. The studios clearly misinterpreted the desires of the black middle class audience! Studio executives were correct that these middle class movie goers want to see images of themselves on screen, but they were and are mistaken if they believe black viewers want to see unsavory images of themselves reflected back to them. Our discussion in Chapter 4 clearly illustrates that black female audiences, especially, want to see an improvement in their cinematic imaging. This observation is further amplified by black critics' resolve to boycott and challenge the media, despite the media's insistence in perpetuating negative images of blacks generally. Moreover, as more and more media watchdog organizations educate the various subgroups into becoming critical consumers of media images (Crier & Roker, 2002), people will likely begin to question their group's representations in the various media. In turn, questioning will likely lead to demands for change in representations of their group.

When this occurs, filmmakers, black and white, will need to become more socially responsible in constructing images of underrepresented groups, particularly those involving black women. As both studies revealed, both sets of filmmakers contribute to the negative imaging of black women. In turn, such imaging has reverberating social consequences for that subgroup of women. This research project, then, takes on importance when representations of black female sexuality are juxtaposed with the debilitating social effects on this subgroup of women. Because of this, change in filmmakers' on-screen imaging is especially needed. But for filmmakers to become responsible in their constructions, they must be helped to recognize their part in the perpetuation of negative beliefs about and attitudes toward black female sexuality.

Academic institutions might want to consider the issue of role diversity as they make book selections and prepare classroom presentations. It is generally agreed that one of the goals of education is to develop self-awareness in students as well as a sense of ethical and social responsibility. Programs designed to train and educate students of filmmaking, therefore, might consider including a curriculum whose goal it would be to develop skills designed to sensitize future filmmakers toward more humane constructions of images of women generally. Such programs should illustrate for future filmmakers the myriad of ways in which filmic images can work to devalue cultural perceptions of women generally, and of black women especially. The focus here on black women's filmic construction arises from our discussion throughout this book that few counter-balancing images are provided them from which the culture at large can view them. Even fewer are offered which audiences, black and white, can interpret as universal, and thus, relate to. Audiences need to see the interior lives of black women in order to get a sense of black women's humanity. Audiences need to begin to get a more realistic glimpse of black women's rich and multifaceted cultural experiences. Presently, such depictions are denied both audiences and black female characters alike. What is left is a one-dimensional, distorted view of these women's lives. Both studies evidence such a representation whether the filmmaker is black or white.

Future filmmakers, hence, must be helped to understand the dynamics between the fictive and the real. They must come to understand and take seriously the symbolic significance of film's imaging on the lived experiences of viewers (Rosen, 1973; Stacey, 1994; Bobo, 1995). The literature on "women" in film suggests that representations of gender are damaging to the personal and lived experiences of females, generally (Mellen, 1975). In contrasting stereotypes of women in film with women's social reality, for example, Rosen (1973) finds that impressionable young women imitate on-screen behavioral trends by mirroring film's obsessive preoccupation with the pursuit of romantic love. She argues that this phenomenon greatly contributes to the development of unrealistic expectations and false values among "women" (p. 105). It would be difficult to over-state that black women are also susceptible to developing such unrealis-tic expectations. Yet, because they aren't depicted on screen as interested in romantic love, imitating such behavioral trends results in devastating consequences for actual black women. The pressure to find a mate can be an unpleasant experience for black women, especially, for cultural ideas of the "feminine" often preclude this choice for many. In the face of this evidence, filmmakers must come to understand how symbolic represen-tations can serve as signals for viewers, influencing how they view them-selves and social "others." Moreover, future filmmakers must be helped to understand that repeated negative images of one cultural group can have devastating effects, potentially alienating that group from the larger society. But such understanding can only occur if educators make these issues a priority in their instructions to future filmmakers.

Recall that female polarization was discussed as a major obstacle for black women in film. It is important for educators to articulate for film students an understanding of the consequences of devaluing women on screen while simultaneously polarizing them such that images of one group are counter-balanced, while a varied definition of the other is sup-pressed. It is particularly important that future male filmmakers, espe-cially, understand that such constructions often can maintain barriers between women and among races, rather than demolish them. One effect of same-gender female polarization is that black and white women have become more and more emotionally segregated as dominant group mem-bers see themselves as having little in common with blacks generally. Specifically, in filmic offerings, gender is much too often presented in the form of female dualism, while race is simultaneously presented as hav-ing less value, as unequal, and often, as negative "other." These two on-screen presentations offer special problems for black women who are at once women and black. As a consequence, this subgroup is dealt a dou-ble blow in the film medium, where they are simultaneously polarized and coded as nonwomen and devalued and treated as negative racial "other." And so, what I am arguing is that gender and racial attitudes must be perceived by future filmmakers, black and white, as not only important to what is presented in film about black female sexuality, but also important to how what is presented might be interpreted by viewers.

It cannot be emphasized enough that film is instrumental in influencing the self-image of viewers as well as effective in directing, lim-iting, and structuring viewers' collective perceptions of diverse subgroups. Therefore, negative sexual construction of black female sexuality on screen has social implications for the human dignity of black women as well as implications for the society at large. The cost to black women in viewing images of themselves as forever trapped in negative filmic roles is the resulting harm done to the self-image of these women. Where it concerns conception of the "feminine," filmmakers need to begin to adopt a more inclusive approach to the beauty model, embracing all color and facial phenotypes as different and equally valued. To help audiences come to perceive black women as human persons, roles for black women must begin to reflect diversity in characterization based on their diverse social experiences, a diversity which should appear as normative and seamless as it often does for other groups of women. Such diverse portrayals certainly would begin to redress the negative imagistic symbols projected onto black women and fostered in viewers' minds.

I previously noted that for those black women who choose to conform to the cultural directive of the "feminine," repeated negative sexual imaging contributes to their being denied participation in acts and rewards of the "feminine." Filmmakers need to construct images such that color effects do not skew applications of the feminine; they need to construct images such that negative behavioral expectations are not always associated with dark-skinned black women particularly. Such cinematic practices are conditions which, if not addressed responsibly, could reinforce "black elitism." Let me reemphasize here that their desire for public self-validation is not simply a question of black women wanting to join in the "cult of true womanhood" for its own sake, nor is it a skewed desire to promote ideals of patriarchy. It is rather a question of being more free to move on to champion other pressing causes specific to their gender and class status. We should be mindful that it is public valuation of white womanhood which has largely aided in whatever social and economic rewards they now enjoy. And it is precisely because they are valued in society that women of the dominant group have been successful in having their gender concerns given public airing.

Arguably, the claim can be made that white women still suffer from sexism with all its insidious byproducts, and so are attempting to move away from the "feminine." And that very well may be! Yet, valuation of their feminine status has allowed them a national voice not rivaled by any other group of women in U.S. history. Public discourse regarding sexism has entered the collective consciousness in a way that same-sex racial issues never have. I argue here that this is because black women have had no social value; no social power; and, thus, have had no collective national voice.

A major reason such is the case is that in this complex issue of female polarization, reactions to white-skin color bias continue to yield negative attitudes toward black women as a group. We might at least begin by acknowledging that regardless of how dignified, educated, and ladylike a black woman is; regardless of how much harmony of grace a black woman possesses; she nonetheless carries with her a social stigma of "whore." The collective body seems trapped in a cultural myopic script of immorality where it concerns perception of black women. Hooks (1981) herself argues that during Black Reconstruction:

> Those black women suffered most whose behaviors best exemplified that of a "lady." A black woman dressed tidy and clean, carrying herself in a dignified manner, was usually the object of mud-slinging by white men who ridiculed and mocked her self-improvement efforts. They reminded her that in the eyes of the white public she would never be seen as worthy of consideration or respect [p. 55].

She argues further that:

> So pervasive was the tendency of whites to regard all black women as sexually loose and unworthy of respect that their achievements were ignored. Even if an individual black female became a lawyer, doctor, or teacher, she was likely to be labeled a whore or prostitute by whites. All black women, irrespective of their circumstances, were lumped into the category of available sex object [p. 58].

Lest the reader speculate that sexual devaluation of black women occurred only during slavery or during the period of Black Reconstruction (1867–1877), St. Jean & Feagin (1998) remind us that the cultural mythos of black women as sexually loose continues to dominate the consciousness of the collective body. In the final analysis, economic freedom, social respectability, social power, a collective voice—even sexual freedom—are all linked to how valuable women are viewed in the culture. This is why, it seems to me, it is imperative that public perception of black women begin to be altered in some small way. Absent reform, film's unrelenting images of black female sexual deviance promise to restrict the personal freedom of actual black women. I am well aware of the potential trap in embracing concepts of the "feminine," but as I see it, this is the place from which black women must start. Possibilities for personal freedom and social movement from this starting point far outweigh any potential threat of black women promoting patriarchal rule.

Just as public validation of a group's value is enriching to that group, so, too, public validation is self-affirming to the individual. The habitual coding of the black female subject as a sexualized being is disaffirming to the self. Until a new definition of the feminine is outlined—better still, until a debunking of the very concept itself occurs—the "masculine" and "feminine" genders are all that cultural members are socialized to internalize; the two are all that mainstream society recognizes. It makes little sense to socialize subgroups into "cultural assimilation" while denying one such group "social integration" (Cripps, 1977). If women's fight is for a fair and just place in the social mainstream, black women cannot now be expected to engage in counteracts of gender resistance. The lack of social value and power hardly affords black women such a luxury. Indeed, if as culturally-valued persons, white women's social reality is still suppressed on screen, black women's social reality doesn't even register on the valuation scale. Therefore, such a resistance would merely reinforce the very negative perceptions these women have for so long been attempting to eradicate. Any mass gender resistance now on their part has the very real potential to provide mainstream society with a further rationale for its continued negative attitudes toward and beliefs about black women. Only when they have the choice of entering into the domain of the "feminine" or rejecting it and so become "valued" social persons can they then join with women of the dominant group in their fight for new definitions of this idea called the "feminine."

That being the case, black women must have a space for expression of their "femininity" in the same way that women of the dominant group now enjoy. That space cannot continue to be relegated to the eternal "hypersexed, unfeminine, nonwoman" category. Without a complete eradication of these false stereotypes, black women will almost certainly continue to be socially devalued and denigrated. As presently played out in the culture and in film, "femininity" for white women carries with it "invisible" privileges from which they continue to benefit (McIntosh, 1998), even as many in this latter group complain on a macro-level. And so they should! But they must also accept that black women have not yet arrived at that public space. Excluded from the feminine class, black women have had no rights as women, for presently, they are relegated, culturally, to the nonwomen category. One devastating result of this cultural portraiture, as we saw previously, is that many black women's chances of securing love and a stable family life are severely arrested. Repeated negative imaging of black women as "unfeminine" locks them into one primary category—the sexual—from which there seemingly is no escape. St. Jean & Feagin (1998) may have put it best when they note that "once created, [negative] stereotypes have a staying power through the generations" (p. 117). When film's vivid images enter the picture, the permanence is further imprinted on viewers' psyche. Such is the power of the moving image! Visual images speak volumes.

It must be noted that despite sweeping social changes of the 1970s, social attitudes have not kept pace with legal and political gains. Perhaps this is because social attitudes extend well beyond the arm of any laws that can be enacted. Where laws can dictate individual social actions, laws cannot legislate private individual attitudes; certainly laws cannot legislate the direction in which a collective attitude will sway! Presently, black and white Americans are legally assimilated, but they remain emotionally segregated. This is why it is not overstating the case to suggest that, in this age of democratic enlightenment, America still faces a moral crisis in its race relations. Most people, on one hand, may be concerned about declining race relations; but on the other hand, they fail simultaneously to protest very loudly or forcefully. Their rhetoric, in fact, lacks the passion needed. Still, no one voice has the power to bring about the kind of change the media can and do. Because the film medium, especially, is such an influential and ritualistic American institution, the industry could go a long way in helping U.S. culture heal. It has the power to take race and gender simultaneously to the center of what it means to be human by presenting black women as realistic human beings. At the very least, film has a social responsibility to reflect truthfully those areas wherein black women have experienced positive social movement. Instead of the dysfunctional images it now feeds viewers which many nonconsciously accept as gospel, film could present black women's experiences as normal. But based on its long history, the film medium tends toward promotion of cultural stereotypes: it feeds on the fears and prejudices of society, effectively reinforcing negative stereotypes of cultural "others." When film becomes an agent of myth-making, intense ambivalence can be one result for the alleged deviant "other."

One issue often overlooked, but which can have a sobering effect for the marginalized "other," is that if people are treated as pariahs long enough, certain group members might respond to the way the world reacts to them by acting out behaviors detrimental to their persons. For how people are perceived by others often can affect not just their self-perception, but their conduct as well (Poussaint, 1983). A sad consequence of the social stigma associated with black women appears in the sexual behaviors of some, who appear to defy their social label by acting in like fashion (Manatu-Rupert, 2000). Despite that some women of the dominant group also engage in improper sexual behaviors, their group's reputation serves to mask such acts, providing group members with a public perceptual cloak of virtue. Any untoward behaviors on a few black women's part, however, work to cast a wide net of doubt onto all women of this group (hooks, 1992, 1995). Such a narrow view reinforces belief in a monolithic tawdry black woman, which in turn adds another layer to negative attitudes already held by the collective body. In the end, it is actual black women who pay a price for the refusal of that collective body to seriously engage in acts of compassion and integrity.

From the point of view of society, the negative imaging has the potential to perpetuate racial and gender conflicts between women, blacks and whites, where social interactions become steeped in disingenuous or hostile exchanges. Certainly, a body of evidence is emerging which suggests that tension between black and white women, for example, is still a major barrier between these two groups generally (Downey, 1993; Russell et al., 1993; Wilson & Russell, 1997; St. Jean & Feagin, 1998; Bell & Nkomo, 2001). One of the major sources of conflict between these women appears to be the devaluation of black women's female status in the culture at large juxtaposed with valuation of white women's assumed right to the "feminine" (Orenstein, 1994; Wilson & Russell, 1997; St. Jean & Feagin, 1998). Ironically enough, despite granting that right to women of the dominant group, film also simultaneously contributes to a dual split among these very women, where some are relegated to the "good girl" category and others to the "bad girl" domain (Mellen, 1973). Mellen argues that women in film are portrayed as "destined to act out sexual roles of either (a) seductive mother, ... (b) castrating bitch, ... or (c) passive, childlike recipient of the brutalities of the male ..." (p. 73). It is reasonable to assume that like most all black women, many white women also suffer unequal treatment as a result of female polarization, though to a lesser degree and with very different consequences. Given that film is a major reinforcer of women's "feminine" role in society, elimination of on-screen images of female polarization should be a goal of filmmakers, black and white.

Elimination of the negative imaging could have positive consequences on a number of levels. Eliminating the negative imaging of women as sex objects could ameliorate cultural perceptions of women generally. As well, it could help in bringing about parity among women. Public markings of respect for differences between women could be a major result of such a change. Elimination of the negative images could also aid in enhancing the physical and psychological well-being of black women especially; it could contribute to deconstructing in the minds of viewers belief in the negative stereotype that black women are endowed with heightened and, thus, deviant sexuality. It could also contribute to dispelling the belief that black women are "accessible" commodities, easily available to any male. Finally, discontinuation of the negative image could contribute to improved relations between social groups, helping to ameliorate both the racial and gender tensions that exist in U.S. culture between women, blacks and whites.

Future Research

In an earlier chapter, I noted that though critics have hit hard at the film industry for its negative cinematic portrayals of black womanhood, little empirical research has been done to provide a clearer understanding of how the images work to impact black women culturally. This absence, coupled with the debate in the black community regarding the direction black cultural products should take, informs my suggestions for future research. First, several more categories should be incorporated into the SBFA instrument which guided this research. Categories of age, social class, empathy, succor, and humor might be useful in adding fuller dimensions to the total sexual orientation of the black female characters in a future study. However, a word of caution regarding the use of humor involving black women might be useful at this juncture.

Earlier on in the preface, I pointed out that a major concern among black media critics is the lack of seriousness often applied to issues involving black cultural life in the media generally (Inniss & Feagin, 1995). Great care and sensitivity, therefore, are needed when introducing humor in the context of black cultural life. For the fact that blacks generally greet humor with a deep sense of appreciation is no reason to pander to audiences' expectations by contriving gags and physical "cut-ups" merely for the sake of laughter, as was the case in the film *Jumping Jack Flash*. Nor should humor be imposed to deflect attention away from serious issues important to black cultural life, as was the case in the film *Made in America*.

A close look at a couple of scenes from *Made in America* helps elucidate this point. In the film, the interracial couple is brought together by the female's 18-year-old daughter who mistakenly believes her father to be the white male (the child was allegedly conceived through artificial insemination). The young woman is confused about her racial identity; but instead of dealing realistically with the issue, the film focuses on the supposed sexual tension between the two adults. And one could even tolerate this plotline had it not been for the manner in which the black woman is coded. Upon returning from their only date, the two are depicted as so entirely centered in their sexuality that they literally pounce on one another, knocking over lamps and pictures on the wall, and generally exhibiting animalistic behaviors as they make their way to the bedroom. These behaviors lack not only delicacy and warmth; they are reminiscent of the buffoonery to which blacks have traditionally been relegated.

But there is an equally disturbing problem. The scene feels awkward and contrived. Such a gratuitous sex theme raises the question: Why does the oversexed black woman emerge in this film? Considering the seriousness of the issues raised in the film, is the requisite sexualized black female not once again a means through which black womanhood cannot—must not be taken seriously? In fact, the awkwardness of the sex scene is such that it reduces viewers into peals of laughter. I would argue that the audience intuitively sensed the incongruity of the genre, which raises the question: Why, given such serious issues, was this film constructed under the genre of "comedy" in the first place? While viewers laughed, they were not laughing with the characters; they were laughing at the buffoonery the characters displayed. Viewers sensed they were not intended to treat these two in any serious way; theirs was a forced, and thus, dishonest, relationship. On the narrative level, the two were coded as interested in each other; yet, on the visual level, they were gratuitously coded as rooted in their biological functioning only. Such exaggerated sexual behaviors once more feed into the cultural belief that black women are sexual beasts, unconcerned with emotions.

In another scene, the message of the "oversexed" black woman is further amplified when the daughter returns from her date and notices the destruction in the room. She lashes out at her mother because the young woman fears a romance between her mother and "father" might end badly, thereby adversely impacting her developing relationship with her "father." But beyond this, the implication is that the daughter has seen this scenario before; that to her, this is normal behavior for her mother. Putting that aside for the moment, the daughter, in a previous scene, has an interethnic date that very night with one of her "father's" employees. But from the onset, the situation is problematic because, here too, the theme of black female hypersexuality surfaces. The manner in which the daughter is dressed is shown to be so sexually provocative that it leads her male school chum to comment disapprovingly on the outfit. Though this male friend's response is sweetly suspect, since he does have a crush on her, the point is well taken. Given that this girl is preparing for a first date with a relative stranger, her mode of dress could be construed as more than suggestive. Indeed, even her mother's tone is mildly disapproving when she comments on the daughter's outfit with the following: "Oh no you don't, Miss Thing. You better go put on a jacket!"

Equally problematic is the fact that this young couple is never shown in a public space on what is their first date. Instead, the only scene shown is that of the pair parked in a secluded area engaged in the act of kissing. As if to crystalize the message of black female hypersexuality, the camera cuts between the scene of the mother's tawdry living room display with the "father," and the scene of the daughter in the act of kissing her date. For a time, an uncomfortable feel exists in the juxtaposition of camera cuts between the two scenes because both mother and daughter are positioned as sexual gender equals. At the same time, the message of hypersexuality is further underscored by the assurance with which the daughter's date approaches her for sex, and his near surprise and definite annoyance when she rebuffs his sexual advances.

The theme of black female hypersexuality continues to play itself out between the two men as they leave the women's home. Their dates having abruptly ended, the worker suddenly notices his boss' disheveled appearance produced from the previous mother/"father" near-sex scene. The worker laughingly comments: "Quite a family, huh, man? Like mother, like daughter, huh? Know what I mean?" Though the film tries to save the situation by having the "father" reply: "Diego, you lay a hand on that girl and I'll kill you, personally," the damage has already been done. The visual image of the mother's earlier nonverbal sexual behaviors has overridden any verbal message offered. That image, especially when considered alongside that of the daughter's accusatory stance against her mother, muddies the picture further and, thus, becomes fixed in viewers' minds. Postman's (1979) reminder that it is the visual images, not the verbal, which contain the most important meanings leads us to draw one major conclusion: that it is the visual messages that audiences tend to remember. As importantly, the larger issue of the daughter's identity crisis gets lost under a barrage of cheap cinematic shenanigans.

But since the issues raised in this film are serious ones (sudden parenting for the male, identity crisis for the daughter, interracial relations for all three, interracial coupling for the "parents"), why is this couple not constructed as individuals who are grappling with emotions involving parenting concerns and possible mating, with all that that entails? Even within the framework of comedy, humor has its high and low rhythm, where dramatic moments are often called for, subject matter dictating. Certainly, the issues outlined above cry out for a certain degree of seriousness. Why then frame them almost entirely in the context of sexual buffoonery?

The use of humor should be organic, a natural occurrence in film, much the way it is for other cultural subgroups. A prime example of humor operating naturally and as an integral part of the cinematic context can be seen in the film *Steel Magnolias*. When all four women friends break out in laughter at the burial site of one of the character's daughter, audiences sense that such laughter is evoked in order to break the heightened and helpless tension all four women are experiencing in that context. Whether or not the filmmaker directed such an act is irrelevant because the laughter is felt as a natural and needed utterance in that moment. It is this form of humor that has too often been lacking in too many media representations of blacks generally; hence, the hue and cry regarding comedic portrayals of blacks in the media generally.

My second suggestion for future research is that the sexual imagery of the black female might be examined from a sociological perspective to better understand her reasons for the sexual behaviors she exhibits. Sexuality has been studied from a variety of perspectives (Marcuse, 1955; Laplanche, 1976; Foucault, 1980). In his analysis of sexuality, for example, Foucault discusses the constraints of sexuality in society. He argues that sexuality is a "transfer point for relations of power" (p. 103), where power can be exercised from numerous positions. Thus, one could use sexuality as a means of resisting domination, for example. Because black women, being both black and women, experience a double jeopardy of daily domination (Beale, 1995; King, 1988), studying the image of black female sexuality from this perspective could provide a deeper understanding of these women's socio-sexual experiences.

My third and final suggestion for future study involves the area of cross-racial gender research. In part, St. Jean & Feagin (1998) have already begun the process by conducting interviews with and facilitating focus groups involving African-Americans to discover their feelings about how the portrayals of blacks in the general media fare. I envision a more specific study which would move beyond their work to include black and white women's responses to images of black women in film. An ethnographic study to discover how black women respond to the negative filmic images of themselves, and their understanding of the culture's response to them, might be compared with white women's response to the same images of black women in films and white women's understanding of black women based on the imaging. Such an effort requires a multidisciplinary approach to help us better understand how each group of women interprets black women's filmic representations. It could also help us identify bridges of understanding between the two groups of women.

Epilogue

At the outset of this book, I mourned the loss of *Sounder* for this study, a film I believe stands as a symbol of what is possible in films featuring black female characters. Although the film is from another time, and there were those who even suggested that the film harkened back to a past portraiture of "gentle" film Negroes (Leab, 1975, p. 260; Bogle, 1989, p. 249), there is a wealth of humanity depicted. Such a universal portrayal gives audiences a rare glimpse into black women's interior lives, images which, in my mind, attempt to represent black women as believable human beings. That this film offered audiences a breadth and depth of the human emotions of black women clearly attests to filmmakers' ability to represent black women in humane terms. Yet, despite the emotional complexity evident in black women's social lives, for example, Hollywood seems crippled by worry that white audiences won't accept positive images of blacks in general (Rhines, 1996; Hacker, 1993). In effect, fear restricts the industry's ability to feature black female subjects on screen as believable human subjects. But what is required is a reassessment of studio executives' assumptions regarding what images will resonate with audiences, and what images audiences will accept.

Clearly, film moguls are the gatekeepers of many of those images that make it onto the screen. But to allow their fears to dictate those images a generic audience is ready for is, at best, problematic. Where it concerns audience response, for too long, too few have spoken for too

201

many. Hollywood has dictated for long enough those imagistic portrayals of cultural "others" audiences want to see. In fact, the debate regarding whether art imitates life or whether life imitates art has for too long lingered in perpetuity. Despite that we are kept distracted by that debate, platitudes won't balance the scales; action will. Hollywood must begin to exhibit some courage by breaking with its old way of representing black women's lived lives, life experiences that are in the process of being debunked. Instead of presenting them as a deviant monolithic group, Hollywood must act boldly by reflecting in its imaging the truth about the diverse cultural experiences of black women. It must assume a proactive stance by presenting a balanced viewing of black women's changing social status.

I am aware that changing behaviors is a challenge. After all, change is not an event; it is a process. Still, what seems clear to me is that change occurs when people want change to happen. For what is daunting is not change itself; rather, people's attitude toward change. Concerned as I am with Hollywood's lack of alteration in the representations of black female sexuality, I am equally concerned with that of black male filmmakers. Change requires conscious monitoring of the self. This point may be especially true where black male filmmakers are concerned. Freire (1970) has already cautioned that change involves more than simply recognizing the oppressive conditions from which individuals seek to escape; change involves that part of the oppressor that is deeply planted within the oppressed, and which knows the relationships of the oppressor. Despite the difficult prospect of overcoming internalized maltreatment, I remain committed to belief in the human spirit to triumph over adversity. Moreover, I believe that, if brought to the realization of one's misrecognition of the "other" and how such misrecognition harms that "other," most people of goodwill eventually do the right thing. Certainly, such a realization holds the promise of broadening the scope of male filmmakers' humanity, if only they listen with that humanity.

We need be mindful that greed or ignorance can be transformed into wisdom, undergirded by compassion and personal integrity. And while reform requires commitment and decisive action, filmmakers are not strangers to change. In their male-inspired creations, both sets of filmmakers have some degree of familiarity with the human potential for change, if only on a cognitive level. As directors of their products, filmmakers often point actors toward the emotional direction the filmmaker envisions. Houseman (1955/56) notes that the finished work reflects the creative vision of filmmakers. Thus, filmmakers have some understanding of the process involved in effecting change. Filmmakers, black and white, must now redeem themselves by acknowledging to the self their part in the perpetuation of the negative imaging and by becoming active agents of transformation in the representation of black women and their sexuality. Likewise, studio executives must relinquish their old fears and prejudices, allowing filmmakers some creative freedom in their construction of "others." For to the extent that they are constrained by studio executives' stereotypic assumptions of black womanhood, it may be that filmmakers' works will continue to advance such pervasive stereotypes when they write, cast, direct, and promote their wares.

Indeed, as we near the end of this first generation of commercial films by black male filmmakers, will the old trend of depicting black female sexuality continue from whence it started in 1986? The second generation of cinematic works is not very far off. While they plan for this second round of films, what definition of black female sexuality will these filmmakers impose upon viewers in these new works? When taken together, will they have charted a new course for black female characters on screen, or will they continue to conform to outdated cultural stereotypes? These questions arise from the findings of both studies which guided this book. Each revealed that black male filmmakers, in particular, are in the habit of presenting lurid and false images of black female sexuality. And I do not believe I am misstating the case when I say that at this very moment, many still do.

If recent works are any indication, the future for black female characters in film seems dubious, indeed! At last viewing, black women were still being sexualized in most films. No matter the alleged social status of the black female characters; no matter their educational background or career achievements, black women's sexual behavior is still coded as falling outside of "appropriate" behaviors for the "feminine." In fact, the black female characters' "feminine" status is still coded as "suspect": either they are coded as depraved sexualized beings, or else they tend to be constructed as characters so lacking in feminine warmth or tenderness that they fail to evoke in viewers "memories" of the "feminine." What many of the so-called newer images of black women do conjure up are cultural memories of Jezebel and Sapphire. This latter figure, the nagging shrew of a black woman, is still coded as a character who constantly diminishes the black male such that he becomes a sympathetic character (hooks, 1981). Sensitive, caring, and strong black women are still absent in most of these newer films. In spite of the many criticisms their films have generated, filmmaker after filmmaker continues in like fashion.

Obviously, black male filmmakers have learned very little about black women and their multifaceted experiences; they have learned very little about black women's socio-sexual experiences in American society. And how tragic this is! It is a tragedy because black male filmmakers fail to see their part in the denigration of black women culturally; they fail to see how their portrayals promote divisiveness between black men and black women; they still fail to see how as cultural producers their works perpetuate the negative imaging of black womanhood. Perhaps the greatest tragedy lies in black male filmmakers' failure to see how lack of transformation in images of black women is, in fact, a missed opportunity for transforming cinematic images of black cultural life and issues; it is a missed opportunity for altering images of blackness, period.

For their part, white male filmmakers appear to be on the fence where representation of images of black female characters—sexual or otherwise—is concerned. These latter filmmakers still seem tentative in presenting roles featuring images of black women as central characters, unless the roles are sexual or "mammy-like." Given the glut of films released since 1995, for example, juxtaposed with the dearth of varied roles for black female characters in their films, it becomes patently clear that the old pattern remains. In fact, the latest release of *The American Film Institute's Greatest Movies of All Times (2001)* names only one film on its list of 100 which features a black female who holds what could be termed a central starring role. But, in March 2002, after seventy-four years, black Americans saw a shift in the Academy Award's tradition—a black female finally won the Best Actress award! Many black women with whom I have discussed the win openly do not view the role for which Halle Berry won the award as a coup. The general consensus is that while such an accolade is far overdue, the role itself is a gross insult to black womanhood, made more so because so few white-produced films feature black women as central figures. "Why this role," many ask, and "why now?" It could be that as more black women fight their way into feminine "visibility," Berry's award is a means of making "formal" that which was before a defacto image—the old oversexed black Jezebel. Suffice it to say that among many black women, deep suspicion abounds! Thus, Berry's starring role notwithstanding, where white filmmakers are concerned, to date, only a mere handful of images of black women as central characters is present in their works. And as for the roles black women occupy, they are, to a large degree, still presented as sexual, as in *Swordfish* and *Monster's Ball*, or "all-knowing" black female characters, as in films such as *Midnight in the Garden of Good and Evil* and *The Matrix*. Much like the constructions by their black male counterparts, white male filmmakers' constructions of black female characters also fail to depict a balanced black woman. Indeed, one might say that much of the filmic coding of black women in white filmmakers' works harken back to the "mammy" figures so prevalent in films of the pre–1970s. That some of these women appear physically different from the image of the old "mammy" only means they are modern versions of that image. What is important is that the behaviors are coded such that they very much become reminiscent of the "mammy" image of the pre-1970s— self-sacrificing to the end. White male filmmakers, too, have learned precious little about black women or their sexuality.

As both studies indicate, it makes little difference that the filmmaker is black or white male; the status quo in films is alive and well, after all, with no balance in depictions of black female subjects. In the end, then, neither set of male filmmakers seems committed to transforming in any substantive way the negative or ambiguous image of black female characters on screen. One might conclude that, where blackness is concerned, not much has changed in American cultural arts.

Yet, it is clear that film can be a transforming instrument. For as a major part of the social ritual in American culture (Jowett & Linton, 1980), film has played a significant role in American life and arts. Film has served not just a major function in how Americans view the world; it has played a significant role in how American viewers see and, therefore, come to relate to one another. As Denzel Washington (2002) so aptly notes, "Technology magnifies the negative and positive in us; it allows us to expose ourselves." Indeed, it is through filmmakers' eyes and as a matter of course that film provides dominant group members with a window through which to view positive images of themselves as reflected in characters' lives. In turn, such reflection provides a psychological space in which these viewers can connect on an emotional level with the vicissitudes of characters' on-screen life experiences.

Such a cathartic force in the lives of dominant group members acts as a powerful tool, for it is here, through this cathartic process, that film allows these viewers expression of deep human feelings, many of which viewers themselves might not otherwise be able to safely express in reality. Perhaps most significant is the overall positive symbolic connection dominant group members have been socialized to nonconsciously align with white actresses, even as they also nonconsciously align negative symbolic connotations with black female subjects on screen. And it is these transactional relationships of positivism between audience and film that now cry out for a fair and humane inclusion of the lived and varied experiences of black female characters by filmmakers, black and white. The overarching question remains thus: just how do filmmakers, black and white male, intend to respond in their next generation of films? Black female viewers—indeed all female viewers—anxiously await filmmakers' next move.

Appendix A: Films in the Two Studies

Only films produced between 1986 and the present that depict black women as sexual or sensual figures are considered relevant to the question framing the studies, since this period saw the emergence of a contemporary American black male–controlled filmmaking culture. Two additional criteria were needed to determine the films' importance and to validate their relevance to both studies.

The first criterion was that the films be "mainstream movies," as defined by their national distribution to commercial film theatres and frequency of rental in videotape form (as determined either by inclusion in *Variety*'s list of "All-Time Box-Office Rental Champs," which ranks films by number of video rentals, or by canvass of Blockbuster video outlets in New York City).

The second was that the films be judged "very important" or "extremely important" to the central question by experienced film critics and scholars, who rated the films on the scale developed for assessing the films' relevance to issues of sexual characterizations (see Appendix B).

The 16 films identified as the sample were all rated 4 ("very important") or 5 ("extremely important").

For each film listed, filmmaker and female African American cast credits are given.

Films by Black Male Filmmakers
for the First Study

1986 *She's Gotta Have It.* Filmmaker, Spike Lee. Stars Tracy Camila Johns.
1991 **Poetic Justice.* Filmmaker, John Singleton. Stars Janet Jackson and Regina King.
1991 **New Jack City.* Filmmaker, Mario Van Peebles. Stars Tracy Camila Johns and Michael Michele.
1995 **Jason's Lyric.* Filmmaker, Doug McHenry. Stars Jada Pinkett and Lisa Nicole Carson.
1995 **Devil in a Blue Dress.* Filmmaker, Carl Franklin. Stars Jennifer Beals/Co-stars Lisa Nicole Carson.

Films by White Male Filmmakers
for the First Study

1991 *Mistress.* Filmmaker, Barry Primus. Stars Cheryl Lee Ralph.
1991 *The Josephine Baker Story.* Filmmaker, Brian Gibson. Stars Lynn Whitfield.
1991 **The Last Boyscout.* Filmmaker, Tony Scott. Stars Halle Berry.
1992 **The Bodyguard.* Filmmaker, Mick Jackson. Stars Whitney Houston/Co-Stars Michel Lamar Ricard.
1992 *Zebrahead.* Filmmaker, Anthony Drazen. Stars N'Bushe Wright.

Films by Black Male Filmmakers
for the Second Study

1997 **Love Jones.* Filmmaker, Theodore Witcher. Stars Nia Long.
1999 **The Best Man.* Filmmaker, Malcolm D. Lee. Stars Nia Long, Monica Calhoun, Melissa DeSousa, and Sanaa Lathan.
2000 *Loving Jezebel.* Filmmaker, Kwyn D. Bader. Stars Nicole Ari Parker.

Films by White Male Filmmakers
for the Second Study

1997 *Jackie Brown*. Filmmaker, Quintin Tarantino. Stars Pam Grier.
2001 *Swordfish*. Filmmaker, Dominic Sena. Stars Halle Berry.
2001 *Monster's Ball*. Filmmaker, Marc Forster. Stars Halle Berry.

*Variety's list of top grossing films.

Appendix B:
Importance of
Sexual Contact
Behaviors in the Films

SCALE: 1   no importance
            2   some importance
            3   sufficiently important
            4   very important
            5   extremely important

She's Gotta Have It	5	*The Bodyguard*	5
Poetic Justice	5	*Zebrahead*	5
New Jack City	4	*Love Jones*	4
Jason's Lyric	5	*The Best Man*	5
Devil in a Blue Dress	4	*Loving Jezebel*	5
Mistress	4	*Jackie Brown*	4
The Josephine Baker Story	4	*Swordfish*	4
The Last Boyscout	4	*Monster's Ball*	5

Bibliography

Anderson, L. (1997). *Mammies No More: The Changing Image of Black Women on Stage and Screen*. Maryland: Rowman & Littlefield Publishers, Inc.

Astone, N. & S. McLanahan. (1991). Family Structure, Parental Practices, and High School Completion. *American Sociological Review, 56*, pp. 309–320.

Atkin, C. (1979). Research Evidence on Mass Mediated Health Communication Campaigns. In D. Nimmo (ed.). *Communication Yearbook, 3*, pp. 655–668. New Brunswick, N.J.: Transaction Books.

Atkins, D. (1992). An Analysis of Television Series with Minority-Lead Characters. *Critical Studies in Mass Communication, 9*, pp. 337–349.

Baker Jr., H. A. (1993). Spike Lee and the Commerce of Culture. In M. Diawara (ed.). *Black American Cinema*. New York: Routledge.

Bandura, A. (1977). *Social Learning Theory*. Englewood Cliffs, N.J.: Prentice-Hall, Inc.

_____ (1986). *Social Foundations of Thought and Action: A Social Cognitive Theory*. Englewood Cliffs, N.J.: Prentice-Hall, Inc.

Basow, S. A. (1980). *Sex-Role Stereotypes: Traditions and Alterations*. Monterey, Calif.: Brooks/Cole Publishing Co.

Beale, F. (1995). Double Jeopardy: To Be Black and Female. In Beverly Guy-Shaftell (ed.). *Words of Fire: An Anthology of African-American Feminist Thought* pp. 146–154. New York: New Press.

Bell, E. L. J. & S. M. Nkomo. (2001). *Our Separate Ways: Black and White Women and the Struggle for Professional Identity*. Cambridge, Mass.: Harvard Business School Press.

Bem, S. L. (1993). *The Lenses of Gender*. New Haven: Yale University Press.

Berelson, B. (1952). *Content Analysis in Communication Research*. Glencoe, Ill.: The Free Press.

211

Berne, E. (1961). *Transactional Analysis in Psychotherapy.* New York: Grove Press.
_____ (1974). *What Do You Say After You Say Hello.* New York: Bantam Books.
Besharov, D. (2002, June 6). *Beyond the Color Line.* Panel Discussion. Book TV/ C-Span 2, Channel 60.
Birdwhistle, R. L. (1970). *Kenesics and Context: Essays on Body Motion Communication.* Philadelphia: University of Pennsylvania Press.
Blakey, W. A. (1974). Everybody Makes the Revolution: Some Thoughts on Racism and Sexism. *Civil Rights Digest, 6*(3), pp. 11–19.
Blauner, R. (1972). *Racial Oppression in America.* New York: Harper & Row.
Blumer, H., & P. Hauser. (1933). *Movies, Delinquency, and Crime.* New York: MacMillan.
Bobo, J. (1992, December). Conference Report. *Available Visions: Improving Distribution of African American Independent Film and Video Conference,* July 24–26. San Francisco Arts Commission.
_____ (1992). The Politics of Interpretation. In G. Dent (ed.). *Black Popular Culture* pp. 65–74. Seattle: Bay Press.
_____ (1995). *Black Women As Cultural Readers: Film and Culture.* New York: Columbia University Press.
Bogle, D. (1973/1989). *Toms, Coon, Mulattoes, Mammies, and Bucks* (expanded edition). New York: The Viking Press.
_____ (1988). *Blacks in American Films and Television: An Encyclopedia.* New York: Garland Press.
Bond, S. & T. Cash. (1992). Black Beauty: Skin Color and Body Images Among African-American College Women. *Journal of Applied Psychology, 22*(11), pp. 874–888.
Boorstin, D. J. (1977) *The Image: A Guide to Pseudo-Events in America.* New York: Atheneum.
Borisoff, D. & D. F. Hahn. (1992). Dimensions of Intimacy: The Interrelationships Between Gender and Listening. *The Journal of the International Listening Association, 6,* pp. 23–41.
Bowser, P. (1981). *Sexual Imagery and the Black Woman in Cinema.* Yearwood, Black Cinema, pp. 42–51.
Boyum, J. (1985). *Double Exposure: Fiction Into Film.* New York: New American Library.
Braxton, G. (1997, February 8). Group Calls for Changes in Portrayal of Blacks on TV. *Los Angeles Times,* pp. A1, A18.
Brownmiller, S. (1975). *Against Our Will: Men, Women and Rape.* New York: Simon & Schuster.
Burgoon, J. K., D. G. Buller, & W. G. Woodall. (1989). *Nonverbal Communication: The Unspoken Dialogue.* New York: Harper & Row.
Butler, J. (1990). *Gender Trouble.* New York: Routledge.
Cash, W. J. (1941). *The Mind of the South.* New York: Knopf.
Cashmore, E. (1997). *The Black Culture Industry.* New York: Routledge.
Cherlin, A. J. (1992). *Marriage, Divorce, Remarriage.* Cambridge Mass.: Harvard University Press.
_____ (1996). *Public and Private Families: An Introduction* (2nd ed.). New York: McGraw-Hill.
Christian, B. (1985). Shadows Uplifted. In J. Newton & D. Rosenfelt (eds.). *Feminist Criticism and Social Change.* New York: Methuen.

Cleaver, E. (1968). *Soul on Ice.* New York: Dell Publishing.
Collins, P. H. (1990). *Black Feminist Thought: Knowledge, Consciousness and the Politics of Empowerment.* N.Y.: Routledge.
Cosby, C. (1994). *Television's Imageable Influences: The Self-Perceptions of Young African-Americans.* Maryland: University Press of America.
Cosby condemns "massacre" of black images depicted by "drive-by" white writers. (1992, October 26). *Jet, 83,* pp. 58–60.
Cose, E. (1993). *The Rage of a Privileged Class.* New York: Harper Collins.
Crier, K. & A. Roker. (2002, January 4). Mind Over Media: Voices from the Middle School. *Court TV in Association with Cable in the Classroom.*
Cripps, T. (1977). *Slow Fade to Black: The Negro in American Film, 1900–1942.* New York: Oxford University Press.
Cruse, H. (1967). *The Crisis of the Negro Intellectual.* New York: Morrow.
Davis, A. Y. (1983). *Women, Race and Class.* New York: Vintage Books.
DeBeauvoir, S. (1974). *The Second Sex.* New York: Vantage.
DeLauretis, T. (1984). *Alice Doesn't: Feminism, Semiotics, Cinema.* Bloomington: Indiana University Press.
DeRougement, D. (1956). *Love in the Western World.* New York: Harper & Row.
Diawara, M. (ed.). (1993). *Black American Cinema.* N.Y.: Routledge.
Dilworth-Anderson, P. (1992, Summer). Extended Kin Networks in Black Families. *Generation, 17,* p. 29.
Dimitrius, J. E. & M. Mazzarella. (1999). *Reading People.* New York: The Ballantine Publishing Group.
Downey, M. (1993, Feb. 23). Interracial Marriages Irk Black Women. *Cleveland Plain Dealer,* Everywoman section, p. C4.
Downey, S. D. (1996). "Feminine Empowerment in Disney's Beauty and the Beast." *Women's Studies in Communication, 19,* pp. 185–212.
Du Bois, W. E. B. (1961). *The Souls of Black Folk: Essays and Sketches.* New York: Fawcette.
Edwards, R. (1998). The Effects of Gender, Gender Role and Values on the Interpretation of Messages. *Journal of Language and Social Psychology, 17,* pp. 52–71.
Ekman, P. (2001). *Telling Lies* (7th edition). New York: Norton & Company.
Ekman, P. & W. V. Friesen. (1969). Nonverbal Leakage and Clues to Deception. *Psychiatry, 32,* pp. 88–106.
Ellison, R. (1952/1989). *Invisible Man* (Reprint). New York: Vintage Books.
Entman, R. (1994). Representation and Reality in the Portrayal of Blacks on Network TV News. *Journalism Quarterly, 71*(3), pp. 509–520.
Erikson, E. H. (1963). *Childhood and Society* (2nd edition). New York: W. W. Norton & Co.
Espenshade, T. J. (1985). Marriage Trends in America: Estimates, Implications, and Underlying Causes. *Population and Development Review, 11,* pp. 193–245.
Everson, W. (1979). *Love in the Film: Screen Romance from the Silent Days to the Present.* Secaucus, N.J.: Citadel Press.
Farley, C. (1993, November 22). Black and Blue. *Time, 42,* pp. 80–81.
Feagin, J. R. (1968). The Kinship Ties of Negro Urbanites. *Social Science Quarterly, 49,* pp. 660–665.
Feagin, J. R. & H. Vera. (1995). *White Racism: The Basics.* New York: Routledge.
Federal Trade Commission (2000, September). *FTC Releases Report on the*

Marketing of Violent Entertainment to Children. http/www.ftc.gov. Retrieved January 8, 2002.

Fine, M. (1995, March 14). Drama's Color Block: "Under One Roof" Bucks the Odds Against Blacks. *USA Today*, 3D.

Foucault, M. (1980). *The History of Sexuality.* New York: Vintage Books.

Frankenberg, R. (1993). *White Women, Race Matters.* Minneapolis: University of Minnesota Press.

Frazier, E. F. (1957). *Black Bourgeoisie.* New York: Free Press.

Freeman-Longo, R. (1998). *Sexual Abuse in America: Epidemic of the 21st Century.* Vermont: Safer Society Press.

Freire, P. (1970). *The Pedagogy of the Oppressed.* New York: Seabury Press.

Freud, S. (1962). *Three Essays on the Theory of Sexuality.* New York: Basic Books.

Freydberg, E. H. (1995). Sapphires, Spitfires, Sluts, and Super-Bitches: Aframericans and Latinas in Contemporary American Film. In K. M. Vaz (ed.). *Black Women in America* pp. 222–243. Thousand Oaks, Calif.: Sage.

Friedman, L. (1991). *Unspeakable Images: Ethnicity and the American Cinema.* Urbana: University of Illinois Press.

Gaines, J. (1997). The Scar of Shame: Skin Color and Caste in Black Silent Melodrama. In V. Smith (ed.). *Representing Blackness: Issues in Film and Video* pp. 61–81. New Brunswick, N.J.: Rutgers University Press.

George, N. (1992). *Buppies, B-Boys, Baps, and Bohos: Notes on Post-Soul Black Culture.* New York: Harper Collins.

_____ (1994). *Blackface: Reflections on African-Americans and the Movies.* New York: Harper Collins.

Gerbner, G. (1967). An Institutional Approach to Mass Communications Research. In L. Thayer (ed.). *Communication: Theory and Research* pp. 429–445. Springfield, Ill.: Charles C. Thomas.

Gianetti, L. (1972). Cinematic Metaphors. *Journal of Aesthetic Education*, October.

Giddings, P. (1984). *When and Where I Enter: The Impact of Black Women on Race and Sex in America.* New York: William Morrow & Company, Inc.

Gilman, S. (1985). *Difference and Pathology: Stereotypes of Sexuality, Race, and Madness.* Ithaca: Cornell University Press.

Gray, H. (1995). *Watching Race: Television and the Struggle for "Blackness."* Minneapolis: University of Minnesota Press.

Guerrero, E. (1993). The Black Image in Protective Custody: Hollywood's Biracial Buddy Films of the Eighties. In M. Diawara (ed.). *Black American Cinema* pp. 237–246. New York: Routledge.

Gutman, H. G. (1976). *The Black Family in Slavery and Freedom, 1750–1925.* New York: Vintage Books.

Hacker, A. (1993, October 18). The Faltering Dream. *The Cronkite-Ward Production*, Discovery Channel.

Hall, R. (1995). The Bleaching Syndrome: African-American's Response to Cultural Domination vis-à-vis Skin Color. *Journal of Black Studies, 26*(2), pp. 172–184.

Hall, S. (1980). Encoding/Decoding. In S. Hall, D. Hobson, A. Lowe, & P. Willis (eds.). *Culture, Media, Language* pp. 128–138. London: Methuen.

_____ (1992). Cultural Studies and Its Theoretical Legacies. In L. Groberg, et al. (eds.). *Cultural Studies* pp. 377–394. New York: Routledge.

_____ (1995). The Whites of Their Eyes. In G. Dines and J. M. Humez (eds.). *Gender, Race, and Class in Media: A Text-Reader* pp. 18–27. Thousand Oaks, Calif.: Sage.

_____ (1997). The Spectacle of the "Other." In S. Hall (ed.). *Representation: Cultural Representations and Signifying Practices* pp. 223–290. London: Sage.

Hanson, C. (1993, April 11). Love in the '90s Means Commitment. *Chicago Tribune*, Womanews section, p. 1.

Harrison, R. P. (1974). *Beyond Words: An Introduction to Nonverbal Communication*. Englewood Cliffs, N.J.: Prentice Hall.

Harvey, A. (1995). The Issue of Skin Color in Psychotherapy with African Americans. *Families and Society, 76*(1), pp. 3–10.

Haskell, M. (1973/1987). *From Reverence to Rape: The Treatment of Women in the Movies* (2nd edition). Chicago: University of Chicago Press.

_____ (1995, May/June). MacLaine: Still Here. *Film Comment, 31*(3), pp. 21–28.

Haste, H. (1993). *The Sexual Metaphor*. Cambridge, Mass.: Harvard University Press.

Hayakawa, S. I., & A. R. Hayakawa. (1990). *Language in Thought and Action* (5th ed.). San Diego: Harcourt Brace Jovanovich, Publishers.

Helford, E. R. (2002). A Galaxy of Our Own: Searching for Black Women in Science-Fiction Film. *Bitch: Feminist Response to Pop Culture, 15*, pp. 34, 37, 88–89.

Henriques, Z. W. & E. Gilbert. (2000). Sexual Abuse/Assault of Women in Prison. In R. Muraskin (ed.). *It's a Crime: Women and Justice* (2nd ed.). New York: Prentice Hall.

Herrnstein, R. J. (1994). *The Bell Curve: Intelligence and Class Structure in American Life*. New York: A Free Press.

Herskovits, M. (1968). *The American Negro*. Bloomington, Ind.: Indiana University Press.

Hines, D. C. (1990). *Black Women in the United States History*, Vol. 2 (rev. ed.). New York: Carlson Publishing.

_____ (ed.). (1993). *Black Women in America: An Historical Encyclopedia, 2*, pp. 1009–1010. New York: Carlson Publishers.

Holsti, O. R. (1969). *Content Analysis for the Social Sciences and Humanities*. Reading, Mass.: Addison-Wesley Publishing Co.

hooks, b. (1981). *Ain't I a Woman: Black Women and Feminism*. Boston, Mass.: South End Press.

_____ (1992). *Black Looks: Race and Representation*. Boston, Mass.: South End Press.

_____ (1995, September). Beyond a Politics of Shape. *Z Magazine*, pp. 26–28.

_____ (1996, January 7). Save Your Breath, Sisters. *New York Times*, p. E19.

Hopson, D. P. & D. S. Hopson. (1990). *Different and Wonderful: Raising Black Children in a Race-Conscious Society*. New York: Prentice Hall.

Houseman, J. (1955/56). How—and What—Does a Movie Communicate? *The Quarterly of Film, Radio, and TV, 10*, pp. 227–238.

Innis, H. (1977). *The Bias of Communication*. Toronto: University of Toronto Press.

Inniss, L., & J. Feagin. (1995). The Cosby Show: The Views from the Black Middle Class. *Journal of Black Studies, 25*, pp. 692–711.

Iverem, E. (1997, May 25). What About Black Romance? *The Washington Post*, pp. G1, G4-G5.

Ivy, D. K., & P. Backlund. (2000). *Exploring Gender Speak: Personal Effectiveness in Gender Communication* (2nd ed.). New York: McGraw Hill.

Janis, I., & S. Feshbach. (1953). Effects of Fear-Arousing Communications. *Journal of Abnormal and Social Psychology, 48*, pp. 78–92.

Jaynes, G. D., & R. M. Williams. (eds.). (1989). *A Common Destiny: Blacks and American Society*. Committee on the Status of Black Americans, National Research Council. National Academy Press.

Johnson, W. (1995, May/June). Message Movies: Do They Deliver? *Film Comment, 31*(3), pp. 39–45.

Jones, J. (1992). The Accusatory Space. In G. Dent (ed.). *Black Popular Culture* pp. 95–98. Seattle: Bay Press.

_____ (1993). The Construction of Black Sexuality: Towards Normalizing the Black Cinematic Experience. In M. Diawara (ed.). *Black American Cinema* pp. 247–256. New York: Routledge.

Jordan, W. D. (1968). *White Over Black: American Attitudes Toward the Negro* [1550–1812]. Chapel Hill: University of North Carolina Press.

Jowett, G, & J. M. Linton. (1980). *Movies As Mass Communication*. Beverly Hills: Sage Publication.

Kaiser Family Foundation (1999, November). *Kids and Media: The New Millennium*. www.kff.org. Retrieved January 8, 2002.

Keen, S. (1991). *Fire in the Belly: On Being a Man*. New York: Bantam Books.

Keith, V. & C. Herring. (1991). Skin Tone and Stratification in the Black Community. *American Journal of Sociology, 3*, pp. 760–778.

Kennedy, L. (1992). The Body in Question. In G. Dent (ed.). *Black Popular Culture* pp. 106–111. Seattle: Bay Press.

King, D. K. (1988, Autumn). Multiple Jeopardy, Multiple Consciousness: The Context of a Black Feminist Ideology. *Signs, 14*(1), pp. 42–72.

Klapper, J. (1960). *The Effects of Mass Communication*. New York: Free Press.

Kracauer, S. (1947). *From Caligari to Hitler*. Princeton: Princeton University Press.

Kroll, J., V. E. Smith, & A. Murr. (1991, June 10). Spiking a Fever. *Time Magazine*, pp. 44–47.

Laplanche, J. (1976). *Life and Death in Psychoanalysis*. Baltimore: The John Hopkins University Press.

Leab, D. (1975). *From Sambo to Superspade: The Black Experience in Motion Pictures*. Boston: Houghton Mifflin Company.

Lerner, G. (1972). *Black Women in White America: A Documentary History*. New York: Vintage Press.

Lerner, H. G. (1989). *The Dance of Intimacy*. New York: Harper & Row Publishers.

Lieberman, M. K. (1986). Some Day My Prince Will Come: Female Acculturation Through the Fairy Tale. In J. Zipes (ed.). *Don't Bet on the Prince: Contemporary Feminist Fairy Tales in North America and England* pp. 185–200. New York: Methuen.

Linton, J. (1978, April). But It's Only a Movie. *Jump Cut, 17*, pp. 16–19.

Lockyer, H, (1967). *The Women of the Bible*. Grand Rapids, Mich.: Zondervan.

Lorber, J. (1994). *Paradoxes of Gender*. New Haven: Yale University Press.

Lorde, A. (1984). Age, Race, Class, and Sex: Women Redefining Difference. In A. Lorde *Sister Outsider: Essays and Speeches* pp.114–123. Trumansburg, N.Y.: The Crossing Press.

Malveaux, J. (1991, Sept.-Oct.). Spike's Spite: Women at the Periphery. *Ms. Magazine*, pp. 78–80.

Manatu, N., & Z. W. Henriques. (in press). Acts of Survival: Economic Inequity Among African-American Women Before and After Imprisonment. In D. Jones-Brown (ed.). *On African-American Women: The Law and the Justice System*. Part of Women and Law Series. Edited by R. Muraskin. Routledge Publishers.

Manatu-Rupert, N. (2000). Media Images and the Victimization of Black Women: Exploring the Impact of Sexual Stereotyping on Prosecutorial Decision Making. In M. Markowitz and D. D. Jones-Brown (eds.) *The System in Black and White: Exploring the Connections Between Race, Crime, and Justice* pp. 181–196. Westport, Conn.: Praeger.

Mapp, E. (1972). *Blacks in American Films: Today and Yesterday*. Metuchin, N.J.: The Scarecrow Press.

Marcuse, H. (1966, c1955). *Eros and Civilization: A Philosophical Inquiry Into Freud*. Boston, Mass.: Beacon Press.

Marketing of Violent Entertainment to Children. (2000, September). *Federal Trade Commission*. http://www.ftc.gov. Retrieved January 8, 2002.

Marshall-Wong, C. (2000). *Challenges to Agency: An Analysis of Black Professional Women in the Workplace and in Their Lived Lives*. (Unpublished dissertation. George Mason University.)

McAdoo, H. P. (1993). Ethnic Families: Strengths That Are Found in Diversity. In H. P. McAdoo (ed.). *Family Ethnicity: Strengths in Diversity*. Newbury Park, Calif.: Sage.

McCall, N. (1994). *Makes Me Wanna Holler*. New York: Random House.

McIntosh, P. (1998). White Privilege: Unpacking the Invisible Knapsack. In P. Rothenberg (ed.). *Race, Class, and Gender* (4th edition) pp. 165–169. New York: St. Martin's Press.

McLean, A. L. (1995, Spring). The Cinderella Princess and the Instrument of Evil: Surveying the Limits of Female Transgression in Two Postwar Hollywood Scandals. *Cinema Journal, 34*(3), pp. 36–56.

McLuhan, M. (1964). *Understanding Media* (2nd edition). New York: New American Library.

Mellen, J. (1973). *Women and Their Sexuality in the New Film*. New York: Horizon Press.

_____ (1975). *Big Bad Wolves: Masculinity in the American Film*. New York: Pantheon.

Methabane, M. (2001, August 22). Interracial Myths Still Nag Couples. *USA Today*, pp. 46–55.

Metz, C. (1974). *Film Language: A Semiotics of the Cinema*. Chicago: Chicago Press.

Meyrowitz, J. (1985). *No Sense of Place*. New York: Oxford University Press.

Mitchell, S. (1993, March 15). Changing Marriage Patterns Add Up to Changing Lifestyles. *Boomer Report*, Lifestyles section, p. 7.

Modleski, T. (1991). *Feminism Without Women: Culture and Criticism in a Post-Feminist Age*. New York: Routledge.

Monroe, S. (1994, March). Hollywood: The Dark Side. *Essence, 24*, pp. 82–84, 127–128.

Morash, M., T. S. Bynum, & B. A. Koons. (1998). *Women Offenders: Programming Needs and Promising Approaches*. (Research in brief). National Institute of Justice. Washington, D.C.: U.S. Department of Justice, Office of Justice Programs.

Morrison, T. (1992). *Playing in the Dark: Whiteness and the Literary Imagination.* New York: Vantage Books.

_____ (1993). *The Bluest Eye.* New York: Plume.

Moynihan, D. P. (1965). *The Negro Family: The Case for National Action.* Washington, D.C.: Government Printing Office.

Mullins, E., & P. Sites. (1984). The Origins of Contemporary Eminent Black Americans: A Three-Generation Analysis of Social Origin. *American Sociological Review,* pp. 672–685.

Mulvey, L. (1989). *Visual and Other Pleasures.* Bloomington: Indiana University Press.

Murray, J. P. (1973). *To Find an Image: Black Films from Uncle Tom to Superfly.* Indianapolis: The Bobbs-Merrill Company, Inc.

Murstein, B., J. Merighi, T. E. Malloy. (1989). Physical Attractiveness and Exchange Theory in Interracial Dating. *The Journal of Social Psychology, 12.* pp. 325–334.

Nafziger, R. O., & D. M. White. (eds.). (1963). *Introduction to Mass Communication Research* (revised edition). Baton Rouge, La.: Louisiana State University.

National Advisory Commission on Civil Disorder. (1968). *Report of the National Advisory Commission on Civil Disorders.* New York: Bantam Books.

National Television Violence Study. (1997). *Issue Briefs.* Studio City, Calif.: Mediascope Press.

Neal, A. & M. Wilson. (1989). The Role of Skin Color and Features in the Black Community: Implications for Black Women and Therapy. *Clinical Psychology Review, 9,* pp. 323–333.

Nielson Media Research (1993). *Some Things You Should Know About Media Violence and Media Literacy.* www.babyboy.com. Retrieved March 6, 2001.

Noble, P. (1970). *The Negro in Film.* N.Y.: Arno Press.

Omolade, B. (1983). Hearts of Darkness. In A. Snitow, C. Stansell, & S. Thompson (eds.). *Powers of Desire* pp. 350–365. New York: Monthly Review Press.

Ong, W. J. (1981). *The Presence of the Word.* Minneapolis: University of Minnesota Press.

Orenstein, P. (1994). *Schoolgirls: Young Women, Self-Esteem, and the Confidence Gap.* New York: Doubleday.

Painter, N. I. (1992). Hill, Thomas, and the Use of Racial Stereotype. In T. Morrison (ed.). *Race-Ing Justice, En-Gendering Power* pp. 201–214. New York: Pantheon Books.

Palmer, P. M. (1983, Spring). White Women/Black Women: The Dualism of Female Identity and Experience in the United States. *Feminist Studies,* 9(1), pp. 151–170.

Parker, L. O. (1999, October 22). The Best Man: A Joyous Occasion. *Washington Post,* pp. 46, 54.

Parks, S. (1995). Seeing Through Our Own Eyes. *Black Film Review* 8(2), pp. 14–15.

Person, E. S. (1988). *Dreams of Love and Fateful Encounters: The Power of Romantic Passion.* N.Y.: W. W. Norton & Company, Inc.

Postman, N. (1979). *Teaching As a Conserving Activity.* New York: Delacorte Press.

Poussaint, A. (1983). Black-on-Black Homicide: A Psychological-Political Perspective. *Victimology, 8*, pp. 161–169.

Radway, J. A. (1984). *Reading the Romance: Women, Patriarchy, and Popular Literature*. Chapel Hill: University of North Carolina Press.

Randolph, L. (1994, May). Life After the Cosby Show: Activist-Actor Celebrates 30 Years of Wedded Bliss, Continues Fight Against Black Stereotypes on TV. *Ebony, 49*, pp. 100–102, 104.

Reddick, L. D. (1944). Educational Programs for the Improvement of Race Relations: Motion Pictures, Radio, the Press and Libraries. *Journal Of Negro Education, 13.*

Reid, M. A. (1988). The Black Action Film: The End of the Patiently Enduring Black Hero. *Film History, 2*, pp. 23–36.

Rhines, J. A. (1996). *Black Film/White Money*. New Brunswick, N.J.: Rutgers University Press.

Rich, A. (1980, Summer). Compulsory Heterosexuality and Lesbian Existence. *Signs, 5*(4), pp. 80–81.

Roberts, D. (1994). *The Myth of Aunt Jemima: Representations of Race and Region*. New York: Routledge.

Robinson, M. (1976). Public Affairs Television and the Growth of Political Malaise. *American Political Science Review, 70*, pp. 425–445.

Robinson, T. (2001). Effects of Reducing Children's Television and Video Game Use on Aggressive Behavior: A Randomized Controlled Trial. *The Journal of the American Medical Association, 285*, p. 1685.

Robinson, T. & J. Ward. (1995). African American Adolescents and Skin Color. *Journal of Black Psychology, 21*(3), pp. 256–274.

Robinson, W. R. (1967). *Man and the Movies*. Baton Rouge, La.: Louisiana State University Press.

Rosen, M. (1973). *Popcorn Venus: Women, Movies and the American Dream*. New York: Coward, McCann & Geoghegan.

Rowe, K. E. (1986). Feminism and Fairy Tales. In J. Zipes (ed.). *Don't Bet on the Prince: Contemporary Feminist Fairy Tales in North America and England* pp. 209–226. New York: Methuen.

Rubin, L. (1998). Is This a White Country, Or What? In P. Rothenberg (ed.). *Race, Class, and Gender* (4th edition), pp. 92–99. New York: St. Martin's Press.

Russell, K., M. Wilson, & R. Hall. (1993). *The Color Complex: The Politics of Skin Color Among African-Americans*. New York: Harcourt Brace Jovanovich.

St. Jean, Y. & J. R. Feagin. (1998). *Double Burden: Black Women and Everyday Racism*. Armonk, N.Y.: M. E. Sharpe.

Sampson, R. J. & J. H. Laub. (1994). Urban Poverty and the Family Context of Delinquency: A New Look at Structure and Process in a Classic Study. *Child Development, 65*, pp. 538.

Schudson, M. (1984). *Advertising, the Uneasy Persuasion: Its Dubious Impact on American Society*. New York: Basic Books.

Schultz, D. & B. Barnes. (1995). *Strategic Advertising Campaigns*. Lincolnwood, Ill.: NTC Business Books.

Sethi, S. C. (1998). Smells Like Racism. In P. Rothenberg (ed.). *Race, Class, and Gender* (4th edition) pp. 154–164. New York: St. Martin's Press.

Shihadeh, E. S. & D. J. Steffensmier. (1994, December). Economic Inequality,

Family Disruption, and Urban Black Violence: Cities As Units of Stratification and Social Control. *Social Forces, 73*, pp. 729–751.

Signorielli, N. (1989). Television and Corruptions About Sex-Roles: Main-streaming Conventionality and the Status Quo. *Sex Roles, 21*(5/6).

Simson, R. (1983). The Afro-American Female: The Historical Context of the Construction of Sexual Identity. In A. Snitow, C. Stansell, & S. Thompson (eds.). *Powers of Desire* pp. 229–235. New York: Monthly Review Press.

Sklar, H. (1998). Imagine a Country. In P. Rothenberg (ed.). *Race, Class, and Gender* (4th edition) pp. 192–201. New York: St. Martin's Press.

Sklar, R. (1975). *Movie-Made America: A Cultural History of American Movies.* New York: Random House.

Smith, B. (1998). *The Truth That Never Hurts.* New Brunswick, N.J.: Rutgers University Press.

Snead, J. A. (1997). Spectatorship and Capture in King Kong: The Guilty Look. In V. Smith (ed.). *Representing Blackness: Issues in Film and Video* pp. 25–45. New Brunswick, N.J.: Rutgers University Press.

Stacey, J. (1994). *Star Gazing: Hollywood Cinema and Female Spectatorship.* New York: Routledge.

Stampp, K. M. (1956). *The Peculiar Institution.* New York: Knopf.

Stanley, R. H. (2003). *Making Sense of Movies.* New York: McGraw Hill.

Staples, R. (1981). *The World of Black Singles: Changing Patterns of Male-Female Relations.* Westport, Conn.: Greenwood Press.

_____ (1987). *The Urban Plantation: Racism and Colonialism in the Post-Civil Rights Era.* California: The Black Scholar Press.

Staples, R., & L. Johnson. (1993). *Black Families at the Crossroads.* San Francisco: Jossey Bass Publishers.

Staples, R. & T. Jones. (1985). Culture, Ideology, and Black Television Images. *Black Scholar, 16*, pp. 10–20.

Taeuber, C. M. (ed.). (1996). *Statistical Handbook on Women in America* (2nd edition). Phoenix, Ariz.: Oryx.

Tannen, D. (1990). *You Just Don't Understand: Women and Men in Conversation.* New York: Morrow.

Tate, G. (1986, December). The Return of the Black Aesthetic: Cult-Nats Meet Freaky-Deke. *Village Voice* (literary supplement).

Taylor, J. (1993). Reaction to Penn et al.'s: On the Desirability of Own Group Preference. *Journal of Black Studies, 19*(3), pp. 333–335.

Tobin, G. (1987). *Divided Neighborhoods: Changing Patterns of Racial Segregation.* Newbury Park, Calif.: Sage Publication.

Tudor, A. (1974). *Image and Influence: Studies in the Sociology of Film.* New York: St. Martin's Press.

United States Commission on Civil Rights. (1990). *The Economic Status of Black Women: An Exploratory Investigation.* N. Zalokar (ed.). Washington, D. C.

Vaz, K. M. (1995). Organization of the Anthology. In K. M. Vaz (ed.). *Black Women in America* pp. xv-xvi. Thousand Oaks, Calif.: Sage.

Villani, S. (2001). Impact of Media on Children and Adolescents: A 10-Year Review of the Research. *Journal of the American Academy of Children and Adolescent Psychiatry, 40*, p. 392.

Wade, T. J. (1996). The Relationships Between Skin Color and Self-Perceived

Global, Physical, and Sexual Attractiveness, and Self-Esteem for African-Americans. *Journal of Black Psychology, 22*(3), pp. 358–373.

Wallace, M. (1979). *Black Macho and the Myth of the Super-Woman.* New York: The Dial Press.

_____ (1990). *Invisibility Blues: From Pop to Theory.* New York: Verso.

_____ (1992). Boyz 'n the Hood and Jungle Fever. In G. Dent (ed.). *Black Popular Culture* pp. 123–131. Seattle: Bay Press.

_____ (1996, May 21). Doin' the Right Thing. (Voice Film Special, pp. 10, 12, 14) *Village Voice, 51*(21).

Warfield, M. (2002, January 21). *A Century of Black Cinema.* Documentary on NBC TV.

Washington, D. (2002, January 21). *A Century of Black Cinema.* Documentary on NBC TV.

Weil, S. (1951). Reflections on the Right Use of School Studies with a View to the Love of God. In S. Weil *Waiting for God* pp. 105–116. New York: Harper Colophon Books.

Welbon, Y. (1992, March). Calling the Shots: Black Women Directors Take the Helm. *Independent,* pp. 18–22.

West, C. (1992). Nihilism in Black America. In G. Dent (ed.). *Black Popular Culture* pp. 37–47. Seattle: Bay Press.

_____ (1993). *Race Matters.* Boston, Mass.: Beacon Press.

West, C. M. (1995, Fall). Mammy, Sapphire, and Jezebel: Historical Images of Black Women and Their Implications for Psychotherapy. *Psychotherapy, 32,* pp. 458–466.

White, R. A. (1983). Mass Communication and Culture: Transition to a New Paradigm. *Journal Of Communication, 33,* pp. 279–301.

Wilkerson, I. (1991, Dec. 2). Black-White Marriages Rise, but Couples Still Face Scorn. *New York Times,* p. B6.

Williams, F. (1984). *The New Communications.* Belmont, Calif.: Wadsworth.

Williams, S. A. (1992). Two Words on Music: Black Community. In G. Dent (ed.). *Black Popular Culture* pp. 164–172. Seattle: Bay Press.

Wilson, M., & K. Russell. (1997). *Divided Sisters.* New York: Anchor Books.

Wilson, W. J. (1996). *When Work Disappears.* New York: Knopf.

Wolfenstein, M., & N. Leites. (1950). *Movies: A Psychological Study.* Glencoe, Ill.: Free Press.

Yamato, G. (1998). Something About the Subject Makes It Hard to Name. In P. Rothenberg (ed.). *Race, Class, and Gender,* (4th edition) pp. 150–154. N.Y.: St. Martin's Press.

Young, M. E. (1993). *Mules and Dragons: Popular Culture Images in the Selected Writings of African-American and Chinese-American Women Writers.* Westport, Conn.: Greenwood Press.

Young, R., & J. D. Young. (eds.). (1993). *African-American Folktales.* Little Rock: August House.

Zolakar, N. (ed.). (1990). *U.S. Commission on Civil Rights: The Economic Status of Black Women-An Exploratory Investigation.* Washington, D.C.

Zook, B. K. (1996, May 21). Still Waiting. (Voice Film Special, p. 6). *Village Voice, 51*(21).

Zwick, E. (2002, February 10). Denzel Washington. *Bravo Profiles.*

Index

Numbers in **bold** refer to photographs.